WHO KNEW?

Gathered AT THE TABLE

OVER 400 RECIPES & 200 TIPS FOR EVERY SEASON

Debra Murray & Bruce Lubin

WHO KNEW?

Gathered AT THE TABLE

• • •

OVER 400 RECIPES & 200 TIPS FOR EVERY SEASON

BLUESTONE BOOKS

Debra Murray
& Bruce Lubin

Cover design by Joanna Williams
Interior originally designed by Quadrum Solutions Pvt. Ltd.
Images used under license by Shutterstock
Author photograph provided by Debra Murray

Bluestone Books
www.bluestonebooks.co

ISBN: 978-1-965636-66-4

Printed and bound in the United States of America

10 9 8 7 6 5 4 3 2 1

Dedication

This book is dedicated to our loyal Who Knew? reader and all those who love finding the best ways to gather at the table.

Table of Contents

Introduction 12

Recipe No. .... Page

Chapter 1 Soups, Sandwiches, and Stews...13

1 Monster Sandwich 14
2 Hot Roast Beef Sandwiches 14
3 Reuben Sandwiches 15
4 Seafood Wraps 15
5 Garden Sandwich Wraps 15
6 Easy Gazpacho 16
7 Cucumber-Lover's Soup 16
8 Chilled Party Soup 17
9 Fresh Avocado Soup 17
10 Vichyssoise 18
11 Cheesy Chicken Soup 18
12 Spinach Soup 19
13 Tomato-Basil Soup 19
14 Tomato-Bacon Soup 20
15 Spicy Tomato Soup 20
16 Quick Borscht 20
17 Calzones 21
18 Turkey Burgers 21
19 Southwestern Burgers 22
20 Provolone-Pepper Burgers 22
21 Potato-Sausage Soup 23
22 Polish Vegetable Stew 23
23 Italian Garbanzo Bean Soup 24
24 Pizza Sandwich 24
25 Crab-Corn Chowder 25
26 Carolina She-Crab Soup 25
27 Rich Cheddar Chowder 26
28 Beer Cheese Soup 26
29 Fiesta Tortilla Soup Con Queso 27
30 Mexican-Style Minestrone Soup 27
31 Cream of Artichoke Soup 28
32 Zesty Black Bean Soup 28
33 Cream of Cauliflower Soup 29

Recipe No. .... Page

34 Welcome Home Soup 29
35 Garlic-Potato Soup 30
36 Cream of Zucchini Soup 30
37 Quick-and-Easy Peanut Soup 30
38 Homemade Tomato Soup 31
39 Tomato-Ravioli Soup 31
40 Chicken-Broccoli Chowder 32
41 Chicken-Sausage Stew 32
42 Northern Chili 33
43 Chicken Chili 33
44 Hot Gobble-Gobble Soup 34
45 Beefy Bean Chili 34
46 Southwestern Soup 35
47 Spaghetti Soup 35
48 Chile Verde Con Carne 36
49 Green Chile Stew Pot (Caldillo) 36
50 Stroganoff Stew 37
51 Oven-Baked Beef Stew 37
52 Ham Bone Soup 38
53 Split Pea Soup 38
54 Creamed Broccoli Soup 39
55 Rich Corn Chowder 39
56 Cod and Corn Chowder 40
57 Seafood Bisque 40
58 Easy Oyster Stew 41
59 New England Clam Chowder 41
60 Italian Minestrone 42
61 Broccoli–Wild Rice Soup 42
62 Ranchero Black Bean Soup 43
63 Creamy Mushroom Soup 43
64 Baked Potato Soup 44
65 Pumpkin Soup 44
66 Zesty Squash Soup 45
67 Johnny Appleseed's Squash Soup 45
68 French Onion Soup 46
69 Curried Zucchini Soup 46

Recipe No. .... Page

70 Southwest Vegetarian Chili 47
71 Cheese-Topped Broccoli Soup 47
72 Eight-Can Soup Bowl 48
73 Creamy Asparagus Soup 48
74 Deluxe Grilled-Cheese Sandwiches.......... 49
75 Get Well Soon Chicken Noodle Soup....... 49
76 Asian-Style Chicken Noodle Soup............ 50
77 Cheesy Chicken and Potatoes 50

Chapter 2 Salads and Sauces 51

78 Chicken-Rice Salad Supreme 52
79 Barbecue Chicken Salad......................... 52
80 Waldorf Salad 53
81 Chef's Salad 53
82 Hawaiian Chicken Salad 54
83 Chicken Tarragon Salad 54
84 Book Club's Favorite Salad 55
85 Aunt Patty's Chicken Salad 55
86 Chicken Caesar Salad............................. 56
87 Spinach-Turkey Salad Supper 56
88 Sweet and Tangy Ham Salad 57
89 Zesty Bean Salad.................................... 57
90 Sweet Tuna Salad 58
91 Tuna and White Bean Salad 58
92 Pasta Plus 59
93 Perfect Pasta Salad 59
94 Colorful Garden Salad 60
95 Fusilli Pasta Salad 60
96 Ready-To-Go Pasta Salad....................... 61
97 Color-Coded Salad 61
98 Broccoli-Noodle Crunch Salad................ 62
99 Black-Eyed Pea Salad 62
100 Artichoke Salad..................................... 63
101 Spinach Salad.. 63
102 Crispy Summer Salad 64
103 Tuna-Veggie Salad 64
104 Shrimp with Watermelon and Avocado 65
105 Smoked Salmon Plate with Horseradish Sauce 65

Recipe No. .... Page

106 Winter Salad 66
107 Seven-Layer Salad................................. 66
108 Super Healthy Salsa............................... 67
109 Italian Salad Dressing Mix 67
110 Homemade Mayonnaise 68
111 Low-Fat Ranch Dressing........................ 68
112 Low-Fat Cream of Chicken Soup Base 69
113 Low-Fat Cream of Mushroom Soup Base 69
114 Low-Fat Cream of Celery Soup Base 70
115 Low-Fat Four-Cheese Blend 70
116 Melty Cheese Sauce 71
117 Low-Fat Sour Cream Substituted............ 71
118 Healthy Chicken Broth 72
119 Healthy Beef Broth................................. 73
120 Homemade Spaghetti Sauce 74
121 Low-Fat Alfredo Sauce 74
122 Readymade Barbecue Sauce 75
123 Sweet-and-Sour Stir-Fry Sauce.............. 75

Chapter 3 Poultry Tonight 76

124 Chicken and Veggie Stir-Fry 77
125 Chicken Tarragon................................... 77
126 Chicken-Broccoli Skillet 78
127 Easy Chicken and Potatoes 78
128 Basic Breaded Chicken.......................... 79
129 Chicken and the Works.......................... 79
130 Tasty Skillet Chicken 80
131 Pimento Cheese-Stuffed Fried Chicken.... 80
132 Parmesan Chicken................................. 81
133 Lemon-Chicken Breeze 81
134 Crunchy Chip Chicken 82
135 Easy Baked Chicken.............................. 82
136 Cheesy Crusted Chicken 83
137 Asparagus Chicken................................ 83
138 Grilled Chicken Cordon Bleu 84
139 Grilled Chicken Fajitas........................... 84
140 Grilled Lemon Chicken........................... 85
141 Classic Chicken Piccata......................... 85

Recipe No. .... Page

142 Chicken with Pine Nuts and Red Peppers.......................................86
143 Almond-Crusted Chicken.......................86
144 Honey-Glazed Chicken 87
145 Stir-Fry Chicken Spaghetti......................87
146 Sweet 'n' Spicy Chicken 88
147 Fast Gobbler Fix 88
148 Creamy Tortellini Supper 89
149 Yummy Barbecued-Grilled Chicken..........89
150 Sweet, Spicy Chicken Thighs..................90
151 Glazed Drumsticks.................................90
152 Chicken Caesar Pizza 91
153 Easy Chicken and Dumplings..................91
154 Spicy Orange Chicken 92
155 Stir-Fry Cashew Chicken........................92
156 Italian Chicken Over Polenta 93
157 Turkey and Rice Olé...............................93
158 Chicken Sausage Pasta 94
159 Pasta-Turkey Salad Supper....................94
160 Super Easy Turkey Treat........................95
161 Tasty Turkey Crunch...............................95
162 Chicken Super Supper...........................96
163 Chicken with White Wine Sauce..............96
164 Chicken Diablo.......................................97
165 Grilled Tequila Chicken 97
166 Salsa-Grilled Chicken.............................98
167 Grilled Lime-Salsa Campsite Chicken.......98
168 Almond Chicken 99
169 Fruited Chicken......................................99
170 Sassy Chicken Over Tex-Mex Corn........100
171 Chili-Chicken Roll-Ups 100
172 Chicken Crunch 101
173 Lemon Dill Chicken 101
174 Springy Chicken...................................102
175 Sweet Pepper Chicken 102
176 Baked Chicken Poupon 103
177 Curry-Glazed Chicken..........................103
178 Montezuma Celebration Chicken 104

Recipe No. .... Page

179 Oven-Fried Chicken 104
180 Apricot-Ginger Chicken.........................105
181 Chicken and Wild Rice 105
182 Quick and Tasty Baked Chicken............106
183 Jalapeño Chicken 106
184 Pineapple-Teriyaki Chicken 107
185 Mandarin Chicken................................107
186 Ranch Chicken 108
187 Ritzy Chicken.......................................108
188 Chicken Cacciatore..............................109
189 Honey-Mustard Turkey Breast...............109
190 Herb-Roasted Turkey 110
191 Turkey Croquettes................................110
192 Grilled Caribbean Turkey 111
193 Simply Delicious Cornish Game Hens 111

Chapter 4 Beef Dinners..............................112

194 Sloppy Joes..113
195 Beef Patties with Mushroom Gravy 113
196 Queso con Carne 114
197 Pasta-Beef Skillet.................................114
198 Skillet Beef and Pasta 115
199 Mexican Beefy Noodles 115
200 Hot 'n' Sour Beef 'n' Noodles 116
201 French Fry Supper 116
202 Bachelor's Beef Skillet..........................117
203 Cheesy Beefy Gnocchi.........................117
204 Hot Tamale Cheese Fiesta 118
205 Stroganoff Made Easy..........................118
206 Thai Beef, Noodles, and Veggies...........119
207 Steak with Creamy Horseradish Sauce ..119
208 Skillet Steak and Veggies 120
209 Savory Steak with Rosemary Root Vegetables 120
210 Grilled Steak with Garlic-Mustard Sauce 121
211 London-in-Asia Broil 121
212 All-the-Trimmings Corned Beef 122
213 Ravioli and More 122

Recipe No. .... Page

214 Cheesy Stuffed Bell Peppers.................123
215 Best Pot Roast Dinner 124
216 Seasoned-Beef Tenderloin.....................124
217 Skillet Sirloin.......................................125
218 Steak and Potatoes 125
219 Italian Steak Extraordinary.....................126
220 Marinated and Grilled London Broil 126

Chapter 5 Pork and Lamb Dinners.............127

221 Rosemary Lamb Chops 128
222 Spicy Lamb Chops with Chickpeas........128
223 Pork Chop Supper................................129
224 Parmesan Covered Pork Chops.............129
225 Pork Chops with Black Bean Salsa........129
226 Peppered Tenderloin.............................130
227 Ham, Corn, and Goat Cheese Omelets..130
228 Italian Sausage and Ravioli....................131
229 Colorful Sausage Supper 132
230 Grilled Garlic-Herb Tenderloin................133
231 Praiseworthy Pork Tenderloin................133
232 Sweet Peach Pork Tenderloin 134
233 Orange Pork Chops..............................134
234 Italian-Style Pork Chops.......................135
235 Onion-Smothered Pork Chops..............135
236 Pork Chops and Apples........................136
237 Apricot Pork Chops 136
238 German-Style Ribs and Kraut................137
239 Oven-Roasted Baby Backs...................137
240 Italian Stuffed Peppers.........................138

Chapter 6 Fish and Seafood.......................139

241 Creamy Noodle Tuna 140
242 Salmon and Green Beans 140
243 Alfredo Salmon and Noodles.................141
244 Red Snapper with Fresh Salsa..............141
245 Orange Roughy with Peppers 142
246 Halibut With Orzo.................................142
247 Pan-Fried Flounder 143
248 Seasoned Fried Fish 143

Recipe No. .... Page

249 Broiled Red Snapper.............................144
250 Grilled Swordfish with Pepper Sauce 144
251 Spicy Baked Fish 145
252 Sea Scallop Stir-Fry 145
253 Supper-Ready Shrimp Salad.................145
254 Skillet Shrimp.......................................146
255 Thai Shrimp-Peanut Noodles 146
256 Shrimp Newburg..................................146
257 Celebration Clams and Linguine............147
258 Red Clam Sauce Over Vermicelli...........147
259 Shrimp Scampi 148
260 Florentine Shrimp and Pasta 148

Chapter 7 Casseroles.................................149

261 Carbonara Skillet Pie............................150
262 Sensational Spaghetti 150
263 Quick Chili Dog Supper........................151
264 Chicken Tetrazzini 151
265 Garden Chicken...................................152
266 Creamy Chicken Enchiladas.................152
267 Discover Green Enchiladas 153
268 Quick Chicken Divan............................153
269 Confetti Orzo 154
270 Chicken Taco Casserole.......................154
271 Divine Chicken Casserole.....................155
272 Speedy Chicken Pie.............................155
273 Chicken Pot Pie 156
274 Gourmet Couscous Salad.....................156
275 Turkey-Stuffed Peppers 157
276 Beefy Mushroom Ravioli.......................157
277 Cornbread-Beef Bake 158
278 Tasty Taco Squares.............................158
279 Italian Chicken and Rice.......................159
280 Dijon Skillet Chicken............................159
281 Spinach Enchiladas..............................160
282 Spicy Vegetable Couscous 161
283 Spinach-Cheese Manicotti....................162
284 Pasta Frittata 162

Recipe No.		Page
285	Quick Chicken Casserole	163
286	Creamy, Cheesy Chicken	163
287	Award-Winning Casserole	164
288	Broccoli Chicken	164
289	Bob's Chicken Bake	165
290	Chicken-Noodle Delight	165
291	Chicken and Dumplings Casserole	166
292	Chicken-Broccoli Deluxe	166
293	Chili Casserole	167
294	Reuben Casserole	167
295	Taco Pie	168
296	Family-Favorite Casserole	169
297	Tator Tot Dinner	169
298	Enchilada Lasagna	170
299	Barbecued Beef Casserole	170
300	Potato-Beef Casserole	171
301	Beef and Broccoli Bake	171
302	Pinto Bean Pie	172
303	Hamburger Heaven	172
304	Cabbage Casserole	173
305	Meatballs and Orzo Casserole	173
306	Pizza Topping Pie	174
307	Penne Pizzazz	174
308	Hot Cheese Squares	175
309	Bacon-Potato Casserole	175
310	Spinach Casserole	176
311	Serious Squash Casserole	176
312	Awesome Butternut Casserole	177
313	Early-Morning Vegetable Lasagna	177
314	Vegetarian Pasta Bake	178
315	Green Bean Casserole	178
316	Zucchini Bake	179
317	Vegetable Frittata	179
Chapter 8 Slow Cooker Favorites		**180**
318	Oregano Chicken	181
319	Sweet-and-Spicy Chicken	181
320	Easy Chunky Chili	182

Recipe No.		Page
321	Chicken Delicious	183
322	Slow Cooker Cordon Bleu	183
323	Chicken 'n' Stuffing Supper	184
324	Chicken Marseilles	184
325	Chicken Breast Deluxe	185
326	Southwestern Chicken Pot	185
327	Honey-Baked Chicken	186
328	White Wine Chicken	186
329	Lemon Chicken	187
330	Alfredo's Chicken	187
331	Imperial Chicken	188
332	Chicken Fajitas	188
333	Arroz Con Pollo	189
334	Chicken Coq au Vin	189
335	Maple-Plum Glazed Turkey Breast	190
336	Turkey Bake	190
337	Turkey Cassoulet	191
338	Sausage and Rice	191
339	Turkey Loaf	192
340	Mac 'n' Cheese Supper	192
341	Enchilada Soup	193
342	Mushroom Meat and Potatoes	193
343	Cheeseburger Supper	194
344	Debra's Favorite Meat Loaf	194
345	Southwest Spaghetti	195
346	Big-Batch Sloppy Joes	195
347	Sweet-and-Sour Slow-Cooker Meatballs	196
348	Beef Tips Over Pasta	196
349	Pot Roast with Veggies	197
350	Sweet-and-Sour Beef	197
351	Savory Steak	198
352	Mushroom Round Steak	198
353	Beefy Onion Supper	199
354	Classic Slow-Cooker Stroganoff	199
355	Swiss Steak	200
356	Spicy Swiss Steak	200
357	Beef Roulades	201

Recipe No. ... Page

358 Herb-Crusted Beef Roast ... 201
359 Old-Time Pot Roast ... 202
360 Smoked Brisket ... 202
361 Shredded Brisket Sandwiches ... 203
362 Beef Ribs and Gravy ... 203
363 Terrific Pork Tenderloin ... 204
364 Spinach-Stuffed Pork Roast ... 204
365 Roasted Red Pepper Tenderloin ... 205
366 Western Pork Supper ... 205
367 Tender Pork Loin ... 206
368 Good-Time Chops, Tators, and Peas ... 206
369 Ranch Pork Chops ... 207
370 Pork Chops and Gravy ... 207
371 Honey-Mustard Pork Chops ... 208
372 Easy Slow Cooker Pork Chops ... 208
373 Country Pork Chops ... 209
374 Deconstructed Pork Chop Pizza ... 209
375 Cranberry-Glazed Pork ... 210
376 Barbecue Pork Roast ... 210
377 Pork and Cabbage Supper ... 211
378 Home-Style Ribs ... 211
379 Mushroom Ham and Rice ... 212
380 Black Bean Soup ... 212
381 Corn-Ham Chowder ... 213
382 Sauerkraut and Bratwurst Supper ... 213
383 Sausage and Beans ... 214
384 Spicy Sausage Soup ... 214
385 Sweet-and-Sour Sausage Links ... 214
386 Navy Bean Soup ... 215
387 Tasty Tuna Bake ... 215
388 Vegetarian Chili ... 216
389 Cheese-Spaghetti and Spinach ... 216
390 Vegetarian Coconut Curry ... 217
391 Harvest Vegetable Casserole ... 217

Chapter 9 Meals in Minutes ... 218

392 Parmesan and Wine Chicken ... 219
393 Chicken Casserole ... 219

Recipe No. ... Page

394 Rush Hour Rice and Chicken ... 220
395 Chicken Couscous ... 220
396 Quick Enchiladas ... 221
397 Chicken Quesadillas ... 221
398 Sweet and Sour Meatballs ... 222
399 Beef Corn Pie ... 222
400 Lightning Meatloaf ... 223
401 Microwaved Rump Roast ... 223
402 Debra's Speedy Swiss Steak ... 224
403 Stuffed Pork Chops ... 224
404 Quick Spare Ribs ... 225
405 Cornbread Casserole ... 225
406 So-Easy Shrimp ... 226
407 Creamed Shrimp over Rice ... 226
408 Vegetarian Tacos ... 227
409 Sweet Potatoes with Black Beans ... 227
410 Broccoli Casserole ... 228
411 Rice and More ... 228
412 Mushroom Burgers ... 229
413 Speedy Zucchini and Fettuccini ... 229

Chapter 10 Microwave Meals ... 230

414 Creamy Microwave Macaroni and Cheese ... 231
415 Microwave Chicken and Yellow Rice ... 232
416 Microwave Pesto Rosé Penne ... 233
417 Microwave Shrimp Divine ... 233
418 Microwave Lemon Butter Salmon ... 234
419 Microwave Thai Shrimp Noodles ... 234
Measurement Equivalents ... 235
Common Substitutions ... 237

Introduction

For years, the two of us have swapped kitchen tricks across studio counters and test kitchens—Debra with her love of delicious, no-fuss cooking, and Bruce with his endless "Who Knew?" shortcuts that make life a little easier. When we joined forces to write *Who Knew? Gathered at the Table*, we realized something wonderful: the meals we rely on with our own families aren't the fancy ones.

They're the ones that get dinner on the table quickly, taste incredible, stretch a tight grocery budget, and turn whatever's already in our pantries into something comforting. So we built this collection to share our favorite secrets with you. Learn how to make smart swaps, how to turn sales and staples into satisfying meals, and how to cook like you knew the answer before anyone in your house could ask, "What's for dinner?"

We wanted this book to feel like a friendly, go-to companion, showing you how to shave minutes off prep, bring flavors to life, and keep dinner joyful instead of stressful. Inside, you'll find meals that practically cook themselves—big weekend soups that carry you through the week, slow-cooker dishes that welcome you home, casseroles that freeze beautifully, and make-ahead favorites perfect for busy nights. There are more than 400 recipes to choose from, and more than 200 signature "Who Knew?" shortcuts (like that holding a stainless-steel spoon as you run your hands under cold water will remove that garlic smell), and what we call "light switch" swaps for when you'd rather have healthier sauces and dressings.

Our hope is that *Who Knew? Gathered at the Table* becomes your dinnertime favorite—one that helps you get to the table faster, eat great food with your loved ones, and enjoy the kind of simple, reliable cooking that makes every day feel a little easier.

CHAPTER 1

Soups, Sandwiches, and Stews

1 Monster Sandwich

This sandwich comes by its name honestly. It's big and will quickly become a family favorite.

½ cup mayonnaise
1 tablespoon horseradish (or regular) mustard
¼ teaspoon garlic salt
1/8 teaspoon black pepper
2 hero buns
1½ pounds roast beef, thinly sliced
3 cups chopped lettuce
1 large red onion, thinly sliced
6–10 ounces provolone cheese, sliced
⅓ cup black olives, chopped

1. Combine mayonnaise, mustard, garlic salt, and black pepper. Cover and set aside for at least 15 minutes.
2. Cut bread in half length-wise and spread mayonnaise mixture on all slices.
3. On bottom slices, layer roast beef, lettuce, onion, provolone cheese, chopped olives, and top slices.
4. Cut each hero in half to make two sandwiches each.

{SERVES 4}

2 Hot Roast Beef Sandwiches

With a little help from your microwave, you can turn a lunch sandwich into a dinner one. Add pickled jalapeño slices for a spicy kick!

1 (12 ounce) loaf French bread
¼ cup creamy dijon-style mustard
¾ pound sliced deli roast beef
8 slices American cheese

1. Split French bread in half and into 4 sandwich rolls.
   Toast slices until just starting to turn brown.
2. On piece of waxed or parchment paper, place onefourth of beef and microwave on HIGH for 1 minute.
   Add one-fourth cheese slices and microwave on HIGH until cheese is melted, about 10–15 seconds. Repeat for three additional sandwiches.
3. Spread mustard on bread slices and construct sandwiches by placing the beef and cheese inside and spread mustard on bottom slice. Line slices of beef over mustard, then add cheese slices over beef.

{SERVES 4}

Who Knew?

If someone accidentally turns on the microwave when it's empty, it can be damaging to the oven. To avoid any problems, just keep a cup of water in the microwave when it is not in use.

3 Reuben Sandwiches

Sometimes, eating dinner at the table isn't always an option when you're in a hurry. These easy sandwiches are our go-to meal for eating on-the-go!

Mayonnaise or mustard (optional)
12 slices dark rye bread
12 slices Swiss cheese
½ pound corned beef, thinly sliced
4 cups sauerkraut, drained

1. Spread mayonnaise or mustard on the bread slices, if desired.
2. On 6 slices of bread, layer 2 slices of cheese, 3–4 slices of corned beef, and lots of coleslaw. Top with remaining bread slices.

{SERVES 6}

4 Seafood Wraps

2 large (9 inch) spinach wraps or tortillas
½ cup mayonnaise
1 (9 ounce) spring salad mix
1 cup finely chopped tomatoes (about 2 medium)
1 bunch scallions, finely chopped
2 (4 ounce) packages albacore tuna steak with lemon and cracked pepper

1. Microwave wraps on HIGH, one at a time, for 10 seconds to soften.
2. Spread thin layer of mayonnaise (about 1 tablespoon) over 1 side of each tortilla.
3. Combine salad mix, tomatoes and scallions in bowl and sprinkle on tortillas.
4. Prepare tuna according to package directions, then crumble and spread evenly over tortillas.
5. Roll or fold over to eat.

{SERVES 4}

5 Garden Sandwich Wraps

4 large (12 inch) spinach wraps or tortillas
¼ cup scallion cream cheese
1 (9 ounce) package salad mix
1 cup finely chopped tomatoes (about 2 medium)
8 thin slices deli turkey or ham (about ¼ pound)

1. Microwave wraps on HIGH, one at a time, for 10 seconds to soften.
2. Spread thin layer of cream cheese (about 1 tablespoon) over 1 side of each tortilla.
3. Spread salad mix and tomatoes over cream cheese. Place 2 slices of turkey or ham on top.
4. Roll or fold over.

{SERVES 4}

6 Easy Gazpacho

Probably the most popular of chilled soups, gazpacho is served in many fine restaurants. Here's an easy, make-at-home version.

2 (28 ounce) cans diced tomatoes
1 seedless cucumber, diced
1 cup chopped red onion
1 cup chopped celery
2 Serrano chili peppers, seeded, coarsely chopped
1 lemon, sliced

1. Work in batches to combine all ingredients plus a little salt and pepper in food processor and pulse until mixture is thick.
2. Garnish with several lemon slices, if desired.

{SERVES 8}

7 Cucumber-Lover's Soup

3 medium cucumbers, peeled and diced
1 (14 ounce) can chicken broth, divided
Dash salt
1 (8 ounce) carton sour cream
3 tablespoons fresh chives, minced
2 teaspoons fresh dill, minced

1. Combine cucumbers, 1 cup of chicken broth, and salt in blender. Cover and process until smooth. Transfer to medium bowl and stir in remaining chicken broth.
2. Whisk in sour cream, chives and dill. Cover and refrigerate before serving. Garnish with dill..

{SERVES 6}

Who Knew? Light Switch

To make this recipe lower in fat, substitute 1¼ cups of our Healthy Chicken Broth for the can of broth and use reduced-fat sour cream.

8 Chilled Party Soup

Though this alcohol-laden recipe isn't family-friendly, it's always a hit at dinner parties! Fresh mint as a garnish is always a nice touch.

3 cups chilled, cubed fresh cantaloupe, divided

3 cups chilled, cubed fresh honeydew melon

2 cups chilled, fresh orange juice

2 cups chilled white wine or champagne

¼ cup chilled lime juice

3 tablespoons honey

1. Puree 2 cups of cantaloupe in food processor or blender and pour into large bowl.
2. Puree honeydew melon and combine with pureed cantaloupe, orange juice, white wine, and lime juice.
3. Pour in honey and mix well. Chop remaining cantaloupe and add to bowl. Serve immediately.

{SERVES 8}

Who Knew?

When selecting limes or lemons at the market, go for the biggest you can find. They tend to be sweeter than their smaller counterparts.

9 Fresh Avocado Soup

3 ripe avocados

4 tablespoons fresh lemon juice

1 (10 ounce) can chicken broth

1 (8 ounce) carton plain yogurt
Chopped chives for garnish
Dash salt and black pepper

1. Peel avocados, remove pits, and add to blender with lemon juice and chicken broth.
2. Process until smooth.
3. Add salt and pepper and refrigerate for several hours. Serve in soup bowls with chopped chives on top.

{SERVES 4-5}

Who Knew? Light Switch

To make this recipe even healthier, substitute 1¼ cups of our Healthy Chicken Broth for the can of broth.

10 Vichyssoise

"Vichyssoise" is a fancy way of saying "potato soup." It's usually served cold, but you can also heat it back up in the microwave.

¼ cup (½ stick) butter
1 onion, chopped
3 medium potatoes, peeled, sliced
1 (14 ounce) can chicken broth
2 cups 2% milk
½ teaspoon black pepper
¼ teaspoon salt

1. Pierce potatoes in several places with fork.
   Microwave on HIGH for 5 minutes per side, turning, until potatoes are tender all the way through. Once cool, peel off skins.
2. Put butter and onion in large casserole dish and microwave, covered, on HIGH for about 3 minutes, until onions are tender.
3. Place 1 potato, along with one-third of the onion mixture and one-third of the chicken broth, in blender.
4. Process until smooth and return to casserole dish. Repeat with remaining potatoes, onion mixture, and chicken broth.
5. Stirring constantly, add milk, pepper, and salt. Cover and refrigerate before serving.

{SERVES 6}

Who Knew? Light Switch

To lower the fat content of this recipe, use 1% or skim milk and substitute 1¼ cups of our Healthy Chicken Broth for the can of broth.

11 Cheesy Chicken Soup

There isn't a kid alive who doesn't love this simple soup!

1 (10 ounce) can fiesta nacho cheese soup
1 (10 ounce) can cream of chicken soup
1 (10 ounce) soup can milk
¾ pound chopped rotisserie chicken breast

1. Mix all ingredients in microwave-safe container.
   Microwave covered on HIGH until heated through, about 10 minutes, stirring every 2 minutes. Make sure mixture does not boil.

{SERVES 4-6}

Who Knew? Light Switch

To make this recipe lower in fat, use skim milk and substitute 1¼ cups of our Low-Fat Cream of Chicken Soup Base for the can of cream of chicken soup.

12 Spinach Soup

2 (10 ounce) packages frozen chopped spinach, cooked

2 (10 ounce) cans cream of mushroom soup

1 cup half-and-half

2 (14 ounce) cans chicken broth

1. Puree spinach, mushroom soup, and half-and-half in blender in batches.
2. Place spinach mixture and chicken broth in microwave-safe container and heat, covered, on

   MEDIUM for 6 minutes, turning halfway through if your microwave doesn't have a turntable.
3. Stir, then microwave on HIGH for 30-second increments until heated through. Do not allow to boil.

{SERVES 6}

Who Knew? Light Switch

To make this recipe low-fat, substitute 2½ cups of our Low-Fat Cream of Mushroom Soup Base for the cans of soup and 2½ cups of our Healthy Chicken Broth for the cans of broth. You can also substitute 1% or skim milk for the half-and-half.

13 Tomato-Basil Soup

Adding basil and onions to this recipe turns an ordinary can of tomato soup into a fresh-tasting palate-pleaser.

2 (10 ounce) cans tomato soup

1 (15 ounce) can diced tomatoes, or 2 fresh tomatoes, chopped

2 teaspoons finely minced onion

2 tablespoons chopped fresh basil

¼ teaspoon black pepper

¼ teaspoon salt

¼ cup cream

1. Combine all ingredients in a microwave-safe container.
2. Microwave on HIGH for 3 minutes, turning halfway through if your microwave doesn't have a turntable.
3. Stir, then microwave on HIGH in 1-minute increments until hot.

{SERVES 4}

14 Tomato-Bacon Soup

Here's another easy way to add a kick to canned tomato soup.

1 (10 ounce) can tomato soup

1 (14 ounce) can stewed tomatoes with celery and peppers

3 slices bacon, cooked and crumbled

1. Combine soup and stewed tomatoes in large casserole dish. Microwave covered on HIGH until heated through, about 8 minutes, stirring every 2 minutes.
2. Pour into soup bowls, sprinkle bacon on top and serve.

{SERVES 4}

15 Spicy Tomato Soup

2 (10 ounce) cans tomato soup

1 (15 ounce) can Mexican stewed tomatoes

1 (4 ounce) can chopped green chilies

1 (10 ounce) can French onion soup

3 slices bacon, cooked, drained, crumbled

1. Combine all ingredients, except bacon, in microwavesafe container.
2. Microwave on HIGH for 3 minutes, turning halfway through if your microwave doesn't have a turntable.
3. Stir, then microwave on HIGH in 1-minute increments until hot.
4. To serve, spoon into bowls and sprinkle crumbled bacon on top.

{SERVES 6}

16 Quick Borscht

1 (15 ounce) jar whole red beets

1 (14 ounce) can beef broth

4 tablespoons sour cream

1. Drain beets and save liquid. Chop beets and combine with beet liquid and broth in microwave-safe container.
2. Heat on HIGH, covered, 6–8 minutes, or until heated through.
3. Refrigerate and serve with dollop of sour cream.

{SERVES 4}

Who Knew? Light Switch

To make this recipe low fat, use reduced-fat beef broth and substitute plain yogurt for the sour cream.

17 Calzones

These calzones can be made with your favorite pizza ingredients. This recipe uses turkey sausage, but try it out with pepperoni, chicken and roasted red peppers, or anything else you can find in your fridge!

½ pound bulk turkey sausage
⅔ cup pizza sauce
1 (10 ounce) package refrigerated pizza dough
½ cup shredded mozzarella cheese

1. Preheat oven to 400°.
2. Brown sausage in skillet, stirring to break up pieces of meat. Drain fat, add pizza sauce, and heat until bubbly.
3. Unroll pizza dough, place on floured surface, and pat into 8 x 12-inch rectangle. Cut into 6 squares.
4. Divide sausage mixture evenly among squares and sprinkle with cheese. Lift one corner of each square and fold over filling to make triangle.
5. Press edges together with tines of fork to seal. Bake for about 12 minutes or until light golden brown. Serve immediately.

{SERVES 6}

18 Turkey Burgers

Using salsa in these turkey burgers not only adds taste, but keeps them moist while they cook. We think this recipe works best with hot chipotle salsa, but feel free to use whichever flavor is your favorite.

2 pounds ground turkey
1 1 (16 ounce) jar salsa, divided
8 slices Monterey Jack or Cheddar cheese
Sesame seed hamburger buns

1. Combine ground turkey with 1 cup salsa in large bowl. Mix well and shape into 8 patties.
2. Place patties on broiler pan and broil for 12–15 minutes. Turn once during cooking. Top each patty with cheese slice and grill just long enough to melt cheese.
3. Place burgers on buns, spoon heaping tablespoon of salsa over cheese and top with remaining half of bun.

{SERVES 8}

Who Knew?

The secret to juicy burgers is simple. Just let them sit, covered, at room temperature for an hour before you cook them. This is safe to do as long as it isn't too hot (over 80°) where they will be resting.

19 Southwestern Burgers

These burgers are perfect for impressing guests at a barbecue. But if you're making them for a quick dinner instead, we've also included broiling instructions below.

8 kaiser buns

2 pounds lean ground beef

1 (1 ounce) packet taco seasoning mix

1 cup salsa, divided

8 slices hot pepper jack cheese

1. Combine beef, taco seasoning, and ¼ cup salsa in large bowl. Shape mixture into 8 patties.
2. To grill, cook patties for about 6 minutes on each side, or until they reach your desired level of doneness.

   To broil in oven, place patties on broiler pan 4 to 5 inches from heat and broil until they cook thoroughly.

   Turn once during cooking.
3. When patties are almost done, place buns cut-side down on grill and heat for 1 or 2 minutes.
4. Place 8 patties on bottom half of buns, top with cheese, and cook for an additional 1 minute or until cheese melts.
5. Top with heaping tablespoon of salsa and top half of bun.

{SERVES 8}

Who Knew?

Trying to get more calcium in your kids' diets? Add a tablespoon or two of powdered milk to the ground beef. They'll never notice the difference, but their bones will.

20 Provolone-Pepper Burgers

¼ cup finely chopped red bell pepper

¼ cup finely chopped onion

½ teaspoon olive oil

¼ teaspoon salt

⅛ teaspoon black pepper

1 pound lean ground beef

2 tomatoes, sliced

4 slices provolone cheese

4 hamburger buns, split

1. Cook bell pepper and onion in olive oil in skillet over medium-high heat until tender.
2. Combine bell pepper, onion, salt, and pepper in bowl.

   Add beef, mix well, and shape into 4 patties.
3. Grill patties over medium-high heat for 5 minutes on each side or until meat is no longer pink.
4. Add cheese and tomatoes and serve on hamburger buns.

{SERVES 4}

Who Knew?

To keep grease from sticking to your fingers when you form the hamburger patties, wet your hands with cold water first.

21 Potato-Sausage Soup

1 pound pork sausage link
1 cup chopped celery
1 cup chopped onion
2 (10 ounce) cans potato soup
¾ cup water
1 (14 ounce) can chicken broth

1. Cut sausage into 1-inch thick diagonal slices. Brown sausage in large heavy soup pot, drain, and place in separate bowl. Leave about 2 tablespoons sausage drippings in skillet and use to sauté celery and onion.
2. Add potato soup, water, chicken broth, and sausage. Boil, reduce heat, and simmer for 20 minutes.

{SERVES 4}

22 Polish Vegetable Stew

We're not sure if this is a traditional Polish recipe, but it's a favorite of our Polish friend Barbara.

1 tablespoon vegetable or canola oil
1 onion, sliced
1 carrot, sliced
2 (15 ounce) cans stewed tomatoes
1 pound kielbasa (Polish sausage), cut into 1-inch slices
1 pound new potatoes, quartered
1 (9 ounce) package coleslaw mix

1. Pour oil into large soup pot. Cook onion and carrot until carrot is tender-crisp.
2. Add tomatoes, sausage, and potatoes. Bring to a boil, reduce heat and simmer for 10 minutes.
3. Stir in coleslaw mix, and cook for additional 8 minutes, stirring occasionally.

{SERVES 6}

Who Knew?

Keep a rubber band wrapped tightly around the top of the handle of all your wooden mixing spoons. Why? Because they keep the spoons from falling into whatever you're stirring. Wrap some rubber bands around your spoons and you can safely rest the spoon on the side of the bowl without it slipping.

23 Italian Garbanzo Bean Soup

1 (16 ounce) package frozen, diced onions and bell peppers

1 tablespoon olive oil

1 pound Italian sausages, sliced

1 (14 ounce) can beef broth

1 (15 ounce) can Italian stewed tomatoes

1 (15 ounce) cans garbanzo beans (chickpeas), rinsed, drained

2 (9 ounce) package coleslaw mix

1. Sauté onions and bell peppers in soup pot with oil over medium until tender-crisp, about 5 minutes. Add Italian sausage and cook until brown.
2. Stir in beef broth, stewed tomatoes, and garbanzo beans. Bring mixture to a boil, reduce heat, and simmer for 20 minutes.

{SERVES 6}

Who Knew?

Enjoy basil or other herbs from your garden all-year-round with this tip: Just chop clean basil leaves, pat dry, and freeze in ice cube trays with enough water to cover the leaves. Then pop into dishes like this one for a fresh, summer taste.

24 Pizza Sandwich

This fun dinner treat also works great as an after-school snack! We suggest using sausage and mushrooms, but you can use your family's favorite pizza toppings.

6 English muffins

1 pound bulk sausage, cooked, drained

1½ cups pizza sauce

1 (4 ounce) can mushrooms, drained

1 (8 ounce) package shredded mozzarella cheese

1. Split muffins and layer ingredients on each muffin half ending with cheese.
2. Place under broiler until cheese melts.

{SERVES 6}

25 Crab-Corn Chowder

1 (2 ounce) packet dry leek soup mix

2 cups milk

1 (8 ounce) can whole kernel corn, drained

½ of 1 (8 ounce) package Velveeta cheese, cubed

1 (7 ounce) can crabmeat, flaked

1. Combine soup mix and milk in large saucepan, cook over medium heat and stir constantly until soup begins to thicken. While still on medium heat, stir in corn and cheese and stir until cheese melts.
2. Just before serving, add crabmeat and stir until heated through.

{SERVES 6}

Who Knew? Light Switch

To make this recipe lower in fat, substitute ¾ cup of our Melty Cheese Sauce for the Velveeta cheese.

26 Carolina She-Crab Soup

We find this recipe tastes best with fresh crabmeat, but it also works with the canned variety.

4 cups milk

¼ teaspoon mace or nutmeg

1 teaspoon grated lemon peel

1 pound fresh crabmeat, flaked

1 (1 pint) carton whipping cream

¼ cup (½ stick) butter

½ cup cracker crumbs
Salt and pepper to taste

2 tablespoons sherry

1. Pour milk, mace, and lemon peel into double boiler and simmer for 5 minutes. Add crabmeat, cream, and butter, and cook over low heat for 15 minutes.
2. Stir in cracker crumbs a little at a time, and season soup with salt and pepper to taste. Cover, remove from heat, and set aside for 5–10 minutes to allow flavors to blend. Add sherry before serving.

{SERVES 6-8}

27 Rich Cheddar Chowder

- 2 (14 ounce) cans chicken broth
- 4 baking potatoes, peeled, diced
- 1 onion, chopped
- 1 cup shredded carrots
- 2 bell peppers (any color), seeded, chopped
- ¼ cup (½ stick) butter
- ¼ cup flour
- 1 (1 pint) carton half-and-half
- 1½ cups milk
- 1 (16 ounce) package shredded sharp Cheddar cheese
- ⅛-¼ teaspoon hot sauce

1. Combine broth, potatoes, onion, carrots, and bell peppers in large soup pot. Bring to a boil, reduce heat, and simmer for 15 minutes.
2. Melt butter in large saucepan, add flour, and stir until smooth. Cook for 1 minute, stirring constantly. Gradually add half-and-half and milk; cook over medium heat and stir constantly until mixture thickens.
3. Add cheese and hot sauce to vegetable mixture and cook just until heated through; do not boil.

{SERVES 6-8}

Who Knew?

It's hard to keep potatoes from slipping out of your hands as you peel them. Screw a corkscrew partway in to keep a raw potato steady—place one hand on the corkscrew handle, one on the peeler.

28 Beer Cheese Soup

- ¼ cup (½ stick) butter
- ¼ cup flour
- 1 (1 pint) carton half-and-half
- 1 (12 ounce) can beer (not light)
- 1 (16 ounce) package Velveeta cheese, cubed
- ¼ teaspoon cayenne pepper
- 2 teaspoons white wine (or regular) Worcestershire sauce
- ¼ teaspoon salt
- Dash hot sauce

1. Melt butter in large soup pot and add flour, stir until smooth, and cook for 1 additional minute. Gradually add half-and-half and beer and cook over medium heat, stirring constantly, until thick.
2. Add cheese and stir until cheese melts. Stir in cayenne pepper,Worcestershire sauce, salt, and hot sauce. Heat, while stirring, until ready to serve.
3. Ladle soup in bowls and serve with crusty bread.

{SERVES 6}

29 Fiesta Tortilla Soup Con Queso

3 (14 ounce) cans chicken broth
2 (15 ounce) cans stewed tomatoes
4 scallions with tops, chopped
1 (7 ounce) can diced green chilies
1 clove garlic, minced
8 corn tortillas
2 tablespoons vegetable or oil
1 (16 ounce) package Mexican Mild–flavor Velveeta cheese, cubed

1. Cut tortillas into long, narrow strips. Fry tortilla strips in hot oil in skillet until strips are crisp, about 10 seconds apiece. Remove from skillet and drain on paper towels.
2. Pour chicken broth, tomatoes, onions, green chilies, and garlic into large saucepan and cook over medium heat.
3. Heat soup to boiling, then reduce heat to low and stir in cheese until it melts.
4. Serve in individual bowls and garnish with tortilla strips.

{SERVES 8}

30 Mexican-Style Minestrone Soup

3 (14 ounce) cans chicken broth
2 (15 ounce) cans stewed tomatoes
4 scallions with tops, chopped
1 (7 ounce) can diced green chilies
1 clove garlic, minced
8 corn tortillas
2 tablespoons vegetable or oil
1 (16 ounce) package Mexican Mild–flavor Velveeta cheese, cubed

1. Cook pasta according to package directions; drain.
2. Combine pasta, vegetables, salsa, beans, chili powder, cumin, and water in large saucepan.
3. Boil, then reduce heat. Simmer for 8–10 minutes, stirring occasionally.
4. When ready to serve, top each serving with Mexican cheese.

{SERVES 6-8}

Who Knew? Light Switch

To make this recipe low-fat, substitute 2 cups of our Super Healthy Salsa for the jar of salsa and 2 cups of our Low-Fat Four-Cheese Blend for the package of cheese.

31 Cream of Artichoke Soup

- **2 shallots, finely chopped**
- **2 tablespoons butter**
- **2 tablespoons flour**
- **1 (14 ounce) can chicken broth**
- **1 ¼ cups artichoke hearts, rinsed, drained, chopped**
- **3 tablespoons fresh minced parsley, divided**
- **1 ¼ cups half-and-half**

1. Sauté shallots in saucepan with butter until they are translucent. Add flour, stir to remove lumps, and remove from heat.
2. Stir in chicken broth, artichoke hearts, and 2 tablespoons parsley. Return to medium heat and cook for 5 minutes.
3. Puree mixture with blender. Strain pureed mixture through coarse sieve and return to clean saucepan.
4. Heat on medium, slowly add half-and-half, and mix thoroughly.
5. Serve hot or cold. Garnish with remaining parsley.

{SERVES 4}

Who Knew?

Don't throw away fresh herbs if you've got more on hand than you need. Just rinse the leaves, air dry, and place (on a single layer) on a plate with a paper towel. Then microwave them in 30-second intervals until they're crunchy (which can take up to 4 minutes). If you store them in an airtight container, they'll last for a year!

32 Zesty Black Bean Soup

- **2 onions, finely chopped**
- **1 tablespoon olive oil**
- **3 teaspoons minced garlic**
- **1 tablespoon chili powder**
- **3 (15 ounce) cans black beans, divided**
- **1 teaspoon ground cumin**
- **1 (14 ounce) can beef broth**
- **1 (16 ounce) package Mexican Mild–flavor Velveeta cheese, cubed**

1. Sauté onions in soup pot with oil over medium heat for 5 minutes. Stir in garlic and chili powder.
2. Puree 1 can beans and add to onion mixture.
   Add remaining beans, cumin, and beef broth.
3. Boil, reduce heat, and simmer for 10 minutes.
   If you like, garnish with shredded cheese or salsa just before serving.

{SERVES 6}

33 Cream of Cauliflower Soup

Even if your family doesn't usually love the taste of cauliflower, they'll love the rich, creamy taste of them in this soup. The smell of garlic and onions cooking in the pan should be enough to get their mouths watering!

1 medium onion, chopped
¼ teaspoon minced garlic
½ tablespoon olive oil
2 (14 ounce) cans chicken broth
1 large cauliflower, cut into small florets
1¼ cups whipping cream Salt and pepper to taste

1. Sauté onion and garlic in oil over medium heat until translucent.
2. Stir in broth and boil over high heat. Reduce to medium heat and add cauliflower. Cook, stirring occasionally, until cauliflower is tender, about 15 minutes.
3. Process soup in batches in blender until smooth and return to pan.
4. Stir in cream and add salt and pepper to taste. Cook over low heat, stirring often, until heated through.

{SERVES 6}

Who Knew?

Add a small amount of lemon juice to the broth to keep the cauliflower whiter during cooking.

34 Welcome Home Soup

2 cups fresh broccoli florets
4-5 large new (red) potatoes, chopped
1 bunch scallions with tops, chopped
2 (14 ounce) cans chicken broth Salt and pepper to taste
Sour cream for garnish

1. Cook vegetables in chicken broth until tender.
   Add salt and pepper to taste.
2. Pour into blender and puree.
3. Pour into soup bowls and garnish with dollop of sour cream.

{SERVES 6-8}

35 Garlic-Potato Soup

4 cups milk

3 cups water

1 (7 ounce) package roasted-garlic instant mashed potatoes

1 (10 ounce) can cream of celery soup

1 (8 ounce) package shredded sharp Cheddar cheese, divided

1 (4 ounce) can chopped pimentos

½ teaspoon black pepper

1. Combine milk and water in soup pot and bring to a boil.
2. Remove from heat, add instant potato mix, and stir with whisk until mixed well. Stir in celery soup and mix well.
3. Stir in half Cheddar cheese, pimentos, and pepper, and stir until cheese melts.
4. Ladle into individual bowls and sprinkle remaining cheese on top of each serving.

{SERVES 6}

36 Cream of Zucchini Soup

1 pound fresh zucchini, grated

1 onion, chopped

1 (14 ounce) can chicken broth

½ teaspoon dried basil

¼ teaspoon salt

⅛ teaspoon black pepper

1 (1 pint) carton half-and-half, divided

1. Combine zucchini, onion, broth, basil, salt, and pepper in saucepan. Bring to a boil and simmer until vegetables are soft.
2. Transfer to food processor or blender and puree.
   Gradually add ½ cup half-and-half and blend.
3. Return zucchini mixture to saucepan and add remaining half-and-half. Heat through, but do not boil

{SERVES 4-6}

37 Quick-and-Easy Peanut Soup

This soup is a treat for any kid (or adult) who loves peanut butter!

¼ cup (½ stick) butter

1 medium onion, finely chopped

2 ribs celery, chopped

2 (10 ounce) cans cream of chicken soup

2 soup cans milk

1¼ cups crunchy peanut butter

1. Melt butter in saucepan and sauté onion and celery over low heat. Add soups and milk and stir until warm.
2. Add peanut butter, stirring constantly, and continue to heat until mixture blends well as is heated through.

{SERVES 4-6}

38 Homemade Tomato Soup

This comfort-food classic tastes great with a little bacon sprinkled on top. (But then again, so does everything!)

- **3 (15 ounce) cans whole tomatoes with liquid**
- **1 (14 ounce) can chicken broth**
- **1 tablespoon sugar**
- **1 tablespoon minced garlic**
- **1 tablespoon balsamic vinegar**
- **¼ teaspoon salt**
- **¾ cup cream, half-and-half, or milk (optional)**

1. Puree tomatoes with hand blender, or in batches with blender. Pour into large saucepan.
2. Add chicken broth, sugar, garlic, balsamic vinegar, and salt. Bring to a boil, reduce heat, and simmer for 15 minutes.
3. If creamier soup is desired, pour in cream and heat until soup is heated through, stirring constantly .

{SERVES 4}

39 Tomato-Ravioli Soup

Convenience foods don't always have to be prepared according to the directions on the package. This recipe takes run-of-the-mill frozen ravioli and turns them into a sophisticated soup.

- **1 (15 ounce) can stewed tomatoes**
- **2 (14 ounce) cans chicken broth**
- **2 small zucchini, sliced**
- **1 teaspoon black pepper**
- **1 teaspoon dried Italian seasoning**
- **¼ teaspoon salt**
- **1 cup cream, half-and-half, or milk (optional)**
- **4 fresh scallions, sliced**

1. Combine tomatoes, chicken broth, pepper, and Italian seasoning in large saucepan. Boil, reduce heat, and add zucchini. Simmer for 5 minutes.
2. Add ravioli and simmer until ravioli are tender, about 8–10 minutes.
3. Sprinkle scallions over each individual serving.

{SERVES 4}

Who Knew?

Place unripe tomatoes in a brown paper bag and leave them on your counter. They'll ripen in a day or two. If they're ripe already, store them in a cool place (around 55°) and they'll keep for five days. In order to keep its membranes intact, you should never refrigerate a tomato!

40 Chicken-Broccoli Chowder

Even kids love broccoli in this rich, thick soup.

- **2 (14 ounce) cans chicken broth**
- **1 bunch fresh scallions, finely chopped, divided**
- **1 (10 ounce) package frozen chopped broccoli**
- **1½ cups dry mashed potato flakes**
- **2½ cups chopped rotisserie chicken**
- **1 (8 ounce) package shredded mozzarella cheese**
- **1 (8 ounce) carton heavy cream**
- **1 cup milk**
- **1 cup water**
- **¼ teaspoon salt**
- **¼ teaspoon black pepper**

1. Combine broth, half scallions, and broccoli in large saucepan. Boil, reduce heat, cover, and simmer for 5 minutes.
2. Stir in dry potato flakes and mix until they blend well.
3. Add chicken, cream, milk, water, salt, and pepper.
   Heat over medium heat, stirring occasionally, until hot, about 5 minutes. Add cheese and stir until melted.
   (If freezing, freeze and thaw before adding cheese.)
4. Ladle into individual soup bowls and garnish with remaining chopped scallions.

{SERVES 8}

41 Chicken-Sausage Stew

- **1 (16 ounce) package frozen stew vegetables**
- **2 pounds rotisserie or deli chicken, cubed**
- **½ pound Italian sausage, sliced**
- **2 (15 ounce) cans Italian stewed tomatoes**
- **1 (14 ounce) can chicken broth**
- **¼ teaspoon cayenne pepper**
- **¼ teaspoon salt**
- **1 cup cooked rice**

1. Combine vegetables, chicken, sausage, tomatoes, broth, cayenne pepper, and salt in large heavy soup pot.
2. Bring to a boil, then reduce heat and simmer for 20 minutes.
3. Stir in cooked rice and simmer for additional 5 minutes.

{SERVES 8}

Who Knew?

To make this recipe lower in fat, substitute 1¾ cups of our Healthy Chicken Broth for the can of chicken broth.

42 Northern Chili

2 onions, coarsely chopped

1 tablespoon olive oil

3 (15 ounce) cans great Northern beans, drained

2 (14 ounce) cans chicken broth

2 tablespoons minced garlic

1 (7 ounce) can chopped green chilies

1 tablespoon ground cumin

3 cups cooked, finely chopped rotisserie chicken

1 (8 ounce) package shredded Monterey Jack cheese

1. Cook onions with oil in large saucepan or pot until tender, but not brown, about 5 minutes.
2. Place 1 can of beans in shallow bowl and mash with fork.
3. Combine mashed beans, 2 remaining cans of beans, chicken broth, garlic, green chilies, and cumin in saucepan. Bring to a boil, then reduce heat, cover, and simmer for 30 minutes.
4. Add chopped chicken, stir to blend well, and heat until chili is heated through.
5. When serving, top each bowl with 3 tablespoons cheese.

{SERVES 6}

Who Knew? Light Switch

To make this recipe lower in fat, substitute 2 cups of our Low-Fat Four-Cheese Blend for the package of Monterey Jack cheese.

43 Chicken Chili

This chili is delicious served with hot, buttered flour tortillas for dipping.

2 pounds boneless, skinless chicken breast halves, cubed

1 (16 ounce) package frozen, chopped onions and bell peppers

1 tablespoon olive oil

2 tablespoons minced garlic

2 tablespoons chili powder

1 tablespoon ground cumin

2 (14 ounce) cans chicken broth

¼ teaspoon salt

3 (15 ounce) cans pinto beans with jalapeños, divided

1. Cook chicken with oil in large soup pot over medium heat, stirring occasionally, for 5 minutes. Add onions and bell peppers and continue to cook until chicken is cooked through, about 5 minutes.
2. Add garlic, chili powder, cumin, broth, and salt. Stir to mix well. Bring to a boil over high heat, then reduce heat to low, cover, and simmer for 15 minutes.
3. Place 1 can beans in shallow bowl and mash with fork.
4. Add mashed beans and remaining 2 cans beans to pot. Bring to a boil, then reduce heat and simmer for 10 minutes.

{SERVES 8}

44 Hot Gobble-Gobble Soup

This turkey soup has a spicy kick to it—not too much, but just right! Use leftover turkey or ask at the deli counter for a large slab that isn't cut into slices.

6-8 cups cooked, chopped turkey
1 (48 ounce) carton + 1 (14 ounce) can chicken broth
4 (10 ounce) cans diced tomatoes with green chilies
2 (15 ounce) cans whole corn, drained
2 large onions, chopped
2 (10 ounce) cans tomato soup
1½ teaspoon garlic powder
1½ teaspoon dried oregano
¼ cup water

1. Combine all ingredients in large soup pot.
2. Bring to a boil, then reduce heat and simmer, stirring occasionally, for 2 hours.

{SERVES 12}

Who Knew? Light Switch

To make this recipe even healthier, substitute 2 quarts of our Healthy Chicken Broth for the carton and can of chicken broth.

45 Beefy Bean Chili

3 pounds ground beef
6 ribs celery, chopped
2 medium onions, chopped
2 bell peppers, seeded, chopped
1 tablespoon minced garlic
2 (15 ounce) cans tomato sauce
3 tablespoons chili powder
4 cups water
½ teaspoon black pepper
1 teaspoon salt
2 (15 ounce) cans pinto beans with liquid
2 (15 ounce) cans black beans with liquid
2-4 cups crushed tortilla chips

1. Cook ground beef in large soup pot over medium heat, stirring occasionally, until meat crumbles and is brown, about 12 minutes.
2. Add celery, onion, bell pepper, and minced garlic.
   Cook until vegetables are tender but not brown, about 8 minutes.
3. Stir in tomato sauce, chili powder, water, salt, and pepper and mix well. Bring mixture to a boil, then reduce heat to low and simmer for 20 minutes.
4. Add beans and simmer for additional 15 minutes.
5. Ladle into individual serving bowls and top each serving with several tablespoons crushed tortilla chips.

{SERVES 12}

46 Southwestern Soup

2 pounds lean ground beef

1 large onion, chopped

3 (15 ounce) cans pinto beans with liquid

2 (15 ounce) can ranch-style beans, drained

2 (15 ounce) cans whole kernel corn with liquid

1 (15 ounce) cans Mexican stewed tomatoes

1 cups water

3 (1 ounce) packets taco seasoning

1. Brown beef and onion in large soup pot, stirring until beef crumbles; drain. Add beans, corn, tomatoes, and water.
2. Bring to a boil, then reduce heat and stir in taco seasoning. Simmer for 25 minutes.

{SERVES 8}

47 Spaghetti Soup

If your family loves spaghetti, they'll love this soup version! To ensure that the noodles don't get too soft, freeze this soup as soon as it cools until you're ready to eat it.

2 quarts water

¼ teaspoon salt

1 (7 ounce) package spaghetti pasta

1 (18 ounce) package frozen, cooked meatballs, thawed

1 (28 ounce) jar spaghetti sauce

1 (15 ounce) can stewed tomatoes

1 cup grated Parmesan cheese

1. In large soup pot, boil water over high heat. Add salt and spaghetti. Reduce heat to medium and cook spaghetti for 6 minutes. Do not drain.
2. When spaghetti is done, add meatballs, spaghetti sauce, and stewed tomatoes and cook until mixture heats through.
3. Add grated Parmesan cheese to individual bowls for garnish.

{SERVES 8}

Who Knew? Light Switch

To make this recipe lower in fat, substitute our Low-Fat Meatballs for the package of frozen meatballs.

48 Chile Verde Con Carne

Chile con carne translates to "chili with meat," and verde refers to the fresh green chilies in this tasty dish.

- 2 quarts water
- ¼ teaspoon salt
- 1 (7 ounce) package spaghetti pasta
- 1 (18 ounce) package frozen, cooked meatballs, thawed
- 1 (28 ounce) jar spaghetti sauce
- 1 (15 ounce) can stewed tomatoes
- 1 cup grated Parmesan cheese

1. In large soup pot, boil water over high heat. Add salt and spaghetti. Reduce heat to medium and cook spaghetti for 6 minutes. Do not drain.
2. When spaghetti is done, add meatballs, spaghetti sauce, and stewed tomatoes and cook until mixture heats through.
3. Add grated Parmesan cheese to individual bowls for garnish.

{SERVES 12}

Who Knew?

To save time, 2 (7 ounce) cans of green chilies may be used instead of roasting fresh green chilies, but the flavor of fresh chilies is the secret to the best chili.

49 Green Chile Stew Pot (Caldillo)

This traditional Mexican dish is called *Caldillo* in Spanish, and is often served on special occasions.

- 4 pounds round steak, cubed
- 3 tablespoons salt, divided
- 2 tablespoons vegetable or canola oil
- 4 medium onions, chopped
- 4 potatoes, peeled, diced
- 4 cloves garlic, minced
- 12-16 fresh green chilies, roasted, peeled, seeded, diced
- 1 teaspoon black pepper Water

1. Sprinkle round steak with 2 tablespoons salt.
2. Heat oil in large skillet over medium-high heat and add meat when hot. Cook, stirring, until meat is brown on all sides, about 12–15 minutes. Add onions, potatoes, and garlic and cook until onions are translucent, about 5–8 minutes.
3. Pour all ingredients from skillet into large stew pot.

   Add chilies, remaining salt, pepper, and enough water to cover all ingredients.
4. Bring to a boil over high heat, then reduce heat to low and simmer until meat and potatoes are cooked through, about 1–2 hours.

{SERVES 12}

50 Stroganoff Stew

- **2 (1 ounce) packets onion soup mix**
- **4 (10 ounce) cans golden mushroom soup**
- **4 (10 ounce) soup canfuls water**
- **4 pounds stew meat**
- **2 (8 ounce) cartons sour cream**
- **6 cups egg noodles, cooked, drained**

1. Preheat oven to 275°.
2. Combine soup mix, mushroom soup, and water and pour over stew meat in roasting pan.
3. Cover tightly and bake for 6 hours.
4. When ready to serve, stir in sour cream, return mixture to oven until it heats through, and serve over noodles.

{SERVES 12}

Who Knew? Light Switch

To make this recipe lower in fat, substitute 2 cups of our Low-Fat Sour Cream Substitute for the cartons of sour cream, and the egg noodles for No Yolks egg noodle substitute.

51 Oven-Baked Beef Stew

- **2 tablespoons flour**
- **½ teaspoon salt**
- **¼ teaspoon black pepper**
- **1 ½ pounds beef chuck, cubed**
- **1 ½ cups chopped onion**
- **½ teaspoon basil**
- **4 potatoes, peeled, cubed**
- **4 carrots, peeled, sliced**
- **½ cup dry red wine**
- **2 (10 ounce) cans tomato soup**
- **2 ½ cups water**

1. Preheat oven to 325°.
2. Combine flour with salt and pepper and pat onto both sides of meat. In large, oven-safe skillet, cook meat on medium-high heat until browned on all sides, about 8–12 minutes. Drain.
3. Add all remaining ingredients; cover and bake for 1 hour.

{SERVES 8-12}

Who Knew? Light Switch

To make this recipe lower in fat, substitute 2 cups of our Low-Fat Sour Cream Substitute for the cartons of sour cream, and the egg noodles for No Yolks egg noodle substitute.

52 Ham Bone Soup

If you don't see them in the case, ask for ham hocks at the deli counter. They may need to fetch them from the back, but they're very inexpensive, and will add an amazing depth of flavor to this simple soup.

4 cups dried navy beans

3 quarts water

1 pound ham hocks
Salt and pepper to taste

1. Cover beans with water and soak overnight.
2. Drain, then place beans in large soup pot with water and ham hocks. Bring to a boil over high heat, then reduce heat to low and simmer until beans are tender, about 2–3 hours.
3. Season with salt and pepper to taste.

{SERVES 8}

Who Knew?

You can make dry beans less gassy by adding fennel seeds to the water while you're soaking them overnight. Use a teaspoon of fennel for every 2 cups of beans.

53 Split Pea Soup

This is a wonderful way to use up leftover ham. If you happen to have a meaty ham bone, you can use that along with, or instead of, the chopped ham.

2 (16 ounce) packages dried green split peas
Water

2 onions, chopped

2 large potatoes, peeled, diced

4 ribs celery, chopped

2 cups cooked, shredded or chopped ham

2 cups shredded carrots

2 teaspoons minced garlic

½ teaspoon salt

¼ teaspoon black pepper

1 (5½ ounce) package seasoned croutons

1. Rinse peas and place in large, heavy soup pot. Fill with water until water is covering the peas by 2 inches. Soak overnight.
2. Drain, then add onions, potatoes, celery, ham, carrots, garlic, salt, and pepper. Fill pot with water until covering all ingredients.
3. Bring to a boil over high heat, then reduce heat to low, cover, and simmer for 2 hours 30 minutes–3 hours, stirring occasionally.
4. Let cool slightly, then blend mixture in food processor or blender in batches.
5. When smooth, return mixture to soup pot, then cover and simmer until heated through, about 5 minutes.

   Garnish with croutons.

{SERVES 12}

54 Creamed Broccoli Soup

- 8 slices bacon
- 6 potatoes, peeled
- 2 small onions, minced
- 4 cups water
- 1½ teaspoon salt
- 2 (10 ounce) packages frozen, chopped broccoli
- ½ cup (1 stick) butter
- 6 tablespoons flour
- 2 (1 pint) cartons cream

1. Fry bacon in deep skillet, drain, and set aside.
2. Shred potatoes with cheese grater. With bacon drippings still in skillet, add potatoes, onion, water, and salt. Cover and cook for 10 minutes. Add broccoli and cook for additional 5 minutes.
3. In separate large saucepan, melt butter and add flour.
   Stir and cook until mixture bubbles.
4. Gradually add cream. Cook, stirring constantly, until it thickens.
5. Stir in potato-broccoli mixture and heat just until heated through.
6. Crumble bacon and sprinkle on top of each serving.

{SERVES 8}

Who Knew?

To easily store unused bacon in the freezer, roll each into a ball and keep in a resealable plastic bag. When you cook the bacon, simply heat it in a microwave for a few seconds, unroll it, and fry away!

55 Rich Corn Chowder

- 8 ears fresh corn
- 6 slices bacon
- 2 small onions, chopped
- 4 red bell pepper, seeded, chopped
- 1½ small baking potatoes, peeled, cubed
- 2 cups water
- ½ teaspoon salt
- 6 teaspoon black pepper
- 2 (1 pint) cartons cream, divided
- 1 tablespoon sugar
- ¾ teaspoon dried thyme
- 1½ tablespoons cornstarch

1. Cut corn from cobs into large bowl and scrape well to remove all milk.
2. Fry bacon in large soup pot over medium heat.
   Remove bacon and save drippings in pan. Crumble bacon and set aside.
3. Cook onion and bell pepper in bacon drippings over medium heat until tender, about 8–10 minutes. Drain.
4. Stir in corn, potatoes, water, salt, and pepper. Bring to a boil over high heat, then cover, reduce heat to low, and simmer for 15 minutes, stirring occasionally.
5. Stir in 3 cups cream, sugar, and thyme.
6. Combine cornstarch and remaining cream and stir until smooth. Gradually add to corn mixture, stirring constantly.
7. Cook on medium-low heat until soup thickens, stirring constantly, about 15 minutes.

{SERVES 12}

56 Cod and Corn Chowder

- 5 cups water
- 2 pounds cod, cut into bite-size pieces
- 4 large baking potatoes, thinly sliced
- 6 ribs celery, sliced
- 2 medium onions, chopped
- 2 (15 ounce) cans whole kernel corn
- ½ teaspoon salt
- ¼ teaspoon black pepper
- 2 (8 ounce) cartons whipping cream
- 12 slices bacon, cooked, crumbled

1. In large soup pot, combine water, cod, potatoes, celery, onion, corn, salt, and pepper. Stir to mix well.
2. Bring to a boil over high heat. Reduce heat to low, cover, and simmer until fish and potatoes are done, about 20 minutes.
3. Stir in cream and heat just until heated through.
4. When ready to serve, sprinkle crumbled bacon over each serving.

{SERVES 12}

57 Seafood Bisque

- 2 pounds new (red) potatoes, washed and chopped into bitesized pieces
- ½ cup (1 stick) butter
- 2 (8 ounce) packages frozen salad shrimp, thawed
- 4 (6 ounce) cans crab, drained, flaked
- 2 teaspoons minced garlic
- 1 cup flour
- 4 (14 ounce) cans chicken broth, divided
- 2 cups milk, cream, or half-and-half
- ½ teaspoon salt
- 1½ cups heavy cream

1. Cook potatoes in boiling water until cooked through, about 10 minutes. Drain.
2. Melt butter in large saucepan over medium heat.
   Add potatoes, shrimp, crab, and garlic and cook for 10 minutes.
3. Stir in flour and cook, stirring constantly, for 3 minutes.
4. Gradually add chicken broth. Cook and stir until mixture thickens.
5. Stir in cream, salt, and pepper, stirring constantly, and cook just until mixture is heated through; do not boil.

{SERVES 12}

58 Easy Oyster Stew

If you want a little snap to this stew, add a pinch or two of cayenne pepper.

- **4 tablespoons butter**
- **6 fresh scallions, finely chopped**
- **2 (12 ounce) cans oysters with liquor**
- **2 (1 pint) cartons whipping cream**
- **4 cups milk**
- **½ teaspoon salt**
- **¼ teaspoon black pepper**

1. Melt butter in soup pot over medium heat. Add scallions and cook, stirring, until tender, about 3 minutes.

   Add oysters, cream, milk, salt, and pepper.
2. Reduce heat to low and cook until oyster edges begin to curl and mixture is hot, but not boiling.

{SERVES 12}

Who Knew?

Always buy milk in cardboard cartons instead of see-though plastic. Translucent containers allow light to seep in, which causes the milk to spoil sooner, and it also destroys up to 40% of the milk's vitamin D. Also, don't store milk on the door of your refrigerator. Items stored there are susceptible to warm air that enters the fridge each time you open it.

59 New England Clam Chowder

This traditional New England clam chowder is not only easy to make, it's very low in fat!

- **1 tablespoon butter**
- **2 large onions, chopped**
- **2 (20 ounce) cans minced clams with liquid**
- **¼ teaspoon black pepper**
- **2 pounds new potatoes, cleaned, diced**
- **2 quarts water**
- **1 teaspoon salt**
- **1 ¼ tablespoon cornstarch**
- **1 ½ cups heavy cream**

1. Melt butter in saucepan over medium-high heat.

   Add onions and cook, stirring, until onions begin to turn translucent, about 10–15 minutes.
2. Add liquid from clams, water, cornstarch, salt, and pepper and mix well. Add potatoes.
3. Bring to a boil, then lower heat to low and simmer, covered, until potatoes are tender, about 10 minutes.
4. Add evaporated milk and clam meat. Cook, stirring, until heated through; do not boil.

{SERVES 10}

60 Italian Minestrone

To make this easy minestrone recipe completely vegetarian, substitute vegetable broth for the beef broth.

¼ cup (½ stick) butter
1 (16 ounce) package frozen onions and bell peppers
3 ribs celery, chopped
2 teaspoons minced garlic
2 (15 ounce) cans diced tomatoes
1 teaspoon dried oregano
1 teaspoon dried basil
¼ teaspoon salt
⅛ teaspoon black pepper
2 (14 ounce) cans beef broth
2 (15 ounce) cans kidney beans, drained
2 medium zucchini, cut in half lengthwise, sliced
1 cup elbow macaroni

1. Melt butter in soup pot over medium-high heat.

   Add onions and bell peppers, celery, and garlic and cook, stirring occasionally, for 2 minutes.
2. Add tomatoes, oregano, basil, salt, and pepper. Bring to a boil, then reduce heat and simmer for 15 minutes, stirring occasionally.
3. Stir in beef broth, beans, zucchini, and macaroni and bring to a boil. Reduce heat and simmer until macaroni is tender, about 15 minutes.

{SERVES 8}

61 Broccoli–Wild Rice Soup

This is a hearty and delicious soup that's full of flavor. Your family will never guess the secret ingredient is cream cheese!

2 (6 ounce) packages chicken-flavored wild rice mix
12 cups water
2 (10 ounce) packages frozen chopped broccoli
4 teaspoons dried minced onion
2 (10 ounce) cans cream of chicken soup
2 (8 ounce) packages cream cheese, cubed

1. Combine rice, rice seasoning packet, and water in large saucepan. Bring to a boil, then reduce heat, cover, and simmer for 10 minutes, stirring once.
2. Stir in broccoli and onion and simmer for 5 minutes.
3. Stir in soup and cream cheese. Cook and stir on low heat until cheese melts.

{SERVES 12}

Who Knew?

To make this recipe lower in fat, substitute 2½ cups of our Low-Fat Cream of Chicken Soup Base for the cans of cream of chicken soup.

62 Ranchero Black Bean Soup

- 2 cups dried black beans
- 2 quarts water
- 2 (48 ounce) cartons beef broth
- 2 large bunches scallions, chopped
- 10 ribs celery, chopped
- 6 cloves garlic, minced
- 1 cup (2 sticks) butter
- 2 bay leaves
- 10 peppercorns
- 1½ teaspoon salt
- ¾ teaspoon cayenne pepper
- 1 cup rice, uncooked

1. Rinse and soak beans in water overnight. Drain, then transfer beans to large saucepan. Add beef broth and cook on high heat until boiling. Reduce heat to low and simmer, covered, for 2 hours.
2. Add butter to separate skillet and cook over mediumhigh heat. When melted, add scallions, celery, and garlic and cook, stirring, until celery is tender, about 8 minutes.
3. Transfer celery mixture to saucepan with beans. Add bay leaves, peppercorns, salt, and cayenne pepper.
4. Simmer covered over low heat for 1 hour. Add rice and continue to cook, stirring occasionally, until beans are tender, about 1 more hour. Add water if liquid level becomes low.
5. Remove bay leaves and peppercorns before serving.

{SERVES 12}

63 Creamy Mushroom Soup

- ½ cup (1 stick) butter
- 6 (8 ounce) packages fresh mushrooms, chopped
- 2 small onions, finely chopped
- 1 cup flour
- 1 (48 ounce) carton chicken broth
- 2 (1 pint) cartons half-and-half
- ½ cup dry white wine
- 1½ teaspoons dried tarragon
- ¼ cup white wineWorcestershire marinade for chicken
- 1 teaspoon salt

1. Melt butter over medium heat in large soup pot.

   Add mushrooms and onions and cook, stirring, until tender, about 8–12 minutes. Add flour and stir or whisk until smooth.
2. Add broth, half-and-half, wine, tarragon,

   Worcestershire marinade, and salt; stir constantly over medium-high heat.
3. Heat until mixture begins to bubble, then reduce heat to medium-low and cook until mixture thickens, stirring often, about 20 minutes.

{SERVES 12}

64 Baked Potato Soup

- **10 large baking potatoes**
- **1½ cups (3 sticks) butter**
- **1⅓ cup flour**
- **12 cups milk**
- **2 (8 ounce) packages shredded Cheddar cheese, divided**
- **2 (3 ounce) packages real bacon bits**
- **2 bunches fresh scallions, chopped, divided**
- **½ teaspoon salt**
- **¼ teaspoon black pepper**
- **2 (8 ounce) cartons sour cream**

1. Preheat oven to 400°. Place potatoes directly on rack and bake for 1 hour, turning halfway through. Remove potatoes and let cool. Cut potatoes in half lengthwise, scoop out flesh, and set aside. Discard potato shells.
2. Melt butter in large soup pot over low heat. Add flour and stir until smooth.
3. Gradually add milk and cook over medium heat, stirring constantly, until mixture thickens.
4. Stir in potatoes, half of cheese, bacon bits, 2 tablespoons scallions, salt, and pepper. Cook until hot, but do not boil.
5. Stir in sour cream and cook just until hot.
6. Spoon into individual soup bowls and sprinkle remaining cheese and scallions over each serving.

{SERVES 12}

Who Knew?

To make this recipe lower in fat, substitute 4 cups of our Low-Fat Four-Cheese Blend for the packages of Cheddar cheese, and 2 cups of our Low-Fat Sour Cream Substitute for the cartons of sour cream.

65 Pumpkin Soup

This decadent soup is perfect for Thanksgiving or another fall feast. If you have sour cream or plain yogurt on hand, scoop a dollop on top of each soup serving for a great garnish.

- **6 tablespoons butter**
- **2 (8 ounce) packages fresh mushrooms, sliced**
- **½ cup flour**
- **2 (32 ounce) cartons vegetable broth**
- **2 (15 ounce) cans cooked pumpkin**
- **2 (1 pint) cartons cream**
- **½ cup honey**
- **2 tablespoons sugar**
- **¾ teaspoon curry powder**
- **½ teaspoon ground nutmeg**

1. Melt butter over medium heat in large saucepan.

   Add mushrooms and cook, stirring occasionally, until mushrooms are tender, about 10–12 minutes.
2. Add flour, stir well until there are no lumps, and gradually add broth. Heat over high heat until mixture starts to bubble, then reduce heat to medium-low and cook until mixture thickens, about 2 minutes.
3. Stir in pumpkin, cream, honey, sugar, curry powder, and nutmeg. Stir constantly until soup is heated through.

{SERVES 12}

66 Zesty Squash Soup

- **¼ cup (½ stick) butter**
- **2 medium onions, finely chopped**
- **¼ cup flour**
- **4 (16 ounce) packages frozen yellow squash, thawed**
- **2 (32 ounce) cartons chicken broth**
- **1 cup water**
- **2 (7 ounce) cans chopped green chilies**
- **½ teaspoon salt**
- **¼ teaspoon black pepper**
- **½ cups whipping cream**

1. Melt butter in large soup pot and sauté onion for 3 minutes, stirring constantly. Stir in flour and cook for 1 minute. stirring until flour is absorbed and not lumpy.
2. Add squash, broth, water, green chilies, salt, and pepper. Bring to a boil over high heat, then reduce heat to low and simmer for 25 minutes.
3. Puree soup in batches in blender until mixture is smooth.
4. Return pureed soup to pot, add whipping cream, and heat just until soup is heated through.

{SERVES 12-16}

67 Johnny Appleseed's Squash Soup

This soup, which is also delicious cold, uses a unique ingredient to help thicken the soup: white bread! You won't believe it until you've tried it.

- **1 large butternut squash**
- **6 tart green apples, peeled, cored, chopped**
- **2 medium onions, chopped**
- **½ teaspoon dried rosemary**
- **½ teaspoon dried marjoram**
- **6 (14 ounce) cans chicken broth**
- **4 slices white bread**
- **½ cup whipping cream**

1. Cut butternut squash in half and scoop out seeds.
2. Combine squash, apples, onions, rosemary, marjoram, broth, and bread in large saucepan. Bring to a boil over high heat, then reduce heat to low and simmer for 45 minutes.
3. Remove squash, scoop out flesh from peel, and discard peel. Add flesh back to mixture.
4. Puree mixture in blender until smooth. Return to saucepan and cook over medium heat for 10 minutes.
5. Just before serving, mix in cream.

{SERVES 12}

68 French Onion Soup

¼ cup (½ stick) butter
8 yellow onions, thinly sliced
2 (32 ounce) cartons beef broth
8 slices French bread, crust trimmed, toasted
8 slices Swiss cheese

1. Melt butter in large soup pot over medium-low heat.
   Add onions and cook until onions are brown, about 20–30 minutes. Scrape onions from bottom of pot and stir occasionally.
2. Add beef broth and cook on medium heat for 1 hour.
3. Just before time to serve, pour soup into individual ovenproof soup bowls. Top with slices of toasted bread and cover with slices of cheese.
4. Place bowls on baking sheet and place under broiler until cheese melts, about 1–2 minutes. Serve immediately.

{SERVES 8}

Who Knew?

If you don't have oven-proof bowls, simply melt the cheese over the toasted bread on a baking sheet, then place in soup bowls and let sit for 1 minute before serving.

69 Curried Zucchini Soup

This delicious soup will make you happy you bought that curry powder! Buy some large garlic-flavored croutons when you find them on sale and save them as a garnish for this recipe.

½ cup (1 stick) butter
6 cups coarsely chopped zucchini
4 ribs celery, thinly sliced
1 tablespoon Italian seasoning
1 teaspoon curry powder
2 (10 ounce) cans cream of potato soup
2 (10 ounce) cans French onion soup
4 cups milk

1. Melt butter in soup pot over medium-low heat.
   Add zucchini, celery, Italian seasoning, and curry powder and stir constantly for 5 minutes.
2. Stir in potato soup, onion soup, and milk. Bring to a boil over medium-high heat, then reduce heat to low and simmer for 10 minutes.

{SERVES 12}

70 Southwest Vegetarian Chili

Sage leaves add a fresh, smoky flavor to this chili that will have your family wondering what your secret ingredient is!

8 scallions, sliced

2 tablespoons minced garlic

1 tablespoon olive oil

4 (15 ounce) cans diced tomatoes with liquid

2 (15 ounce) cans pinto beans, rinsed, drained

1⅛ teaspoons cayenne pepper

3 tablespoons chili powder

2 teaspoons ground cumin

½ teaspoon salt

9 fresh sage leaves, chopped

1. Sauté scallions and garlic with olive oil in large saucepan over medium heat for 3 minutes. Add tomatoes, beans, cayenne pepper, chili powder, cumin, coriander, and salt.
2. Heat chili to boiling over high heat, then reduce heat to low and simmer for 25 minutes, stirring several times throughout cooking time.
3. Add sage, and cook for 3 more minutes.

{SERVES 8}

71 Cheese-Topped Broccoli Soup

1 (48 ounce) carton plus 1 (32 ounce) carton chicken broth

2 cups water

4 ribs celery, sliced

2 medium onions, chopped

2 medium baking potatoes, peeled, chopped

2 (16 ounce) packages frozen, chopped broccoli

1 (1 pint) carton cream

1 cup milk

½ teaspoon salt

½ teaspoon black pepper

2½ cups grated Parmesan cheese

1. Combine broth, water, celery, onions, and chopped potatoes in large, heavy soup pot.
2. Bring to a boil over high heat, then reduce heat to low and simmer, covered, until vegetables are tender, about 20 minutes.
3. Stir in broccoli and continue to simmer until broccoli is tender, about 15 minutes.
4. Stir in cream, milk, salt, and pepper.
5. Heat on medium, stirring constantly, until soup is heated through. (Do not boil.) Ladle into individual soup bowls and sprinkle with Parmesan cheese.

{SERVES 12}

72 Eight-Can Soup Bowl

It doesn't get much easier than this! Stock up when these items are on sale, because you can keep them almost indefinitely. Throw in some cooked chicken for a heartier soup.

2 (14 ounce) cans chicken broth

2 (10 ounce) cans cream of chicken soup

2 (15 ounce) cans ranch-style beans

2 (10 ounce) cans tomatoes with green chilies

1 large bag tortilla chips, crushed coarsely

1 (12 ounce) package shredded four-cheese blend

1 (8 ounce) carton sour cream

1. Combine broth, chicken soup, beans, and tomatoes with green chilies in saucepan. Simmer for 30 minutes.
2. Serve over tortilla chips and top with cheese and sour cream.

{SERVES 12}

Who Knew? Light Switch

To make this recipe lower in fat, substitute 1¼ cup of our Low-Fat Cream of Chicken Soup Base for the can of cream of chicken soup, 3 cups of our Low-Fat Four-Cheese Blend for the package of four-cheese blend, and 1 cup of our Low-Fat Sour Cream Substitute for the carton of sour cream.

73 Creamy Asparagus Soup

4 tablespoons butter

2 onions, finely chopped

2 red bell peppers, seeded, chopped

1 pound asparagus, chopped

4 (10 ounce) cans cream of chicken soup

2 cups milk, cream, or half-and-half

2 teaspoons lemon juice

½ teaspoon dried tarragon

½ teaspoon salt

¼ teaspoon black pepper

1. Melt butter in soup pot over medium-high heat. Add onion and bell pepper and cook, stirring, for 3 minutes.

   Add asparagus and continue to cook, stirring, until all vegetables are tender. Remove from heat.
2. Pour mixture into food processor or blender and blend until smooth.
3. Return onion-asparagus mixture to soup pot and add chicken soup, milk, lemon juice, tarragon, salt, and pepper.
4. Cook on medium-high heat, stirring constantly, until soup is heated through. Do not boil.

{SERVES 12}

74 Deluxe Grilled-Cheese Sandwiches

These grilled-cheese sandwiches taste particularly good with chipotle-flavored mayonnaise, if you can find it!

¼ cup (½ stick) butter, softened

8 slices 7-grain bread

½ cup chipotle (or regular) mayonnaise

8 slices sharp Cheddar cheese

8 slices crisp bacon, crumbled

1 avocado, pitted, skinned, and thinly sliced

1. Spread softened butter on thick slices of 7-grain bread. Place up to 4 slices, butter-side down, in heavy skillet. (You may have to make sandwiches in batches.)
2. Spread each piece of bread with 1 tablespoon mayonnaise and 1 slice cheese.
3. Sprinkle with 2 tablespoons crumbled bacon and avocado slices. Top with second slice of cheese.
4. Spread 1 tablespoon mayonnaise on each slice of remaining bread and butter on the reverse side.

   Place butter-side up on top of sandwich.
5. Heat skillet on medium-high and cook for about 2 minutes or until bottom slice of bread toasts light brown.
6. Turn sandwich over and cook for an additional 2 minutes or until cheese melts completely.

{SERVES 4}

75 Get Well Soon Chicken Noodle Soup

2 (14 ounce) cans chicken broth

2 boneless, skinless chicken breast halves, cubed

2 carrots, peeled and chopped

2 ribs celery, chopped

1 bay leaf

½ (8 ounce) package medium egg noodles

1 Salt and pepper to taste

1. Combine broth, chicken, carrots, celery, and bay leaf in large saucepan. Bring to a boil, then reduce heat and simmer until chicken is cooked through, about 5–10 minutes.
2. Stir in noodles and cook for 10 minutes or until noodles and vegetables are done; stir often.
3. Remove bay leaf and serve with salt and pepper.

{SERVES 4-6}

76 Asian-Style Chicken Noodle Soup

3 cups water

2 medium stalks bok choy with leaves, thinly sliced

1 (8 ounce) package baby carrots

1 red bell pepper, seeded, chopped

1 rotisserie chicken, boned, skinned, cubed

1 (3 ounce) package chicken-flavor ramen noodles

1. Boil water in soup pot and add bok choy, carrots, and bell pepper. Cook until vegetables are tender, about 3 minutes.
2. Reduce heat to medium and add chicken and ramen noodles, including seasoning packet. Simmer for
3. minutes; stir occasionally. Stir in flavor packet from noodles and serve immediately.

{SERVES 8}

Who Knew?

How do you keep your cutting board from sliding around when you're trying to chop? It's easy—just dampen a paper towel, place it on your counter, and put the board on top. It won't move again!

77 Cheesy Chicken and Potatoes

1 (20 ounce) package frozen hash browns with peppers and onions, thawed

1 tablespoon olive oil

1 tablespoon minced garlic

2 ½ cups chopped, cooked rotisserie chicken

1 bunch scallions, sliced

⅓ cup chicken broth or water

1 cup shredded Cheddar cheese

1. Cook potatoes in a little oil in large skillet over medium-high heat for 7 minutes, turning frequently.
2. Add garlic, chicken, scallions, and broth and cook for 5–6 minutes. Remove from heat and stir in cheese. Serve immediately right from skillet.

{SERVES 4-6}

CHAPTER 2

Salads and Sauces

78 Chicken-Rice Salad Supreme

2 (5 ounce) cans premium chunk chicken breast

2 (9 ounce) packages whole grain brown ready-rice

⅔ cup sun-dried tomatoes

2 ripe avocados, peeled, diced

¾ cup dijon-style mustard vinaigrette dressing.

1. Drain chicken, separate into chunks and save broth.
2. Prepare microwave rice pouches according to package directions.
3. Combine chicken, rice, tomatoes, and avocado in large bowl.
4. Gently stir dressing into chicken-rice mixture and refrigerate for 2 hours before serving.

{SERVES 8}

79 Barbecue Chicken Salad

Here's a quickie with an "it took a long time" flavor.

¾ cup ranch dressing

3 tablespoons barbecue sauce

2 tablespoons salsa

3 boneless, skinless chicken breast halves, grilled and sliced into strips

1 (9 ounce) package romaine lettuce

1 (15 ounce) can seasoned black beans, rinsed, drained

12-15 cherry tomatoes

1. Combine ranch dressing, barbecue sauce, and salsa in bowl. Refrigerate and set aside.
2. Place chicken strips, cut-up romaine, black beans and cherry tomatoes in bowl. Toss enough dressing with salad to lightly coat.

{SERVES 8}

Who Knew?

To make this recipe low-fat, use our Low-Fat Ranch Dressing and our Readymade Barbecue Sauce.

80 Waldorf Salad

Use one green apple and one red apple in this salad for a great look and taste!

1 pound deli chicken, cubed
2 apples, chopped
1 cup (about 2 ribs) chopped celery
1 (6 ounce) package shredded lettuce
½ cup chopped walnuts
2 (6 ounce) cartons plain yogurt
½ cup mayonnaise

1. Place chicken, apples, celery, lettuce, and walnuts in a large mixing bowl.
2. Stir in yogurt and mayonnaise and toss to mix well.

   May be served room temperature or refrigerate for several hours. Serve over shredded lettuce.

{SERVES 6}

Who Knew?

The quickest way to "chop" walnuts and other nuts is to place them in a sealed plastic bag, then roll over them with a rolling pin. (This is also a clean, easy way to break up graham crackers or vanilla wafers to make a pie crust!)

81 Chef's Salad

2 (10 ounce) packages romaine lettuce
2 ½-3 cups chopped rotisserie chicken
2 hard-boiled eggs, quartered
2 tomatoes, chopped
1 (8 ounce) package shredded Colby cheese
1 small red onion, chopped
Salad dressing

1. Combine all ingredients in a large salad bowl and top with your favorite dressing.

{SERVES 5}

82 Hawaiian Chicken Salad

- ¾ cup mayonnaise
- ½ cup poppy seed salad dressing
- 3 cups diced chicken breasts, cubed (about 1½ pounds)
- 1 tablespoon olive oil
- 1 (20 ounce) can pineapple chunks, well-drained
- 1 cup red grapes, halved
- 1 cup chopped celery
- ½ cup salted peanuts

1. Combine mayonnaise and poppy seed dressing; set aside.
2. Cook chicken cubes in large skillet with hot oil, stirring occasionally, until brown (about 8–10 minutes).

   Let cool.
3. Combine chicken, pineapple, grapes, and celery in bowl and toss.
4. Top with mayonnaise-poppy seed dressing and toss.
5. Just before serving, sprinkle peanuts over top of salad.

{SERVES 8}

83 Chicken Tarragon Salad

- ⅔ cup mayonnaise
- 1 tablespoon lemon juice
- 2 tablespoons white wine vinegar
- 1¼ teaspoons dried, crumbled tarragon
- 1 cups chopped cooked rotisserie chicken
- 1 cup chopped celery
- 1 cup chopped pecans
- ¾ cup chopped cucumbers

1. Combine mayonnaise, lemon juice, vinegar, and tarragon in bowl and mix well. Set aside.
2. Combine chicken, celery, pecans, and cucumbers in bowl. Toss with dressing and serve.

{SERVES 5}

Who Knew?

To make this already low-fat recipe even healthier, try using our Homemade Mayonnaise!

84 Book Club's Favorite Salad

½ cup mayonnaise
1 tablespoon orange juice
2 tablespoons red wine vinegar
1 teaspoon chili powder
¼ teaspoon salt
⅛ teaspoon black pepper
1 cup red grapes, halved
1 cup green grapes, halved
1 cup chopped celery
⅔ cup whole walnuts
small red onion, chopped
½ of one rotisserie-cooked chicken
2 cups red-leaf lettuce, chopped

1. Combine mayonnaise, orange juice, vinegar, chili powder, salt, and pepper in bowl and mix well.
2. In separate, large bowl, combine red and green grapes, celery, walnuts, and onions. Toss with dressing.
3. Cut chicken into strips, and add to mixture until dressing coats all ingredients. (You will use about ½ of one chicken—we prefer to use white meat.)
4. Place lettuce on serving plates and place salad mixture on top.

{SERVES 6-8}

85 Aunt Patty's Chicken Salad

3 cups chopped rotisserie chicken
1 cup celery
1 ½ cups green grapes, halved
¾ cup cashew nuts
¾ cup mayonnaise
1 cup chow mein noodles

1. Combine chicken, celery, grapes, and cashew nuts in bowl and toss with mayonnaise. Just before serving, mix in noodles.
2. Serve on cabbage leaves or bread.

{SERVES 6}

86 Chicken Caesar Salad

3 cups chopped rotisserie chicken
1 cup celery
1 ½ cups green grapes, halved
¾ cup cashew nuts
¾ cup mayonnaise
1 cup chow mein noodles

1. Cook chicken cubes in large skillet with hot oil, stirring occasionally, until brown (about 8–10 minutes).
   Let cool.
2. Combine chicken, salad greens, cheese, and croutonsin large bowl.
3. When ready to serve, toss with salad dressing.

{SERVES 4}

Who Knew?

Want a super-crispy salad? Try preparing it in a metal bowl and then placing it in the freezer for one minute before serving.

87 Spinach-Turkey Salad Supper

2 (8 ounce) packages baby spinach
⅓ cup whole walnuts
⅓ cup dried cranberries
2 apples, sliced
¾ pound deli smoked turkey, cubed
½ cup honey-mustard salad dressing

1. Combine spinach, walnuts, dried cranberries, apples, and turkey in large salad bowl.
2. Toss with salad dressing

{SERVES 4}

88 Sweet and Tangy Ham Salad

3 cups cooked, chopped ham
¾ cup chopped celery
1 cup small curd cottage cheese,
1 drained
1 cup chopped cauliflower florets
1 cup chopped broccoli florets
Honey-mustard salad dressing
Lettuce leaves

1. Combine ham, celery, cottage cheese, cauliflower, and broccoli in large bowl.
2. Toss with salad dressing.
3. Serve on lettuce leaves.

{SERVES 4}

89 Zesty Bean Salad

You can use any salad dressing for this bean-based dinner salad. If you go for a creamy option like ranch, add a couple of tablespoons of lemon juice before mixing it in.

1 (15 ounce) can kidney beans
1 1 (15 ounce) can pinto beans
1 1 (16 ounce) package frozen whole
1 kernel corn, thawed, drained
1 medium red onion, chopped
2 2 cups cubed deli ham (about pound)
1 (8 ounce) bottle salad dressing

1. Rinse and drain kidney and pinto beans and place in salad bowl.
2. Add corn, onion, and ham; mix well.
3. Toss with salad dressing and refrigerate until ready to serve. (You may want to wait awhile for the flavors to blend.)

{SERVES 4}

Who Knew?

Chopping onions or garlic doesn't have to leave your hands smelling bad anymore! You'll clean up instantly if you wash your hands in a splash of mouthwash. The alcohol in mouthwash removes odors instantly!

90 Sweet Tuna Salad

- **½ (8 ounce) bottle sweet honey Catalina salad dressing**
- **½ cup mayonnaise**
- **1 (6 ounce) can tuna in water**
- **1 apple, cored, chopped**
- **1 (10 ounce) package frozen green peas, thawed, drained**
- **1 red bell pepper, chopped**
- **3 cups shredded lettuce (about 1/3 of 1 head)**

1. Combine dressing and mayonnaise in bowl and set aside.
2. In separate bowl, combine tuna, add apple, peas, and bell pepper.
3. Pour dressing mixture over salad and toss to blend.
4. Serve over bed of shredded lettuce.

{SERVES 6}

91 Tuna and White Bean Salad

If you don't have any capers, use a few green, pitted olives for this fresh-tasting salad.

- **1½ tablespoons extra virgin olive oil**
- **3 tablespoons lemon juice**
- **½ teaspoon salt**
- **¼ teaspoon black pepper**
- **2 (6 ounce) cans tuna, drained**
- **1 (15 ounce) can cannelloni beans, drained and rinsed**
- **1 (12 ounce) jar roasted red peppers, drained and quartered**
- **2 tablespoons capers**

1. Combine oil, lemon juice, salt, and pepper in bowl. Mix until blended well.
2. In large bowl, combine remaining ingredients. Toss with oil mixture.

{SERVES 4}

Who Knew?

A great way to get discounts on the products you love is with a little praise! Simply go to the company's website, find the "contact us" section, and write something nice. Don't be surprised if you get a coupon or trial size product shortly thereafter!

92 Pasta Plus

- 1 (16 ounce) package rainbow rotini (spiral) pasta
- 2 cups small fresh broccoli florets
- 1 cup baby carrots, halved lengthwise
- 1 ½ red bell peppers, seeded, julienned
- ½ of 1 medium red onion, chopped
- ⅔ of 1 (16 ounce) bottle peppercorn ranch salad dressing

1. Microwave water on HIGH in covered microwave-safe dish until boiling. Add pasta and cook until tender, about 10 minutes. Drain, rinse, and let cool.
2. Place pasta in large salad bowl and add broccoli, cauliflower, carrots, and bell pepper.
3. Pour about three-fourths of dressing over salad and toss. Add remaining fourth if needed. Cover and refrigerate for 1–2 hours.

{SERVES 6}

Who Knew?

When using only part of a red, green, or yellow pepper, cut it from the bottom or the sides, leaving the seeds attached, and it will remain moist for longer. Place it in a resealable plastic bag and use within 4 days.

93 Perfect Pasta Salad

- ¾ cup mayonnaise
- 2 tablespoons white wine vinegar
- 1 tablespoon dijon-style mustard
- 1 teaspoon sugar
- ¾ teaspoon garlic salt
- ⅛ teaspoon black pepper
- 1 (8 ounce) package cavatappi (corkscrew) pasta
- 2 cups fresh broccoli florets
- ½ cup shredded carrots
- ½ cup chopped red bell pepper
- ½ cup chopped red onion

1. Combine mayonnaise, vinegar, mustard, sugar, garlic, salt, and pepper in large bowl. Set aside in refrigerator.
2. Prepare pasta in microwave according to package directions. Drain, but reserve some water. Let pasta cool.
3. In reserved pasta water, microwave broccoli on HIGH until tender, about 2 minutes.
4. Combine pasta, broccoli, carrots, bell pepper, and onion and toss with dressing until coated well.

{SERVES 4}

94 Colorful Garden Salad

To make this bright salad even more colorful, use multi-colored tortellini pasta.

1 (8 ounce) package tortellini pasta

1 tablespoon olive oil

1 (8 ounce) can cut green beans, drained

1 cup diced carrots

1 cup cherry tomato halves

1 yellow bell pepper, seeded, julienned

1 (8 ounce) package Cheddar cheese, cubed

1 (8 ounce) bottle zesty Italian dressing

1. Prepare pasta in microwave according to package directions. Drain, rinse, and let cool. Transfer to bowl and drizzle oil over tortellini.
2. Add green beans, carrots, tomatoes, bell pepper, and cheese and toss.
3. Pour dressing over salad and toss to make sure dressing coats all ingredients. Cover and refrigerate for several hours before serving.

{SERVES 4}

Who Knew?

When using only part of a red, green, or yellow pepper, cut it from the bottom or the sides, leaving the seeds attached, and it will remain moist for longer. Place it in a resealable plastic bag and use within 4 days.

95 Fusilli Pasta Salad

1 (16 ounce) package fusilli (spiral) pasta

1 (16 ounce) package frozen broccoli and cauliflower

1 (8 ounce) package mozzarella cheese, cubed

1 (8 ounce) bottle of Catalina salad dressing

1. Prepare pasta in microwave according to package directions. Drain and let cool.
2. Cook vegetables in microwave according to package directions. Drain and cool.
3. Combine pasta, vegetables, and cheese chunks in large bowl.
4. Toss with Catalina dressing. Refrigerate several hours before serving.

{SERVES 6}

96 Ready-To-Go Pasta Salad

This pasta salad uses pepperoni—a great way to get some meat in your meal without having to cook anything!

1 (16 ounce) package rotini (spiral) pasta

12 cherry tomatoes, halved, drained

4 fresh scallions, sliced

1 (4 ounce) can sliced ripe olives

¾ cup chopped green bell pepper

¾ cup sliced pepperoni, halved

1 (8 ounce) package cubed mozzarella cheese

1 cup Italian vinaigrette salad dressing

1. Prepare pasta in microwave according to package directions. Drain, rinse, and let cool. Transfer to bowl and drizzle oil over tortellini.
2. Add green beans, carrots, tomatoes, bell pepper, and cheese and toss.
3. Pour dressing over salad and toss to make sure dressing coats all ingredients. Cover and refrigerate for several hours before serving.

{SERVES 6-8}

97 Color-Coded Salad

1 (16 ounce) package tri-colored fusilli (spiral) pasta, cooked, drained

1 red bell pepper, chopped

1 small zucchini, chopped

1 cup broccoli florets

1 cup Caesar salad dressing

1. Combine all ingredients in bowl.
2. Toss with salad dressing.
3. Refrigerate until ready to serve.

{SERVES 4}

Who Knew?

Finished with that bottle of salad dressing? Clean out the inside and peel off the label, and now you've got a brand-new vase! It'll be great for smaller bouquets, and no one will notice the difference—just tie some yarn or ribbon around the screw top and set your flowers in place.

98 Broccoli-Noodle Crunch Salad

This unique salad is super crunchy and super tasty. And it will stay crispy in the refrigerator for days!

¾ cup olive oil

½ cup white vinegar

½ cup sugar

2 (3 ounce) packages chickenflavored ramen noodles

1 cup slivered almonds

1 cup dry-roasted sunflower seeds

1 (12 ounce) package broccoli slaw

1. Combine olive oil, vinegar, sugar, and 1 seasoning packet from the ramen noodles package. Mix well and set aside.
2. Break up ramen noodles (but do not cook) and mix with almonds, sunflower seeds, and broccoli slaw.
3. Pour dressing over noodle mixture and mix well.

{SERVES 8}

Who Knew?

Save the stems from broccoli you've used in other meals throughout the week, then use them to make this scrumptious salad. Just substitute the broccoli slaw for about 2 cups of grated broccoli stems.

99 Black-Eyed Pea Salad

This nutritious salad is especially good with jalapeño black-eyed peas, if you can find them.

⅓ cup olive oil

⅓ cup white vinegar

3 tablespoons sugar

¼ teaspoon garlic powder

½ teaspoon salt

2 (15 ounce) cans black-eyed peas (preferably jalapeño flavored), drained

1 ripe avocado, peeled, chopped

1 medium red onion, chopped

1 cup chopped celery

1 red bell pepper, seeded, chopped

1 green bell pepper, seeded, chopped

1. Combine olive oil, vinegar, sugar, garlic powder, and salt in a small bowl and mix well. Refrigerate for at least 15 minutes.
2. Mix remaining ingredients in large bowl.
3. Pour dressing over salad and mix well.

{SERVES 6}

100 Artichoke Salad

This rich meal is no Jell-O salad! The garlic and herbs give it a complex taste that will have guests asking for your recipe. For a pretty finish, sprinkle a little paprika over the salad and place olives and radishes in the center of the ring.

- **1 (1 ounce) packet unflavored gelatin**
- **¾ cup water, divided**
- **1 cup mayonnaise**
- **1 (14 ounce) can hearts of artichoke, well drained**
- **½ (10 ounce) package frozen green peas, thawed**
- **2 tablespoons lemon juice**
- **1 (4 ounce) jar chopped pimentos**
- **1 bunch scallion with tops, finely chopped**
- **1 ½ cups shredded mozzarella cheese**
- **1 teaspoon Italian herb seasoning**
- **½ teaspoon garlic powder**
- **½ teaspoon salt Lettuce**

1. Soften gelatin in ¼-cup cold water in bowl. Boil remaining water and mix into gelatin. Add mayonnaise and stir until smooth.
2. Remove any spikes or tough leaves from artichoke hearts, chop, and stir into gelatin.
3. Add all remaining ingredients except lettuce, pour into ring mold, and refrigerate.
4. When solid and ready to serve, slip a knife around edges to loosen from mold. Unmold onto a serving plate lined with lettuce..

{SERVES 8}

Who Knew?

When preparing any recipe with gelatin in hot summer months, add a teaspoon of white vinegar to the mix. It will help keep your salads and desserts firm.

101 Spinach Salad

This nutritious salad is especially good with jalapeño black-eyed peas, if you can find them.

- **½ cup sugar**
- **¼ cup white wine vinegar**
- **⅓ cup olive oil**
- **2 teaspoons poppy seeds**
- **1 (10 ounce) bag baby spinach**
- **1 cup fresh sliced strawberries**
- **1 (3 ounce) package slivered almonds**
- **½ cup crumbled feta cheese**

1. Combine sugar, vinegar, olive oil, and poppy seeds and mix well; set aside.
2. Combine remaining ingredients and toss with dressing.

{SERVES 6}

102 Crispy Summer Salad

The walnuts and sunflower seeds in this colorful salad provide a satisfying crunch.

2 (8 ounce) packages baby spinach, stems removed

1 small head cauliflower, cut into small florets

1 red bell pepper, seeded, cut in strips

¾ cup whole walnuts

½ cup toasted, salted sunflower seeds

1 cups ham, chopped
Raspberry or strawberry vinaigrette dressing to taste

1. Combine spinach, cauliflower, bell pepper strips, walnuts, sunflower seeds, and ham in large salad bowl.
2. Toss with dressing to taste.

{SERVES 6}

Who Knew?

Avoid wet, limp salads by placing an inverted saucer in the bottom of the salad bowl before you throw in all your veggies. The excess water that is left after washing the vegetables and greens will drain under the saucer and leave the greens high and dry.

103 Tuna-Veggie Salad

1 (8 ounce) package maruzze (shell) pasta

2 small yellow squash, chopped

2 small zucchini, chopped

1 (15 ounce) can pinto beans, rinsed, drained

1 (11 ounce) can corn, drained

1 (12 ounce) can tuna, drained

1 cup creamy Italian salad dressing

¼ teaspoon salt

⅛ teaspoon black pepper

1. Prepare pasta in microwave according to package directions. Drain, rinse, and let cool.
2. Place squash and zucchini in microwave-safe container with a small amount of water and microwave on HIGH until tender (about 8 minutes), stirring every 2 minutes. Drain well.
3. Combine pasta, squash, zucchini, beans, corn, tuna, salt, and pepper in large bowl. Refrigerate until cool.
4. Pour salad dressing over mixture and toss to mix well. Refrigerate for at least 15 minutes more.

{SERVES 6-8}

104 Shrimp with Watermelon and Avocado

It may seem like an odd combination, but once you taste this dish you'll see how well these three ingredients work together.

- **1 pound shrimp, cooked, peeled, and deveined**
- **4 cups chopped watermelon**
- **1 medium red onion, sliced**
- **½ cup fresh cilantro leaves**
- **2 avocados, peeled, pitted, and chopped**
- **½ teaspoon salt**
- **¼ teaspoon black pepper**

1. Mix ingredients well in large salad bowl and serve.

{SERVES 4-5}

105 Smoked Salmon Plate with Horseradish Sauce

Smoked salmon on sale? Buy some for a simple, healthy dinner.

- **1 tablespoon prepared horseradish**
- **1 tablespoon coarse-grain mustard**
- **¼ cup lemon juice**
- **½ cup sour cream**
- **¼ teaspoon salt**
- **⅛ 1/8 teaspoon black pepper**
- **1 pound smoked salmon, thinly sliced**
- **2 cucumbers, sliced**
- **2 bunches watercress, stems trimmed**

1. In bowl, combine horseradish, mustard, lemon juice, sour cream, salt, and pepper until well blended.
2. Place salmon, cucumbers, and sprigs of watercress on serving plates. Place large dollop of sour cream mixture on each place and serve with bagel chips or crackers.

{SERVES 4-6}

106 Winter Salad

When you need a quick "something" to take to a friend, this is it! It can be kept in the refrigerator for a week and is a really good dinner salad to have on hand.

½ cup olive oil

¾ cup white vinegar

¾ cup sugar

¾ teaspoon garlic powder

2 teaspoons salt

1 teaspoon black pepper

1 (15 ounce) can cut green beans, drained

1 (15 ounce) can black-eyed peas, drained

1 (15 ounce) can white corn, drained

1 (4 ounce) jar chopped pimentos

1 red bell pepper, seeded, chopped

1. Combine olive oil, vinegar, sugar, garlic powder, salt, and pepper in a small bowl and mix well. Refrigerate for at least 15 minutes.
2. Combine all other ingredients. Cover with dressing and mix well to coat.

{SERVES 6-8}

107 Seven-Layer Salad

Serve this salad in a glass bowl, which allows those enjoying it to see the layers!

1 (10 ounce) package fresh spinach, torn into pieces, divided

1 cup sliced fresh mushrooms

1 (10 ounce) box frozen green peas, thawed

3 ribs celery, sliced

1½ cups shredded Cheddar and Monterey Jack cheese blend, divided

1½ cups mayonnaise

1½ cups sour cream

1 bunch scallions, chopped

2 teaspoons sugar

½ teaspoon seasoned salt

1 teaspoon black pepper

4 eggs, hard-boiled, grated

1 red bell pepper, seeded, chopped

1 cucumber, sliced

1. Layer half of the spinach in bottom of large bowl, then place mushrooms, peas, celery, and half of the Cheddar cheese on top.
2. To make the dressing, combine mayonnaise, sour cream, scallions, sugar, seasoned salt, and pepper in bowl. Dribble half of mixture over top of cheese.
3. Next layer remaining spinach, eggs, bell pepper, cucumber, and remaining Cheddar cheese. Spreadremaining dressing on top.
4. If possible, cover and refrigerate overnight to let flavors blend.

{SERVES 4-6}

108 Super Healthy Salsa

Once you've tried this fresh salsa, you may never go back to canned! This recipe is for medium salsa, but make it as mild or as spicy as you wish by adjusting the amount of jalapeño pepper.

4-5 medium to large tomatoes
½ of 1 jalapeño pepper
½ of 1 medium red onion, chopped
1 clove garlic, chopped
¼ cup chopped fresh cilantro
¼ teaspoon salt
⅛ teaspoon black pepper

1. Chop tomatoes in bite-sized chunks. Place in bowl and add remainder of ingredients.
2. If a less-chunky salsa is desired, remove half of tomato mixture and puree in blender until smooth. Add back in.
3. Keep in airtight container in refrigerator until ready to use.

{Yields 2–4 cups.
2 cups = 1 (16 ounce) jar salsa}

109 Italian Salad Dressing Mix

This mix is a delicious, homemade substitute for a packet of Italian dressing. It also gives you the ability to omit the sugar or salt according to your diet.

1 teaspoon carrot, grated, then finely chopped
1 teaspoon red bell pepper, finely minced
2 teaspoons sugar
¾ teaspoon lemon pepper
¼ teaspoon dried parsley flakes
¼ teaspoon garlic powder
⅛ teaspoon onion powder
⅛ teaspoon ground oregano
1 teaspoon salt
⅛ teaspoon black pepper

1. Preheat oven to 250º.
2. Place carrot and bell pepper on baking ban and heat in oven until dry, but not brown, about 45–60 minutes.
3. Combine dried carrot and bell pepper with the other ingredients in small bowl; mix well. Store in airtight container.
4. To make into dressing, mix with ¼ cup vinegar, then slowly add ½ cup oil and mix until well blended.

{Yields approximately 2 tablespoons.
2 tablespoons = 1 (1 ounce) packet Italian dressing mix}

110 Homemade Mayonnaise

Did you know you can make your own mayonnaise? All it takes is a lot of blending and a little taste-testing to make sure you get it the way you like it! For this recipe, we use extra virgin olive oil rather than vegetable oil to lower the fat content.

1 large egg brought to room temperature
1 tablespoon white wine vinegar
1 teaspoon Dijon-style mustard
⅛ teaspoon salt, plus additional to taste
1½ cups extra virgin olive oil
White or black pepper to taste
Lemon juice to taste

1. Place egg, vinegar, mustard, and 1/8 teaspoon salt in food processor or blender. Blend until well-mixed.
2. With machine running, slowly add oil, several drops at a time, until mixture thickens.
3. Add more salt, pepper, and lemon juice to taste and mix well.
4. Keep refrigerated in airtight container.

{Yields approximately 2 cups. 4 cups = 1 (32 ounce) jar mayonnaisea}

Who Knew?

Did you know that white and brown eggs are nutritionally identical? Don't pay more for one kind over the other!

111 Low-Fat Ranch Dressing

Here's a recipe for delicious low-fat ranch dressing that doesn't skimp on the flavor.

⅓ cup nonfat Greek-style yogurt
⅓ cup milk
3 tablespoons mayonnaise
2 tablespoons apple cider vinegar
1 teaspoon Dijon mustard
1 tablespoon finely chopped fresh chives
1 garlic clove, minced
½ teaspoon salt
¼ teaspoon black pepper

1. Combine all ingredients in bowl and mix until blended well.
2. Refrigerate for 30 minutes before using.
3. Store in airtight container in refrigerator.

{Yields approximately 1 cup. 2 cups = 1 (16 ounce) bottle dressing}

112 Low-Fat Cream of Chicken Soup Base

This recipe makes 9 soup can–sized portions of condensed soup to use as a base in casseroles and other dishes. To eat as a meal, simply add an additional 1¼ cups water in step 2.

2 cups nonfat dry milk powder
¾ cup cornstarch
¼ cup reduced sodium chicken bouillon granules
¼ teaspoon onion powder
½ teaspoon ground thyme
½ teaspoon dried basil
⅛ teaspoon black pepper

1. Combine milk powder, cornstarch, chicken bouillon, onion powder, thyme, basil, and black pepper and mix until blended. Keep in an airtight container until ready to use.
2. To make 1 can's worth of condensed soup, combine 1/3 cup of mixture and 1¼ cups water in saucepan. Cook, stirring, until mixture thickens.

{Yields 11¼ cups.
1¼ cup = 1 (10 ounce) can condensed soup}

113 Low-Fat Cream of Mushroom Soup Base

This recipe makes 2 soup can–sized portions of condensed soup to use as a base in casseroles and other dishes. To eat as a meal, simply add an additional 2½ cups water to this recipe.

2 tablespoons olive oil
2½ cups chopped crimini, white, portabella, and/or morel mushrooms
1 tablespoon butter or margarine
2 tablespoons flour
½ ½ cup vegetable stock
1½ 1½ cups 1% or 2% milk
1 teaspoon salt
¼ teaspoon black pepper

1. Heat olive oil over medium-high heat until hot, then add mushrooms. Cook, stirring frequently, until mushrooms are soft, about 3–5 minutes.
2. Remove mushrooms and add butter or margarine to any remaining olive oil. When melted, add flour and mix well to form a roux.
3. Add remaining ingredients and cook over medium heat, stirring constantly, until mixture thickens, about 7 minutes.
4. Pour into blender and blend until smooth.
5. Store in airtight container in refrigerator until ready to use.

{Yields 2 cups.
1¼ cup = 1 can condensed soup}

114 Low-Fat Cream of Celery Soup Base

This easy recipe makes 2 soup can–sized portions of condensed soup to use as a base in casseroles and other dishes. To eat as a meal, simply add an additional 2½ cups water to this recipe.

2½ cups chopped celery
1 tablespoon butter or margarine
2 tablespoons flour
½ cup vegetable stock
1½ cups 1% or 2% milk
1 teaspoon celery salt or table salt
¼ teaspoon black pepper

1. Place celery in microwave-safe container and heat on HIGH, covered, until celery is tender 2–3 minutes.
2. Melt butter in saucepan over medium heat. Add flour and mix well to form a roux.
3. Add celery and remaining ingredients and cook over medium heat, stirring constantly, until mixture thickens, about 7 minutes.
4. Pour into blender and blend until smooth.
5. Store in airtight container in refrigerator until ready to use.

{Yields 2 cups.
1¼ cup = 1 (10 ounce) can condensed soup}

115 Low-Fat Four-Cheese Blend

Low-fat cheese blends are great for their waistline-saving properties, but often sacrifice taste. This four-cheese blend uses a mixture of reduced-fat cheese and cheeses that are naturally low in fat to give you fewer calories with a richer taste. You'll also save a bundle by grating the cheese yourself!

1 cup grated low-fat sharp Cheddar cheese
1 cup grated jalapeño Cheddar cheese
1 cup part-skim mozzarella cheese
1 cup grated smoked Gouda cheese

1. Combine grated cheese and toss to mix thoroughly. Store refrigerated in airtight container until ready to use.

{Yields 4 cups.
2 cups = 1 (8 ounce) package shredded cheese}

Who Knew?

Want to know the easiest way to clean a cheese grater? Before you begin grating, spray it with vegetable oil, which will make it less sticky. Afterward, rub the crusty heel from a stale loaf of French bread over the grater, and your clean-up is finished!

116 Melty Cheese Sauce

No cheese sauce can really compare to the creamy, melty quality of Velveeta cheese—but maybe that's a good thing, because we'd have to have a laboratory in our home! This cheese sauce at least comes close, and it's richer in flavor. Use low-fat cheese and it will save you a lot of calories.

2 tablespoons butter or margarine

2 tablespoons flour

2 cups skim milk

1 teaspoon white wine or lemon juice

2 cups grated Cheddar cheese (use reduced-fat if desired)

1 teaspoon salt

1. Melt butter in saucepan over medium heat. Add flour and mix well to form a roux.
2. Add milk and wine or lemon juice and cook, stirring constantly, until sauce thickens, about 7–10 minutes.

   Make sure sauce does not boil.
3. Remove from heat; add Cheddar cheese and salt and mix until cheese is melted. If necessary, warm over low heat to melt cheese.
4. Let cool to room temperature and store in airtight container in refrigerator until ready to use.

{Yields 4 cups.
2 cups = 1 (8 ounce) package shredded cheese}

Who Knew?

Most reduced-fat Cheddar will take longer to melt than regular Cheddar, so make sure to grate it finely. You may also want to add it gradually while stirring constantly over low heat.

117 Low-Fat Sour Cream Substituted

¾ cup low-fat cottage cheese

¼ cup non-fat plain yogurt

2 tablespoons skim milk

2 tablespoons lemon juice

1. Add ingredients to blender or food processor and blend until smooth.
2. Refrigerate for at least 4 hours before serving.

{Yields approximately 1 cup.
1 cup = 1 (8 ounce) carton sour cream}

118 Healthy Chicken Broth

Chicken broth is so easy to make, we start a pot of it every time we're having a whole chicken. Just put your scraps in the pot along with a few vegetables, and you'll have low-fat alternative to the canned stuff that's practically free!

4-5 pounds of chicken parts, including necks, backs, and meaty bones

1 large onion, quartered

2 large carrots, peeled and halved

4 stalks celery, leafy tops intact, halved

2 cloves garlic

1 bay leaf

½ tablespoon whole black peppercorns

4 quarts cold water

1. Place all ingredients in large soup pot. Cook on high until boiling, then reduce heat to low and cook, stirring occasionally, for 3 hours.
2. Pour broth through a strainer, saving the liquid only.
   Place in refrigerator until cool and fat congeals at top.
3. Skim fat; store broth in refrigerator or freezer until ready to use.

{Yields approximately 3 quarts.
1¾ cups = 1 (15 ounce) can}

Who Knew?

Don't worry about peeling the onion before you put it in the soup pot—the onion skin will give your soup a richer brown color.

119 Healthy Beef Broth

Cheap beef parts are not usually as easy to come by at the butcher's as cheap chicken parts, but if you've just prepared a roast or your family has just devoured some short ribs, save the bones to make this super cheap broth. Or ask at the deli counter for what they have available!

2 pounds meaty beef soup bones (beef shanks or short ribs)

1 medium onion, quartered

2 carrots, peeled, quartered

2 celery ribs with leaves, halved

¼ cup warm water

6 cups cold water

2 bay leaves

1 garlic cloves

4 whole peppercorns

1 teaspoon dried thyme or oregano

1. Preheat oven to 450º.
2. Place soup bones in roasting pan. Bake uncovered for 30 minutes. Add onion, carrots, and celery and bake for additional 30 minutes.
3. Transfer to large soup pot. Add warm water to roasting pan and stir to loosen browned material at bottom of pan. Transfer water and juices to soup pot.
4. Add cold water, bay leaves, garlic, peppercorns, and thyme or oregano. Cook on high heat until boiling, then reduce heat to low and simmer for 4 hours.
5. Pour broth through a strainer, saving the liquid only.

   Place in refrigerator until cool and fat congeals at top.

3. Skim fat; store broth in refrigerator or freezer until ready to use.

{Yields approximately 1 quart.
1¾ cup = 1 (15 ounce) can}

120 Homemade Spaghetti Sauce

This recipe uses carrots rather than sugar to neutralize the acidity of the tomatoes.

1 cup olive oil

4 medium yellow onions, finely chopped

4 garlic cloves, minced

1 tablespoon tomato paste

2 (32 ounce) cans crushed tomatoes

½ cup vegetable broth or water

2 carrots, peeled and grated

1 tablespoon dried oregano

1 tablespoon Italian seasoning

1 teaspoon salt

½ teaspoon black pepper

½ teaspoon crushed red pepper flakes (optional)

1. Heat oil in large saucepan over medium-high heat.

   When hot, add onions. Cook, stirring, until onions just begin to turn translucent, about 5 minutes. Add garlic and tomato paste and continue to cook, stirring, until tomato paste begins to brown.
2. Add tomatoes, broth, carrots, oregano, Italian seasoning, and salt and mix well. Heat until bubbling, then reduce heat to low and simmer, stirring occasionally, for 1 hour.
3. Add black pepper and red pepper flakes (if desired).

**{Yields approximately 6 cups.
1¾ cups = approximately 1 (16 ounce) jar spaghetti sauce}**

121 Low-Fat Alfredo Sauce

It's hard to make a cream-based sauce low fat, but this recipe gets a little help from some reduced fat cream cheese.

2 tablespoons butter or margarine

1 garlic clove, minced

2½ tablespoons flour

2 cups skim milk

½ of 1 (8 ounce) package light cream cheese, softened

½ cup grated Parmesan cheese

½ teaspoon salt

¼ teaspoon black pepper

1. Melt butter or margarine in saucepan over medium heat. Add garlic and cook, stirring, until garlic begins to turn translucent, about 1 minute.
2. Add flour and mix well to form roux.
3. Add milk and cook, stirring constantly, over mediumhigh heat. When mixture begins to bubble, reduce heat to low and continue stirring constantly until mixture thickens, about 5 minutes.
4. Add cream cheese, Parmesan cheese, salt, and pepper. Stir until cheese melts.
5. Store in airtight container in refrigerator.

**{Yields approximately 3 cups.
1¾ cups = approximately 1 (16 ounce) jar alfredo sauce}**

122 Readymade Barbecue Sauce

Making your own barbecue sauce won't save you much on calories, but it's easy to make with ingredients you already have on hand! You'll never buy an expensive bottle again.

1 tablespoon vegetable or canola oil
1 medium-size onion, minced
2 cloves garlic, minced
2 cup ketchup
¼ cup tomato sauce
6 cup water
2 tablespoons cider vinegar
1 tablespoonsWorcestershire sauce
4 teaspoon hot sauce, or more to taste
1 teaspoon beef bouillon granules
1 tablespoons dark brown sugar, or more to taste
2 tablespoons mustard
Pinch of cayenne pepper
½ teaspoon salt
½ teaspoon black pepper

1. Heat oil in saucepan over medium-high heat.
   When hot, add onion and garlic and cook until tender, about 3–5 minutes.
2. Add remaining ingredients. Bring to a boil, then reduce heat to low. Simmer for 20 minutes, stirring frequently. If sauce begins to stick to bottom of saucepan, add more water and mix well.
3. Store in airtight container in refrigerator.

{Yields 2 cups.}

123 Sweet-and-Sour Stir-Fry Sauce

Making your own stir-fry sauce is another great way to save money on bottles of condiments! Use pineapple juice in your recipe if you'd like to avoid refined sugar.

1 tablespoon cornstarch
1 tablespoons water
⅓ cup white vinegar
Juice from 1 (4 ounce) can pineapple chunks or rings
¼ cup sugar
½ teaspoon minced ginger
1 teaspoon minced garlic
1 tablespoon soy sauce
2 tablespoons ketchup

1. Combine cornstarch and water and mix well to dissolve cornstarch. Set aside.
2. In saucepan, combine remaining ingredients. Cook on high, stirring constantly, until sugar dissolves and mixture begins to boil.
3. Reduce heat to medium-low and add cornstarchwater mixture. Stir until mixture begins to thicken.
4. Let cool and store in refrigerator until ready to use.

{Yields approximately 1 cup.}

CHAPTER 3

Poultry Tonight

124 Chicken and Veggie Stir-Fry

- 3 boneless, skinless, chicken breast halves, cut in strips
- 1 tablespoon olive oil
- ½ teaspoon minced garlic
- 1 (3 ounce) package chicken-flavored ramen noodles
- 1 (16 ounce) package frozen broccoli, cauliflower, and carrots, thawed
- 1 (10 ounce) package frozen peas, thawed
- ⅔ cup sweet-and-sour sauce
- 1 tablespoon soy sauce
- ⅛ teaspoon black pepper

1. Cook chicken strips in large skillet with oil over medium heat, stirring occasionally, until brown (about 12–15 minutes).
2. Add garlic, vegetables, and peas. Cook, stirring, until vegetables are tender, about 5 minutes.
3. Add sweet-and-sour sauce, soy sauce, and pepper.
   Mix to stir and heat through.
4. Serve over rice.

{SERVES 4}

Who Knew? Light Switch

Save money by using our Sweet-and-Sour Stir-Fry Sauce rather than buying a bottle at the store.

125 Chicken Tarragon

Even if you're not familiar with the name "tarragon," you will probably recognize its scent and flavor. Tarragon works wonders in this recipe!

- 1 (8 ounce) package egg noodles
- 2 cups water
- 1 cup dry white wine
- 1 teaspoon dried tarragon leaves
- 1 (1 ounce) packet dry vegetable soup mix
- 4 boneless, skinless chicken breast halves

1. Cook noodles according to package directions, drain, and set aside.
2. Pour water into large skillet. Heating over medium heat, add wine and tarragon and bring to boil. Stir in dry soup mix and boil for 5 minutes.
3. Add chicken and reduce heat. Cover and simmer for 15 minutes or until juices run clear.
4. Arrange noodles on serving dish. Use slotted spoon to remove chicken and place on top of noodles. Cover with foil to keep warm.
5. Boil juices in skillet until liquid reduces to ½ cup, about 5–10 minutes. Heat for 3 to 4 minutes more and pour over chicken.

{SERVES 4}

126 Chicken-Broccoli Skillet

3 cups cubed chicken (about 1 pound)

1 tablespoon olive oil

1 (16 ounce) package frozen broccoli florets

1 (8 ounce) package shredded Cheddar cheese

¼ cup water

⅔ cup mayonnaise

1. Cook chicken cubes in large skillet with oil, stirring occasionally, until brown (about 12–15 minutes).
2. Add broccoli, cheese, and water.
3. Cover and cook over medium heat, stirring occasionally, until broccoli is tender-crisp and cheese melts. Turn off heat.
4. Stir in mayonnaise and heat through. Serve over rice.

{SERVES 4}

Who Knew?

If you like dry, fluffy rice, try this trick as soon as the rice is done cooking: Wrap the lid with a cotton dishtowel and set it on the pot for about 15 minutes. The cloth will absorb the steam.

127 Easy Chicken and Potatoes

1½ pounds new potatoes, quartered

1 tablespoon olive oil

1 teaspoon salt

1-1½ pounds chicken breasts

¼ cup dry white wine

2 tablespoons butter, divided

2 tablespoons rosemary
Salt and pepper to taste

1. Preheat oven to 425°.
2. Cook potatoes in hot oil over medium-high heat, stirring occasionally, until golden brown, about 15 minutes. Sprinkle with salt.
3. Transfer to baking sheet and bake for 10 minutes.
4. Cook chicken in skillet over medium-high heat, turning occasionally, until cooked through, about 3–5 minutes per side. Remove chicken and place on serving dish; keep warm.
5. Add wine to skillet, reduce heat to low, and simmer for 2 minutes, stirring constantly. Add 1 tablespoon of butter and whisk until combined. Add remaining butter and whisk until combined. Add rosemary and salt and pepper to taste.
6. Add potatoes to serving dish and spoon wine-butter mixture over top.

{SERVES 4}

128 Basic Breaded Chicken

Here's a great way to dress up chicken breasts. Learn this recipe and you'll use it again and again!

1 pound chicken breasts
2 large eggs
1 tablespoon Dijon mustard
1 cup dry bread crumbs
2 cups finely grated Parmesan cheese
½ teaspoon salt
¼ teaspoon black pepper
2 tablespoons olive oil

1. Rinse chicken and pat dry. Place chicken between two pieces of waxed paper and roll with rolling pin until ½-inch thick.
2. In small bowl, combine eggs and mustard and whisk until well blended.
3. In separate bowl, combine bread crumbs, Parmesan cheese, salt, and pepper.
4. Dip chicken breasts, one at a time, into egg mixture, then bread crumb mixture, coating each time.
5. Heat olive oil in skillet over medium-high heat.

   Add half of chicken breasts and cook, turning halfway through, until cooked through, about 3–5 minutes per side. Transfer to plate and repeat with remaining chicken breasts, adding more oil if necessary.

{SERVES 4}

Who Knew?

If you're having trouble getting the breading to stay on, here are a few tips you can try. First, make sure that the food that is to be breaded is very dry. Let the eggs heat up to room temperature before you use them. And use homemade breadcrumbs! Not only are they less expensive, but they stick better than store-bought because of their uneven texture.

129 Chicken and the Works

3 boneless, skinless chicken breast halves
1 tablespoons olive oil
½ (10 ounce) cans cream of chicken soup
1 cups water
1 cups instant white rice
1 (10 ounce) package frozen green peas, thawed

1. Brown chicken in large, 12-inch skillet with oil.

   Reduce heat, cover and simmer for about 15 minutes.

   Transfer chicken to plate and keep warm.
2. Add soup and water, and mix well. Heat to boiling and stir in rice and green peas.
3. Top with chicken breasts, then cover and simmer over low heat for about 10 minutes.

{SERVES 6}

130 Tasty Skillet Chicken

5 large boneless, skinless chicken breast halves
2 tablespoons olive oil
1 green bell pepper, seeded, julienned
1 red bell pepper, seeded, julienned
2 small yellow squash, seeded, julienned
1 (16 ounce) bottle chunky salsa

1. Cut chicken breasts into thin strips. Sauté in large skillet with a oil for 5 minutes over medium-high heat.

   Add peppers and squash and cook for an additional 5 minutes or until peppers are tender-crisp and chicken is cooked through.
2. Stir in salsa, lower heat to medium-low, and simmer for 10 minutes. Serve over rice.

{SERVES 5}

Who Knew? Light Switch

To make this recipe even lower in fat, substitute 2 cups of our Super Healthy Salsa for the jar of salsa.

131 Pimento Cheese-Stuffed Fried Chicken

"What can we make with pimento cheese?" you may wonder. This recipe is our answer.

½ cup milk
1 large egg, beaten
2 cups seasoned breadcrumbs
1 teaspoon salt
2 teaspoons black pepper
4 boneless, skinless chicken breast halves
Olive oil
1 (16 ounce) carton pimento cheese

1. Preheat oven to 350°.
2. Combine milk and egg in shallow bowl and mix well.

   In separate shallow bowl, combine breadcrumbs, salt, and pepper.
3. Dry chicken breasts with paper towels, then dip one-by-one in milk mixture, then dredge in breadcrumbs.
4. Pour oil to 1/8-inch in large skillet and heat on medium-high heat. Once hot, cook until golden brown, about 10–12 minutes on each side. Remove from oil and drain on paper towels.
5. Transfer chicken to sprayed, 9 x 13-inch baking sheet. Hold chicken with tongs and cut slit in one side of each chicken breast to form pocket. Spoon about ¼ cup pimento cheese into each pocket and bake until cheese melts, about 3 minutes.

{SERVES 4}

132 Parmesan Chicken

- **1 (8 ounce) packet Italian salad dressing mix**
- **½ cup grated Parmesan cheese**
- **¼ cup flour**
- **¾ teaspoon garlic powder**
- **5 boneless, skinless chicken breast halves**

1. Preheat oven to 375°.
2. Combine salad dressing mix, Parmesan cheese, flour, and garlic in shallow bowl.
3. Moisten chicken with a little water and coat with cheese mixture. Place in sprayed, 9 x 13-inch baking pan.
4. Bake for 25 minutes or until chicken is light brown and juices run clear.

{SERVES 6}

133 Lemon-Chicken Breeze

- **4-6 boneless, skinless chicken breast halves**
- **2-3 tablespoons flour**
- **½ cup (1 stick) butter**
- **2½ tablespoons olive oil**
- **½ cup dry white wine**
- **¼ cup lemon juice**
- **4 tablespoons chopped parsley**
- **⅛ teaspoon salt**

1. Preheat oven to 350°.
2. Turn each piece of chicken on its side and slice into 3 thin slices. Dredge each slice in flour.
3. Melt butter in skillet with oil over medium-high heat.

   When hot, add chicken and brown on all sides. Remove chicken and drain on paper towels.
4. Add wine, lemon juice, and parsley to skillet and mix.
5. Place chicken breasts in sprayed, 9 x 13-inch baking dish and pour warm lemon mixture over chicken.
6. Bake until sauce seeps into chicken, about15 minutes.

{SERVES 4-6}

134 Crunchy Chip Chicken

1½ cups crushed sour-cream-and-onion potato chips
1 tablespoon dried parsley
1 egg, beaten
1 tablespoonWorcestershire sauce
1 tablespoon water
4 large boneless, skinless chicken breast halves
¼ cup vegetable oil

1. Combine potato chips and parsley in shallow bowl.
2. In separate shallow bowl, combine beaten egg, Worcestershire sauce, and water.
3. Dip chicken pieces in egg mixture, then dredge chicken in potato chip mixture.
4. Heat oil in heavy skillet and fry chicken pieces in skillet, turning once, until golden brown or juices run clear, about 10 minutes on each side.

{SERVES 4}

Who Knew? Light Switch

For a lower fat version of this recipe, substitute the sour-cream-and-onion potato chips for 1½ cups panko bread crumbs (which can often be found in the "ethnic" aisle) and 1 teaspoon onion powder.

135 Easy Baked Chicken

You'll need to bake this chicken for more than 30 minutes, but with a prep time of about 5 minutes, it's so easy we included it here.

6 boneless, skinless chicken breast halves
½ cup (1 stick) butter, melted
Cornbread stuffing mix with seasoning, crushed

1. Preheat oven to 350°.
2. Dip chicken breasts in melted butter, then roll in cornbread stuffing mix to coat.
3. Place is shallow baking pan and bake for 45 minutes.

{SERVES 6}

136 Cheesy Crusted Chicken

¾ cup mayonnaise (not light)

½ cup grated Parmesan cheese

5-6 boneless, skinless chicken breast halves

1 cup Italian breadcrumbs

1. Preheat oven to 375°.
2. Combine mayonnaise and cheese in bowl. Place chicken breasts on sheet of wax paper and spread mayonnaise-cheese mixture over chicken. Sprinkle heavily with breadcrumbs on both sides.
3. Place chicken on sprayed, 9 x 13-inch baking pan so pieces do not touch. Bake for 20 minutes (25 minutes if chicken pieces are fairly large).
4. Serve as is, or slice chicken pieces and place on serving platter.

{SERVES 6}

Who Knew? Light Switch

It's easy to turn any of these meals into a "TV dinner." Just place the leftover meat along with any veggies or potatoes on a paper plate, then insert it into a freezer bag and freeze! Later on, you can poke a few holes in the bag and heat up in your microwave.

137 Asparagus Chicken

1 (8 ounce) package egg noodles

1 (1 ounce) packet hollandaise sauce mix

2 large boneless skinless chicken breasts, cut into strips
Olive oil

1 tablespoon lemon juice

1 pound asparagus (about 14–17 spears), bottoms removed

1. Prepare egg noodles and hollandaise sauce according to package directions. Set aside.
2. Cook chicken strips in large skillet with oil, stirring occasionally, until brown (about 12–15 minutes).
3. Add hollandaise sauce and lemon juice. Cover and cook for 5 minutes, then add asparagus spears. Cook until asparagus is tender, about another additional

5 minutes, stirring occasionally.

4. When ready to serve, place chicken asparagus mixture over noodles.

{SERVES 6}

138 Grilled Chicken Cordon Bleu

6 boneless, skinless chicken breast halves
6 slices Swiss cheese
6 thin slices deli ham
3 tablespoons olive oil
1 cup seasoned breadcrumbs

1. Flatten chicken to ¼-inch thickness. Place 1 slice each cheese and ham on each piece of chicken to within ¼-inch of edges.
2. Fold in half and secure with toothpicks. Brush chicken with oil and roll in breadcrumbs.
3. Grill, covered, over medium-hot heat for 15–18 minutes or until juices run clear.

{SERVES 6}

Who Knew?

When grilling chicken, always grease the rack well. Why? Because as the bird cooks, the collagen in the skin turns into a sticky gelatin, which will cause it to stick to the rack.

139 Grilled Chicken Fajitas

6 boneless, skinless chicken breast halves
¼ cup sesame seeds
⅛ teaspoon cayenne pepper
½ teaspoon salt
1 red or green bell pepper
1 medium onion
12 flour tortillas

1. Pound chicken breasts between pieces of wax paper to flatten.
2. Mix together sesame seeds, cayenne pepper, and salt. Sprinkle both sides of chicken with sesame seed mixture.
3. Slice bell pepper into strips and slice onion twice to make 3 thick slices.
4. Grill chicken breasts, bell pepper, and onion over charcoal fire. Cook for about 5 minutes on each side, or until chicken is browned and juices run clear. Cut chicken breasts into thin strips.
5. To assemble, warm each tortilla on grill for about 1 minute, then place several strips chicken, bell pepper, and onion in center of tortilla. Fold over and serve.

{SERVES 6}

Who Knew?

Traditional fajitas do not include sour cream or other fixings, but you don't have to be traditional! Try serving with cheese, guacamole or chopped avocado, sour cream, and/or salsa.

140 Grilled Lemon Chicken

- **2 teaspoons garlic salt**
- **1 tablespoon freshly grated lemon peel**
- **2 teaspoons dried thyme leaves**
- **½ teaspoon black pepper**
- **6 boneless, skinless chicken breast halves**

1. Combine garlic salt, lemon peel, thyme leaves, and pepper in small bowl. Heat coals and spray grill.
2. Sprinkle seasoning mixture over chicken breasts. Grill chicken for 3-5 minutes or until chicken is no longer pink and juices run clear. Turn once during cooking.

{SERVES 6}

Who Knew?

If you don't have garlic salt, you can substitute 2/3 teaspoon salt and 1⅓ teaspoon garlic powder.

141 Classic Chicken Piccata

- **5-6 boneless, skinless chicken breast halves**
- **2-3 tablespoons flour**
- **2 tablespoons olive oil**
- **3 tablespoons butter**
- **1 clove garlic, minced**
- **1 (1 pound) fresh mushrooms, sliced**
- **1 (14 ounce) can chicken broth**
- **½ cup dry white wine**
- **Juice from 1 lemon (about 3–4 tablespoons lemon juice)**
- **2 tablespoons capers**

1. Rinse chicken, pat dry, and flatten to about ¼-inch thick with rolling pin. Dredge in flour, coating well.
2. Pour oil and butter in large skillet and heat over medium-high heat. Place chicken in skillet and brown on all sides. Remove from skillet and keep warm.
3. Sauté garlic and mushrooms until tender. Add broth, wine, and lemon juice and simmer for several minutes.
4. Return chicken to skillet and coat with liquid.

   Add capers and simmer until chicken is done and juices run clear.

{SERVES 5-6}

Who Knew?

If you don't have a rolling pin on hand, reach for a zucchini. The chicken won't stick, and it's not as unseemly as using a shampoo bottle.

142 Chicken with Pine Nuts and Red Peppers

¾ pound boneless chicken breasts
1 tablespoon extra virgin olive oil
1 (14 ounce) can chicken broth
1 (8 ounce) can whole kernel corn, drained
½ of 1 (12 ounce) jar roasted red peppers, drained and chopped
¼ cup pine nuts, toasted

1. Preheat oven to 325°.
2. Chop chicken into cubes and brown in saucepan with oil for 5 minutes over medium-high heat, stirring frequently.
3. Add chicken broth, corn, and bell peppers. Cover and simmer for 10 minutes.
4. Spoon into sprayed, 7 x 11-inch baking dish, top with pine nuts, and bake for 15 minutes.

{SERVES 6}

143 Almond-Crusted Chicken

This recipe is a little more complicated than others in this chapter, but you'll love its sophisticated taste.

1 egg
1 teaspoon water
¼ cup seasoned breadcrumbs
1 cup slivered almonds
4 boneless, skinless chicken breast halves
1 teaspoon minced garlic
⅓ cup finely chopped onion
2 tablespoons canola oil
1 cup white wine
¼ cup teriyaki sauce
1 (5 ounce) package grated Parmesan cheese

1. Preheat oven to 375°.
2. Place egg and water in shallow bowl and beat.
   In another shallow bowl, combine breadcrumbs and almonds.
3. Dip each chicken breast in egg, then in almond mixture, and place in sprayed, 9 x 13-inch baking pan.
   Bake for 20 minutes.
4. Meanwhile, make sauce by first sautéing garlic and onion in saucepan with oil until they begin to turn translucent. Then add wine and teriyaki sauce.
5. Bring to a boil, then reduce heat and simmer until mixture reduces by half, about 10 minutes.
6. Remove chicken from oven and sprinkle Parmesan cheese over each breast. Cook for additional 5–10 minutes or until almonds and cheese are golden brown.
7. Pour sauce over chicken and serve.

{SERVES 4}

144 Honey-Glazed Chicken

This delightfully sweet chicken goes great with couscous or rice.

4 boneless, skinless chicken breast halves
Dash salt and pepper
1 tablespoon olive oil
1 (20 ounce) can pineapple chunks with juice
½ cup refrigerated dijon-style honey-mustard
1 green bell pepper, thinly sliced
1 red bell pepper, thinly sliced
1 (10 ounce) box couscous

1. Cut chicken breasts into strips, add a little salt and pepper and brown in large skillet with olive oil.
2. Add juice from pineapple, cover and simmer for 15 minutes.
3. Add honey-mustard, bell pepper slices and pineapple chunks to chicken. Bring to a boil, reduce heat, cover and simmer for additional 15 minutes.

{SERVES 4}

145 Stir-Fry Chicken Spaghetti

1 pound boneless, skinless chicken breast halves
¼ teaspoon salt
¼ teaspoon black pepper
1 tablespoon olive oil
1½ cups sliced mushrooms
1½ cups bell pepper strips
1 cup sweet-and-sour stir-fry sauce
1 (16 ounce) package spaghetti
¼ cup (½ stick) butter

1. Season chicken with salt and pepper and cut into thin slices. Brown chicken slices in large skillet with oil and cook for 5 minutes on medium-low heat. Transfer to plate and set aside.
2. In same skillet, stir-fry mushrooms and bell pepper strips for 5 minutes (add more olive oil if necessary). Add chicken strips and sweet-and-sour sauce and stir until ingredients are hot.
3. Prepare spaghetti according to package directions.

   While spaghetti is still hot, drain well, add butter and stir until butter melts. Place in large bowl and toss with chicken mixture. Serve hot.

{SERVES 5}

Who Knew? Light Switch

Save money by using our Sweet-and-Sour Stir-Fry Sauce rather than buying a bottle at the store.

146 Sweet 'n' Spicy Chicken

With so many brands of salsa these days, it's often easy to find one that's on sale. Grab the cheapest you can find for the "spicy" half of this recipe.

1 pound boneless, skinless chicken breast halves, cubed

1 (1 ounce) packet taco seasoning

1 tablespoon olive oil

1 (16 ounce) jar chunky salsa

1 cup peach preserves
Rice or noodles, cooked

1. Place chicken cubes in large, resealable plastic bag, add taco seasoning, and toss to coat.
2. Brown chicken in skillet with olive oil until chicken starts to brown, about 8 minutes.
3. Add salsa and preserves to skillet, mix well, and bring mixture to a boil.
4. Reduce heat, cover, and simmer until juices run clear.

Serve over rice or noodles.

{SERVES 4}

147 Fast Gobbler Fix

½ pound boneless, skinless chicken breasts, cubed

1 tablespoon olive oil

1 (16 ounce) package frozen, chopped onions and bell peppers

2 (3 ounce) packages chickenflavored ramen noodles

4 cups water

2 (10 ounce) cans cream of chicken soup

1. Cook chicken cubes over medium heat in soup pot with oil, stirring occasionally, until brown (about 10–15 minutes).
2. Add onions and peppers and cook until tender, but not brown. Add ramen noodles with seasoning packet and water. Cook for 5 minutes or until noodles are tender.
3. Stir in chicken soup. Heat, stirring constantly, until heated through. Serve as soup or over rice.

{SERVES 6}

Who Knew? Light Switch

To make this recipe low fat, substitute 2½ cups of our Low-Fat Cream of Chicken Soup Base for the cans of soup.

148 Creamy Tortellini Supper

- 1 pound chicken breasts
- 2 tablespoons olive oil
- 1 (9 ounce) package cheese tortellini (thaw if frozen)
- 1 (10 ounce) package frozen green peas, thawed
- 1 (8 ounce) package cream cheese with chives and onion
- ½ cup sour cream

1. Cook chicken in large skillet with oil over medium heat, turning once or twice, until chicken is slightly browned and juices run clear. Remove from skillet and keep warm.
2. Cook cheese tortellini according to package directions. When draining, place peas in colander and pour hot pasta water over green peas to warm. Return tortellini and peas to saucepan.
3. Combine cream cheese and sour cream in smaller saucepan and heat on low, stirring continuously, until cheese melts. Spoon mixture over tortellini and peas and toss with heat on low.
4. Spoon tortellini and peas in serving bowl and place chicken on top. Serve hot.

{**SERVES 6**}

149 Yummy Barbecued-Grilled Chicken

- 6 boneless, skinless chicken breast halves
- 3 cups ketchup
- ½ cup packed brown sugar
- ¼ cupWorcestershire sauce
- 2 tablespoons vinegar
- 1 teaspoon hot sauce
- 2 teaspoons salt
- ½ teaspoon black pepper

1. Rinse chicken and pat dry with paper towels.
2. Combine ketchup, brown sugar,Worcestershire sauce, vinegar, hot sauce, salt and pepper in saucepan and mix well. Bring to a boil, reduce heat to low, and cook for 15 minutes.
3. Fire up grill and smoke chicken over mesquite wood, if possible. Cook chicken for 8–10 minutes per side or until juices are clear, basting frequently with sauce.
4. Serve with remaining sauce for dipping.

{**SERVES 6**}

Who Knew?

Always leave 30 percent of your grill empty when cooking. Next time a flare up occurs, it's easy to move your dinner out of harm's way and prevent charring.

150 Sweet, Spicy Chicken Thighs

Dark meat chicken sometimes gets a bad name because it contains more fat than white meat, but it has lots of benefits, too. Dark meat stays moister, so you'll know it will be tender, and it is usually cheaper than white meat.

1 pound boneless, skinless chicken breast halves, cubed

1 (1 ounce) packet taco seasoning

1 tablespoon olive oil

1 (16 ounce) jar chunky salsa

1 cup peach preserves
Rice or noodles, cooked

1. Preheat oven to 425°.
2. Line 10 x 15-inch shallow baking pan with heavy foil and set metal rack in pan.
3. Combine chili powder, salt, pepper, honey, and lemon juice in bowl.
4. Brush mixture over chicken thighs and place on rack in baking pan. Turn thighs to coat completely.
5. Bake, turning over once, until juices run clear, about 30 minutes.

{SERVES 5-6}

151 Glazed Drumsticks

½ cup hoisin sauce

2 tablespoons light soy sauce

1 teaspoon minced garlic

1⅓ pound chicken drumsticks

1. Combine hoisin sauce, soy sauce and garlic in bowl and mix well. Set aside.
2. Place chicken legs in a single layer in sprayed, 9 x 13-inch baking dish and broil for 5 minutes.

   Turn chicken and broil for an additional 5 minutes on opposite side.
3. Remove from heat and preheat oven to 325°.
4. Brush chicken with sauce, leaving some for basting.
5. Bake until glaze bubbles and browns, about 20 minutes. During baking time, brush legs with remaining sauce once or twice.

{SERVES 8}

152 Chicken Caesar Pizza

It may seem strange to put salad on a pizza, but pizza with greens is actually quite common around Italy.

1 (12 inch) Italian pizza crust
1 (8 ounce) package shredded mozzarella cheese
1 (6 ounce) package cooked chicken breast strips
2 cups shredded lettuce
3 fresh scallions, sliced
½ (8 ounce) bottle Caesar dressing

1. Preheat oven to 400°.
2. Top pizza crust with mozzarella cheese and bake for 8 minutes or until cheese melts.
3. Combine chicken strips, lettuce, onions, and cheese in bowl. Pour Caesar dressing over salad and toss.
4. Top hot pizza with salad and cut into wedges.
   Serve immediately.

{SERVES 4}

153 Easy Chicken and Dumplings

For this recipe, use an inexpensive rotisserie chicken from your local supermarket, or ask the butcher to cut you a slab of chicken rather than slicing it.

3 cups cooked, chopped chicken (about 1 pound)
2 (10 ounce) cans cream of chicken soup
3 teaspoons chicken bouillon granules
4½ cups water
1 (8 ounce) can refrigerated buttermilk biscuits

1. Combine chicken, soup, bouillon granules, and water in large soup pot or large, heavy pan. Boil mixture and stir to mix well.
2. Separate biscuits and cut in half; cut again making 4 pieces out of each biscuit. Drop biscuit pieces one at a time into boiling chicken mixture and stir gently.
3. When all biscuits are in pot, reduce heat to low, simmer, and stir occasionally for 15 minutes.

{SERVES 8}

Who Knew? Light Switch

To make this recipe low fat, substitute 2½ cups of our Low-Fat Cream of Chicken Soup Base for the cans of soup and use low-fat biscuits.

154 Spicy Orange Chicken

Chicken fingers aren't just for kids! Here's a great way to jazz them up for adults.

- **¾ cup orange marmalade**
- **1 tablespoon canola oil**
- **1 tablespoon soy sauce**
- **1½ teaspoons lime juice**
- **½ teaspoon minced ginger**
- **½ teaspoon cayenne pepper**
- **1 pound chicken tenders**
- **2 tablespoons canola oil**
- **2 tablespoons soy sauce**
- **1 (16 ounce) package frozen stir-fry vegetables, thawed**

1. To make sauce, combine marmalade, oil, soy sauce, lime juice, minced ginger and cayenne pepper in saucepan and mix well. Let heat while preparing chicken.
2. Lightly brown chicken tenders in oil in large skillet over medium-high heat. Add soy sauce and cook for an additional 3 minutes.
3. Add stir-fry vegetables and cook for about 5 minutes or until vegetables are tender-crisp.
4. Pour warm sauce over stir-fry chicken and vegetables.

   Mix well and serve over rice or chow mein noodles.

{SERVES 6}

Who Knew?

If you don't have orange marmalade, you can substitute frozen, concentrated orange juice (that has been thawed) and a bit of orange or lemon zest (peel).

155 Stir-Fry Cashew Chicken

- **1 tablespoon olive oil**
- **1 pound chicken tenders, cut into strips**
- **1 (16 ounce) package frozen broccoli, cauliflower, and carrots**
- **1 (8 ounce) jar stir-fry sauce (teriyaki or another flavor)**
- **⅓ cup cashew halves**
- **1 (12 ounce) package chow mein noodles**

1. Place oil in large skillet or wok over high heat. When hot, add chicken and cook, stirring frequently, for 4 minutes.
2. Add vegetables and cook for additional 4 minutes or until vegetables are tender. Stir in stir-fry sauce and cashews and cook until mixture is hot. Serve over chow mein noodles.

{SERVES 6}

156 Italian Chicken Over Polenta

2 ½ cups water
¾ cup cornmeal
½ teaspoon salt
⅔ cup grated Parmesan cheese
1 pound frozen chicken tenders, each cut in half
1 tablespoon extra virgin olive oil
1 onion, chopped
1 (15 ounce) can Italian stewed tomatoes
⅔ cup pitted Kalamata olives
Salt and pepper to taste

1. To make polenta, bring water to a boil in medium saucepan. Stir in cornmeal and salt and cook, stirring occasionally, until mixture starts to thicken. Stir in Parmesan cheese.
2. Place chicken in large skillet with oil.
3. Add onion and cook covered over medium-high heat for about 8 minutes, turning halfway through.
4. Add tomatoes and olives, cover and cook for additional 8 minutes or until chicken is done.
5. Spoon polenta onto serving plates and top with chicken and sauce.

{SERVES 6}

157 Turkey and Rice Olé

This one-dish meal can be served over rice or in tortillas as wraps.

1 pound ground turkey
1 (5½ ounce) package Mexican rice mix
2 cups water
1 (15 ounce) can black beans, rinsed, drained
1 cup chunky salsa
Flour tortillas (optional)

1. Brown turkey in large skillet, stirring occasionally and breaking up large pieces. Add rice mix and water.
2. Bring to a boil, reduce heat, and simmer until rice is tender, about 8 minutes. Stir in beans and salsa and cook just until mixture is hot.
3. If desired, warm tortillas and spoon mixture inside.

{SERVES 6}

158 Chicken Sausage Pasta

1 (16 ounce) package rigatoni (tube) pasta
1 tablespoon olive oil
1 (1 pound) package chicken sausages, sliced
1 cloves garlic
2 red bell pepper, seeded, chopped
1 teaspoon salt
¼ teaspoon red pepper flakes
⅛ cup grated Parmesan cheese
¾ cup pitted Kalamata olives
Salt and pepper to taste

1. Cook pasta according to package directions.
2. Heat oil in skillet. When hot, add bell pepper, sausage slices. Cook over medium heat until bell pepper is tender and sausage is cooked through, about 7 minutes. Add garlic, salt, and red pepper flakes 1 minute before end of cooking time.
3. Toss with pasta to coat. Serve with Parmesan cheese.

{SERVES 4}

159 Pasta-Turkey Salad Supper

This is a great recipe for when deli turkey is on sale. Our favorite kind is hickory-smoked cracked-pepper, but you can use any variety.

1 (12 ounce) package tri-color spiral pasta
1 (4 ounce) can sliced ripe olives, drained
1 cup fresh broccoli florets
1 cup fresh cauliflower florets
2 small yellow squash, sliced
1 cup halved cherry tomatoes
1 (8 ounce) bottle Parmesan ranch dressing
1 pounds hickory-smoked crackedpepper turkey breast, cooked, sliced

1. Cook pasta according to package directions. Drain and rinse in cold water. Add olives, broccoli, cauliflower, sliced squash, and tomatoes and combine in large salad bowl.
2. Toss with dressing. Place thin slices of turkey breast, arranged in rows, over salad. Serve immediately.

{SERVES 8}

160 Super Easy Turkey Treat

1 pound ground turkey
1 (10 ounce) can tomato soup
1 (10 ounce) can tomato bisque soup
1 cup chunky salsa
8 (6-inch) corn tortillas, cut into 1-inch pieces
¼ cup water
1 cup shredded Mexican four-cheese blend, divided

1. Preheat oven to 375°.
2. Cook ground turkey in large skillet over medium-high heat, stirring often, until turkey is light brown. Drain.
3. Stir in soups, salsa, tortillas, water, and half cheese.
4. Spoon into sprayed, 7 x 11-inch glass baking dish.
5. Cover and bake for 35–40 minutes. Remove from oven and sprinkle with remaining cheese.

{SERVES 4-6}

Who Knew? Light Switch

To make this recipe lower in fat, try using our Super Healthy Salsa and Low-Fat Four-Cheese Blend!

161 Tasty Turkey Crunch

It doesn't get much easier than this yummy dish that's reminiscent of Thanksgiving. If you don't have any leftover turkey, ask at the deli counter for a slab of turkey (rather than slices).

1 (8 ounce) package noodles
2½ cups cooked, diced turkey (about 1 pound)
1 (1 ounce) packet chicken gravy, prepared
2 cups crushed round buttery crackers

1. Preheat oven to 350°.
2. Cook noodles according to package directions; drain.
3. Spread noodles into sprayed, 2-quart baking dish.

   Place turkey on top of noodles, cover with gravy, and top with cracker crumbs.
4. Bake for 35 minutes.

{SERVES 6}

162 Chicken Super Supper

- **5 boneless, skinless chicken breast halves**
- **5 slices onion**
- **5 potatoes, peeled, quartered**
- **1 (10 ounce) can cream of celery soup**
- **¼ cup water**

1. Preheat oven to 325°.
2. Place chicken breasts in sprayed, 9 x 13-inch baking dish. Top chicken with onion slices and place potatoes around chicken.
3. Heat soup with water in saucepan over medium heat for 5 minutes.
4. Pour soup over chicken and vegetables. Cover and bake for 1 hour 10 minutes.

{SERVES 5}

Who Knew? Light Switch

To make this dish lower in fat, substitute 1¼ cups of our Low-Fat Cream of Celery Soup Base for the can of soup.

163 Chicken with White Wine Sauce

- **¼ cup (½ stick) butter**
- **4 large boneless, skinless chicken breast halves**
- **1 cup diced celery**
- **½ cup seeded, diced green or red bell pepper**
- **½ cup minced onion**
- **1½ cups white wine**

1. Melt butter in large skillet over medium-high heat, and brown chicken on all sides, about 5 minutes per side.
2. Remove chicken and set aside.
3. Sauté celery, bell pepper, and onion in saucepan until tender, about 5–8 minutes. Pour in wine and stir.
4. Return chicken to skillet, cover, and cook over medium heat until juices run clear, about 15 minutes.

   While cooking, baste with pan juices several times.

{SERVES 4}

Who Knew?

Old white wine can be used for more than just cooking! Use white wine to wipe down your shower doors and bathroom title. Its low alcohol content makes it perfect for soap scum, while remaining non-toxic.

164 Chicken Diablo

Cumin, one of our favorite spices, gives this chicken a rich, smoky flavor.

6 boneless, skinless chicken breast halves

1 (8 ounce) package cream cheese, softened

1 (16 ounce) jar salsa

2 teaspoons ground cumin

1 bunch fresh scallions with tops, chopped

1. Preheat oven to 350°.
2. Pound chicken breasts to flatten.
3. Beat cream cheese in bowl until smooth; add salsa, cumin, and onions.
4. Place heaping spoonful of cream cheese mixture on each chicken breast. There will be leftover mixture for later.
5. Roll up each breast so cream cheese mixture is wrapped in center.
6. Place chicken rolls seam-side down in sprayed, 7 x 11-inch baking dish. Spoon remaining cream cheese mixture over rolls.
7. Cover and bake for 30 minutes. Uncover and continue baking until chicken rolls are light brown.

{SERVES 6}

Who Knew? Light Switch

To save money and make this recipe even healthier, substitute 2 cups of our Super Healthy Salsa for the jar of salsa.

165 Grilled Tequila Chicken

½ cup lime juice

¼ cup tequila

1½ teaspoons chili powder

1½ teaspoons minced garlic

1 teaspoon seeded jalapeño pepper, very finely chopped

6 boneless chicken breast halves

¼ teaspoon salt

⅛ teaspoon black pepper

1. Combine lime juice, tequila, chili powder, garlic, and jalapeño pepper in large resealable plastic bag.
2. Add chicken breasts, seal bag, and turn to coat.
   Refrigerate for 10 hours or overnight.
3. Remove breasts from marinade and sprinkle with salt and pepper. Discard marinade.
4. Grill chicken breasts skin-side down for 5–7 minutes.
   Turn over and grill until cooked through, about 10 minutes.
5. Remove to platter, cover, and let stand for 5 minutes before serving.

{SERVES 6}

166 Salsa-Grilled Chicken

4-5 boneless, skinless chicken breast halves
1 (16 ounce) jar thick-and-chunky salsa, divided
¼ cup soy sauce
1 tablespoon Dijon-style mustard

1. Pound chicken to about ½-inch thick.
2. Combine half of salsa, soy sauce, and mustard in large bowl. Add chicken to bowl, coat with marinade, and marinate for 2–3 hours in refrigerator.
3. Grill over hot coals, flipping as needed, until juices run clear. Top with remaining salsa.

{SERVES 4-5}

Who Knew? Light Switch

To save money and make this recipe even tastier, use 1 cup of our Super Healthy Salsa rather than jarred salsa for the garnish.

167 Grilled Lime-Salsa Campsite Chicken

Even if you don't have a campfire (or a charcoal grill), this recipe tastes delicious using a propane or countertop grill.

¼ cup olive oil
1 (10 ounce) jar green chili salsa
1½ tablespoons lime juice
½ teaspoon sugar
1 tablespoon minced garlic
1 teaspoon ground cumin
½ teaspoon oregano
6 boneless, skinless chicken breast halves

1. Combine oil, salsa, lime juice, sugar, garlic, cumin, and oregano in bowl and mix well. Add chicken breasts and marinate for 3–4 hours.
2. Cook over hot coals, turning occasionally, until juices run clear, about 10–15 minutes.

{SERVES 6}

Who Knew?

Mincing garlic is usually a sticky mess, but it doesn't have to be! Just sprinkle the garlic with a few drops of olive oil beforehand. The oil will prevent the garlic from sticking to your hands or the knife.

168 Almond Chicken

We love the tiny taste of bourbon in this dish! Don't worry, the alcohol cooks off, so it's safe for the kids, too!

- **3 tablespoons butter**
- **4 boneless, skinless chicken breast halves**
- **1 (6 ounce) can frozen orange juice concentrate, thawed**
- **½ teaspoon salt**
- **¼ teaspoon black pepper**
- **2 tablespoons bourbon**
- **½ cup chopped, salted almonds, toasted**

1. Melt butter in skillet. Add chicken and cook over medium heat, flipping once, until brown on both sides, about 10 minutes. Reduce heat to low.
2. Add orange juice, salt, and pepper. Cover and cook over medium heat for 25 minutes. Spoon sauce over chicken twice while it cooks. Remove chicken to serving platter and keep warm.
3. Add bourbon to sauce in skillet and cook, stirring occasionally, for 10 minutes.
4. Pour mixture over chicken and serve over rice.
   Sprinkle with almonds.

{SERVES 4}

Who Knew?

One of the easiest—and certainly one of the most fun—ways to toast nuts is in a popcorn air popper. Place the almonds for this recipe into the popper and plug it in for 60 seconds. The nuts will be perfectly browned on all sides!

169 Fruited Chicken

- **6 large boneless, skinless chicken breast halves**
- **½ cup (1 stick) butter, melted**
- **⅔ cup flour**
- **½ teaspoon salt**
- **¼ teaspoon black pepper**
- **¼ teaspoon paprika**
- **1 (15 ounce) can chunky fruit cocktail with juice**

1. Preheat oven to 350°.
2. Dip chicken in butter, then in flour. Place in sprayed, 9 x 13-inch baking dish. Sprinkle with salt, pepper, and paprika.
3. Bake for 45 minutes.
4. Pour fruit and half juice over chicken. Bake for additional 20 minutes.

{SERVES 6}

170 Sassy Chicken Over Tex-Mex Corn

- **2 teaspoons garlic powder**
- **1 teaspoon ground cumin**
- **⅔ cup flour**
- **1½ teaspoons salt**
- **4 boneless, skinless chicken breast halves**
- **1 tablespoon olive oil**
- **2 tablespoons water**
- **1 (10 ounce) can chicken broth**
- **1½ cups hot salsa**
- **1 (11 ounce) can Mexicorn**
- **1 cup rice, cooked**

1. Combine garlic powder, cumin, flour, and salt in shallow bowl.
2. Cut chicken breasts in half lengthwise. Then dip in lour mixture, coating all sides.
3. Pour oil in heavy skillet over medium-high heat. Brown each chicken breast on both sides (about
2 minutes per side), reduce heat, and add water to skillet.
4. Cover and simmer for 15 minutes. Transfer chicken to foil-lined baking pan and place in oven at 250° to keep warm.
5. Using the same skillet, combine broth, salsa, and corn and cook for 10 minutes. Stir in rice until well mixed.
6. To serve, spoon corn mixture on platter and place chicken breasts over corn.

{SERVES 4}

Who Knew? Light Switch

To save money and make this recipe even healthier, substitute 1¼ cups of our Healthy Chicken Broth for the can of chicken broth, and 2 cups of our Super Healthy Salsa for the jar of salsa.

171 Chili-Chicken Roll-Ups

- **8 boneless, skinless chicken breast halves**
- **1 teaspoon salt**
- **½ teaspoon black pepper**
- **2 (4 ounce) cans diced green chilies**
- **1 (8 ounce) package shredded Cheddar cheese**
- **½ cup (1 stick) butter, melted**
- **2 cups crushed tortilla chips**

1. Place each chicken breast on wax paper and flatten to about ¼-inch thickness with rolling pin or mallet. Sprinkle with salt and pepper.
2. Place 1/8 of green chilies and 1/8 of cheese evenly in center of each chicken breast. Carefully roll each chicken breast so no chilies or cheese seep out, and secure with toothpicks.
3. Place chicken rolls in small baking dish, and refrigerate or freeze.
4. When ready to bake, thaw chicken rolls and preheat oven to 350°.
5. Dip each chicken roll in melted butter, then in crushed tortilla chips.
6. Bake until heated through, about 25–30 minutes.

{SERVES 8}

172 Chicken Crunch

Here's another recipe that uses super-healthy corn flakes as a low-fat breading.

3-4 boneless, skinless chicken breast halves

½ cup Italian salad dressing

½ cup sour cream

2½ cups crushed corn flakes

1. Place chicken in resealable plastic bag; add salad dressing and sour cream. Seal and refrigerate 1 hour.

   Remove chicken from marinade and discard marinade.
2. When ready to bake, preheat oven to 375°.
3. Dredge chicken in corn flakes, and place in sprayed, 9 x 13-inch baking dish.
4. Bake for 45 minutes.

{SERVES 4-6}

Who Knew?

We love making this marinade with our Low-Fat Sour Cream Substitute and our Italian Salad Dressing Mix.

173 Lemon Dill Chicken

3 tablespoons butter

5-6 boneless, skinless chicken breast halves

2 cups water

½ teaspoon salt

2 teaspoons dried dill weed

1 tablespoon lemon juice

¼ teaspoon black pepper

1. Melt butter in skillet over medium-high heat.

   Place chicken breast halves in skillet and cook over medium-high heat until brown on both sides, about 3–5 minutes per side.
2. Stir water, salt, and dill weed into skillet; bring to a boil.
3. Reduce heat to low, cover, and simmer, stirring occasionally, until chicken is cooked through, about 25–30 minutes.
4. Add lemon juice and pepper and cook for 5 minutes more.
5. Serve over white or brown rice.

{SERVES 6}

174 Springy Chicken

- **4-5 boneless, skinless chicken breast halves**
- **1 tablespoon oregano**
- **¾ teaspoon garlic powder**
- **½ cup (1 stick) butter, melted**

1. Rub chicken with oregano and garlic powder and marinate in refrigerator for 3–4 hours.
2. When ready to bake, preheat oven to 325°.
3. Place chicken in sprayed, 9 x 13-inch baking dish and pour melted butter on top.
4. Cover and bake for 1 hour.

{SERVES 5}

Who Knew?

Don't worry if you're missing a spice other ingredient you as prepare tonight's dinner. Just head over to RecipeTips.com, where you'll find all sorts of substitutions (and healthier options) so you can keep your meal on schedule!

175 Sweet Pepper Chicken

- **6-8 boneless, skinless chicken breast halves**
- **2 tablespoons vegetable or canola oil**
- **⅓ cup cornstarch**
- **⅔ cup sugar**
- **½ cup packed brown sugar**
- **1 teaspoon chicken bouillon granules**
- **1 (15 ounce) can pineapple chunks with juice**
- **1 ½ cups orange juice**
- **½ cup vinegar**
- **¼ cup ketchup**
- **2 tablespoons soy sauce**
- **¼ teaspoon ground ginger**
- **1 red bell pepper, seeded, thinly sliced**

1. Preheat oven to 325°.
2. Place chicken breast halves in skillet with oil and cook over medium-high heat until brown on both sides, about 3 minutes per side. Place in sprayed, 10 x 15-inch baking dish.
3. Combine cornstarch, sugar, brown sugar, and bouillon granules in large saucepan and mix well.
4. Drain pineapple and set aside juice. Add pineapple juice, orange juice, vinegar, ketchup, soy sauce, and ginger to cornstarch mixture and mix well.
5. Cook on high heat, stirring constantly, until mixture thickens. Pour sauce over chicken breasts.
6. Bake for 45 minutes.
7. Remove from oven, add pineapple chunks and bell pepper, and bake for additional 15 minutes.

{SERVES 8-10}

176 Baked Chicken Poupon

- 2 tablespoons Dijon-style mustard
- 2 tablespoons olive oil
- 1 teaspoon garlic powder
- ½ teaspoon Italian seasoning
- 4 boneless, skinless chicken breast halves

1. Preheat oven to 375°.
2. Combine mustard, oil, garlic powder, and seasoning in resealable plastic bag. Add chicken breasts and marinate for 15 minutes.
3. Place chicken in sprayed, 9 x 13-inch baking pan.
4. Bake for 35 minutes.

{SERVES 4}

177 Curry-Glazed Chicken

- 3 tablespoons butter
- ⅓ cup honey
- 2 tablespoons Dijon-style mustard
- 1½ teaspoons curry powder
- 4 boneless, skinless chicken breast halves

1. Preheat oven to 375°.
2. Melt butter in 9 x 13-inch baking pan.
3. Mix honey, mustard, and curry powder in pan with butter.
4. Add chicken to pan and turn until chicken is coated with butter mixture.
5. Bake for 50 minutes, basting twice with liquid in pan. Serve over rice.

{SERVES 4}

Who Knew?

Before using a measuring cup to measure out sticky liquid like honey, coat the inside with vegetable oil or nonstick cooking spray. The liquid will pour out easily.

178 Montezuma Celebration Chicken

- **6 boneless, skinless chicken breast halves**
- **1 green bell pepper, seeded, cut in rings**
- **1 (16 ounce) jar hot salsa**
- **⅔ cup packed brown sugar**
- **1 tablespoon mustard**
- **½ teaspoon salt**

1. Preheat oven to 350°.
2. Place chicken breasts in sprayed, 9 x 13-inch baking dish without breasts touching each other. Cover with bell pepper rings. Combine salsa, brown sugar, mustard, and salt in bowl and spoon over each piece of chicken.
3. Cover and bake for 35–40 minutes. Uncover and continue baking for additional 10–15 minutes to let chicken breasts brown slightly.

{SERVES 6}

Who Knew? Light Switch

To save money and make this recipe even healthier, substitute 2 cups of our Super Healthy Salsa for the jar of salsa. Add a pinch of cayenne pepper for kick.

179 Oven-Fried Chicken

- **⅔ cup fine dry breadcrumbs**
- **⅓ cup grated Parmesan cheese**
- **½ teaspoon garlic salt**
- **½ cup Italian salad dressing**
- **6 boneless, skinless chicken breast halves**

1. Preheat oven to 350°.
2. Combine breadcrumbs, cheese, and garlic salt in shallow bowl. Pour salad dressing in separate shallow bowl. Dip chicken in dressing and dredge in crumb mixture.
3. Place chicken in 9 x 13-inch sprayed baking pan.
4. Bake for 50 minutes.

{SERVES 6}

Who Knew? Light Switch

To save money and make this dish even more delicious, try using our Italian Salad Dressing Mix!

180 Apricot-Ginger Chicken

2 teaspoons ground ginger

½ cup Italian dressing

4 boneless, skinless chicken breast halves

⅔ cup apricot preserves

1. Combine ginger and Italian dressing; place in large resealable plastic bag.
2. Add chicken to bag. Marinate in refrigerator overnight, turning occasionally.
3. When ready to bake, preheat oven to 350°.
4. Remove chicken from refrigerator and reserve ¼ cup marinade. Place chicken in shallow baking dish. Bake, covered, for 35 minutes.
5. Pour reserved marinade in saucepan, bring to boil over medium-high heat, and cook, stirring, for 1 minute.

   Remove from heat and stir in apricot preserves.
6. Brush chicken with marinade mixture and return to oven for additional 10 minutes.

{SERVES 4}

Who Knew? Light Switch

To save money and make this recipe even tastier, try using our Italian Salad Dressing Mix!

181 Chicken and Wild Rice

For a thicker sauce in this dish, spoon 3 tablespoons sauce into small bowl and stir in 2 tablespoons flour. Mix well and add back to rest of sauce. Heat over low heat, stirring constantly until sauce thickens.

1 (6 ounce) package long-grain and wild rice mix

4-5 boneless, skinless chicken breast halves

1 tablespoon olive oil

2 cans French onion soup

¾ cup water

1 red bell pepper, seeded, julienned

1 green bell pepper, seeded, julienned

1. Cook rice according to package directions in saucepan. Keep warm.
2. Brown chicken breasts on both sides with oil in over medium-high heat, about 3 minutes per side.
3. Add soup, water, and bell peppers. Reduce heat to medium-low. Cover and cook for 15 minutes.
4. To serve, place rice on serving platter with chicken breasts on top. Transfer onion soup sauce into a gravy boat, and pour over chicken and rice when ready to eat.

{SERVES 5}

182 Quick and Tasty Baked Chicken

This is an easy dish to stick in the oven while you're also baking a casserole!

4 boneless, skinless chicken breast halves

1 (10 ounce) can Italian tomato soup

2 tablespoonsWorcestershire sauce

1 teaspoon garlic powder

1½ tablespoons packed brown sugar

1. Preheat oven to 350°.
2. Place chicken breasts in sprayed, 7 x 11-inch baking dish.
3. Combine tomato soup,Worcestershire sauce, garlic, and brown sugar in small bowl and mix well. Spoon over chicken.
4. Bake for 1 hour.

{SERVES 4}

Who Knew?

If you only have "regular" tomato soup, simply add a teaspoon of oregano and/or basil to this recipe.

183 Jalapeño Chicken

The sour cream and white wine balance out the spiciness of this festive dish.

5-6 boneless, skinless chicken breast halves

¼ cup olive oil

¼ cup white wine

1 (1 pint) carton sour cream

1 tablespoon flour

1 clove garlic, minced

½ teaspoon salt

¼ teaspoon black pepper

½ teaspoon ground cumin

1 (7 ounce) can whole jalapeño peppers

1 (12 ounce) package shredded Monterey Jack cheese

1 onion, sliced in rounds

1. Preheat oven to 325°.
2. Cook chicken on with oil in skillet over medium-high heat, flipping once, until both sides are brown, about 3 minutes per side. Place in 9 x 13-inch baking dish.
3. Combine wine, sour cream, flour, garlic, salt, pepper, cumin, and jalapeño peppers in blender. Blend until smooth to make sauce.
4. Pour sauce over chicken breasts, sprinkle with cheese, and top with onion rings.
5. Cover and bake for 1 hour.

{SERVES 6}

184 Pineapple-Teriyaki Chicken

You'll fall in love with the sweet taste of pineapple mixed with the teriyaki sauce in this delectable dinner!

6 boneless, skinless chicken breast halves

½ red onion, sliced

1 green bell pepper, seeded, sliced

1 cup teriyaki marinade

1 (15 ounce) can pineapple rings with juice

1. Preheat oven to 350°.
2. Place chicken in sprayed, 9 x 13-inch baking dish and arrange vegetables over chicken.
3. Mix teriyaki marinade with juice from canned pineapple. Pour over vegetables and chicken.
4. Bake for 35 minutes. Spoon juices over chicken once during baking.
5. Place pineapple rings on top of chicken and return to oven for additional 10 minutes.

{SERVES 6}

185 Mandarin Chicken

1 (11 ounce) can mandarin oranges, drained

1 (6 ounce) can frozen orange juice concentrate

1 tablespoon lemon juice

⅔ cup water

1 tablespoon cornstarch

4 boneless, skinless chicken breast halves

2 tablespoons garlic-and-herb seasoning

2 tablespoons butter

Water, as necessary

1. Combine oranges, orange juice concentrate, lemon juice, water, and cornstarch in saucepan. Cook on medium heat, stirring constantly, until mixture thickens. Set aside.
2. Sprinkle chicken breasts with seasoning and place in skillet with butter. Cook until brown on each side, about 7 minutes per side.
3. Lower heat and spoon orange juice mixture over chicken. Cover and simmer for 20 minutes, adding a little water if sauce gets too thick.

{SERVES 4}

Who Knew?

Who needs a spoon rest when you're at the stove cooking? Just rest your spoon on a piece of bread, which will catch all the juices and bits of food. Toss the bread when you're done cooking and clean-up is a cinch!

186 Ranch Chicken

6 boneless, skinless chicken breast halves

1 (1 ounce) packet ranch buttermilk salad dressing mix

1 cup buttermilk

½ cup mayonnaise

2-3 cups crushed corn flakes

1. Preheat oven to 350°.
2. Pat chicken pieces dry and place on paper towels.
3. Combine ranch dressing mix, buttermilk, and mayonnaise in shallow bowl and mix well.
4. Dip chicken pieces in dressing and cover well. Roll each piece in corn flakes and coat all sides well.
5. Place chicken pieces in sprayed, 9 x 13-inch baking dish. Make sure they do not touch each other. Bake for 1 hour.

{SERVES 6-8}

Who Knew?

Want to cook once and eat twice? Next time you're preparing boneless, skinless chicken breasts, make a few extra, toss in a freezer bag with some Caesar dressing, and refrigerate. Tomorrow night, warm them in the microwave, toss over salad greens, shave a little Parmesan cheese on top, and dinner is ready!

187 Ritzy Chicken

You'll be surprised what a different taste the sour cream gives this melt-in-your mouth chicken dish.

⅓ (12 ounce) box round buttery crackers, crushed

¼ teaspoon black pepper

6 boneless, skinless chicken breast halves

1 (8 ounce) carton sour cream

1. Preheat oven to 350°.
2. Combine cracker crumbs and pepper in dish or pie plate.
3. Dip chicken in sour cream, then roll in cracker crumbs.
4. Place chicken in sprayed, 9 x 13-inch baking dish.
5. Bake for 55 minutes.

{SERVES 6}

Who Knew? Light Switch

To make this recipe lower in fat, substitute 1 cup of our Low-Fat Sour Cream Substitute for the carton of sour cream.

188 Chicken Cacciatore

You don't need to use the oven to make a whole chicken! This stovetop supper is perfect for when the oven's full.

1 (2 pound) broiler-fryer chicken, cut up
1 tablespoons butter
½ tablespoons butter
½ tablespoons butter

1. Quarter chicken and sprinkle with salt and pepper.
2. Place in large skillet with oil on medium-high heat.
   Add sliced onions, then cook until chicken is browned, about 3 minutes on each side. Heat 10 minutes more, flipping halfway through.
3. Add stewed tomatoes, tomato sauce, oregano, and celery seed. Bring mixture to a boil, then reduce heat to low and simmer for 20 minutes.
4. Serve over hot pasta.

{SERVES 6}

Who Knew?

Reusable plastic containers are perfect for keeping leftovers, but tomato sauce will often stain clear plastic. To keep this from happening, simply spray the container with non-stick cooking spray (or vegetable oil) before storing tomato-based dishes like this one.

189 Honey-Mustard Turkey Breast

½ cup maple syrup
1 cup honey
1 teaspoon dry mustard
¼ cup red wine vinegar
1 (4 pound) bone-in turkey breast

1. Combine syrup, honey, mustard, and vinegar in saucepan and bring to a boil.
2. Reduce heat and simmer until glaze is thick, about 20 minutes. Reserve 1 cup.
3. Place turkey breast in roasting pan and pour remaining glaze over turkey. Bake until cooked through, about 1½ –2 hours.
4. Slice turkey and serve with heated, reserved glaze. Let sit 15 minutes.

{SERVES 8}

190 Herb-Roasted Turkey

½ cup maple syrup
1 cup honey
1 teaspoon dry mustard
¼ cup red wine vinegar
1 (4 pound) bone-in turkey breast

1. Preheat oven to 325°.
2. Combine poultry seasonings, paprika, garlic powder, nutmeg, salt, and pepper in small bowl.
3. Rinse turkey under cold water and pat dry. Place onion wedges in turkey cavity and rub about half of rub mixture inside.
4. Place turkey breast-side up on shallow roasting pan lined with heavy foil. Spread oil over outside of turkey.

   Sprinkle remaining rub mixture over turkey. Add ½ cup water to roasting pan.
5. Cover loosely with heavy foil and bake until meat thermometer inserted in breast reaches 175°, about3 hours 30 minutes. Let stand for 15 minutes before carving. Reserve pan juices for gravy.
6. Combine gravy mix and flour in saucepan. Slowly stir in pan drippings and remaining water, stirring constantly.
7. Bring to a boil, then reduce heat and stir constantly until mixture thickens.

{SERVES 16-20}

191 Turkey Croquettes

If you don't have any leftover turkey to use for this recipe, ask for a slab of unsliced turkey at your market's deli counter.

1 ½ cups cooked, chopped turkey
1 (10 ounce) can cream of chicken soup
1 cup stuffing mix
2 eggs
1 tablespoon minced onion
1 cup flour
Vegetable or canola oil

1. Combine turkey, soup, stuffing mix, eggs, and onion in bowl and refrigerate for several hours.
2. Divide mixture and shape into patties or balls.
3. Dredge croquettes in flour and fry in vegetable or canola oil until brown, about 1–2 minutes.

{SERVES 6}

Who Knew?

To make this recipe lower in fat, substitute 1¼ cup of our Low-Fat Cream of Chicken Soup Base for the can of cream of chicken soup.

192 Grilled Caribbean Turkey

These turkey tenderloins have a wonderful sweet-and-spicy Caribbean flavor. If you can't find raspberry-chipotle sauce, you can just use regular chipotle sauce with a little raspberry or other jam added in.

2 tablespoons jerk seasoning

1½-2 pounds turkey tenderloins

1 tablespoon fresh, chopped rosemary

1½ cups raspberry-chipotle sauce, divided

1. Rub jerk seasoning evenly over tenderloins.
2. Sprinkle with rosemary and press seasonings into meat. Cover and refrigerate for 1–2 hours.
3. Grill tenderloins with lid closed over medium-high heat for 5–10 minutes on each side.
4. Baste with half raspberry-chipotle sauce. Let tenderloins stand for 10 minutes before slicing.
5. Serve with remaining raspberry-chipotle sauce.

   Serve over mashed potatoes or rice.

{SERVES 6}

193 Simply Delicious Cornish Game Hens

For the most part, Cornish game hens are a rare treat in our house. But if you happen to find them on sale, here's a simple, delicious way to prepare them.

2 (2 pound) Cornish game hens

¼ cup olive oil

2 teaspoons paprika

2 tablespoons black pepper

1 tablespoon salt

1. Preheat oven to 350°.
2. Wash and dry hens and place in sprayed baking pan.

   Rub hens with oil.
3. Sprinkle paprika, pepper, and salt over each.
4. Bake until juices run clear, about 1 hour 30 minutes–2 hours.

{SERVES 4}

Who Knew?

Poultry must be thoroughly cleaned inside and out before cooking, in order to remove any residue that may be left from the slaughtering process. If you detect a slight "off" odor when you open the package, rinse the bird under cool water, then submerge in a solution of water plus 1 tablespoon lemon juice or vinegar and 1 teaspoon salt per cup of water. Then refrigerate 1–4 hours before cooking.

CHAPTER 4

Beef Dinners

194 Sloppy Joes

- **1 pound lean ground beef**
- **¼ cup chopped onion**
- **¼ cup chopped green bell pepper**
- **¾ cup ketchup**
- **1 teaspoon prepared yellow mustard**
- **1 tablespoon brown sugar**
- **½ teaspoon garlic powder**
- **½ teaspoon salt**
- **¼ teaspoon black pepper**
- **4 hamburger buns**

1. In skillet, cook ground beef, onion, and bell pepper over medium heat until beef is browned and onion and pepper are tender, about 8 minutes.
2. Stir in the ketchup, mustard, brown sugar, garlic powder, salt, and pepper. Reduce heat to low and simmer for 20 minutes.
3. Serve in hamburger buns.

{SERVES 4}

195 Beef Patties with Mushroom Gravy

Serve this richly delicious dish over pasta or rice, but for a special treat, serve over mashed potatoes or hot biscuits.

- **1 pound lean ground beef**
- **¼ cup chili sauce**
- **1 egg, beaten**
- **⅔ cup crushed corn flakes**
- **1 teaspoon black pepper**
- **½ tablespoon vegetable or canola oil**
- **½ (10 ounce) cans cream of mushroom soup**
- **2 cup water**
- **½ teaspoon salt**

1. Combine ground beef, chili sauce, egg, corn flakes, salt, and pepper in bowl and mix well. Shape into 4 patties, about ¾-inch thick.
2. Place patties with oil in skillet and brown on each side over high heat, about 2 minutes per side.
3. Reduce heat, cover, and simmer until cooked through, about 10 minutes.
4. Combine soups with water in bowl and mix well.
5. Spoon mixture over patties and simmer for an additional 10 minutes or until heated through.

{SERVES 4}

Who Knew?

To make this recipe low-fat, substitute 2½ cups of our Low-Fat Cream of Mushroom Soup Base for the cans of soup.

196 Queso con Carne

Queso con Carne means "cheese with meat," and what could be tastier? This dish works great as a meal with rice or alone as a party appetizer.

- **1 pound lean ground beef**
- **¼ (8 ounce) package cream cheese**
- **1 (16 ounce) jar salsa**
- **⅔ (15 ounce) can black beans, rinsed, drained**
- **1 Tortilla chips (preferably scoops)**

1. Cook beef, stirring frequently, in large skillet over medium-high heat. When browned, drain.
2. Stir in cream cheese, salsa, and black beans, and cook, stirring, until cream cheese is melted and beans are warm.
3. Serve with tortilla chips.

{SERVES 8}

Who Knew?

Spray your stovetop with a tiny bit of cooking spray before simmering or sautéing. If your pot boils over or your pan starts splattering, it's easy to clean up the mess with just a wipe of a damp paper towel.

197 Pasta-Beef Skillet

- **1 pound lean ground beef**
- **1 small onion, chopped**
- **1 teaspoon minced garlic**
- **1 (15 ounce) can Italian stewed tomatoes**
- **1 cup water**
- **1 (12 ounce) package penne (tube) pasta**
- **1 (8 ounce) package shredded Cheddar cheese**
- **1 cup crushed tortilla chips**

1. Cook beef, onion, and garlic, stirring frequently, in large skillet over medium-high heat.
2. When beef is browned, drain and stir in tomatoes, water, and pasta. Cover and cook until pasta is tender, about 15 minutes.
3. Sprinkle cheese over top, cover, and cook over medium-low heat just until cheese melts. Sprinkle with chips and serve immediately.

{SERVES 8}

198 Skillet Beef and Pasta

4½ cups water
1 (14 ounce) can beef broth
1 (8 ounce) package rotini (spiral) pasta
1 pound lean ground beef
2 (11 ounce) cans Mexicorn (or regular corn), drained
1 (12 ounce) package Mexican Mild–flavor Velveeta cheese, cubed
Salt and pepper to taste

1. Bring water and beef broth to a boil. Add pasta and reduce heat. When pasta is tender, drain and set aside.
2. Cook beef, stirring frequently, in large skillet over medium-high heat. When browned, drain.
3. Stir in corn and cheese and cook on low heat until cheese melts.
4. Gently stir cooked pasta into beef mixture until pasta is coated.
5. Spoon mixture into serving bowl and add salt and pepper to taste.

{SERVES 8}

Who Knew?

Cook pasta only until it is slightly chewy (what the Italians call *al dente*, or "to the tooth"). Always use plenty of water, and keep the water at a rapid boil—the pasta needs to move around as it cooks, to keep it from sticking together.

199 Mexican Beefy Noodles

1 pound ground beef
1 (1 ounce) packet taco seasoning mix
½ cup water
1 (15 ounce) can Mexican stewed tomatoes
1 (15 ounce) can pinto beans with liquid
1 (16 ounce) package fettuccini pasta
1 bunch fresh scallions, sliced
Salt and pepper to taste

1. Cook beef, stirring frequently, in large skillet over medium-high heat. When browned, drain.
2. Add taco seasoning and water and simmer for 15 minutes. Stir in stewed tomatoes and pinto beans.
3. Cook noodles in saucepan according to package directions and place on serving platter. Spoon beef mixture over noodles and sprinkle with sliced scallions.

   Add salt and pepper to taste.

{SERVES 8}

200 Hot 'n' Sour Beef 'n' Noodles

- 1 pound ground beef
- 1 tablespoon vegetable or olive oil
- 1 (3 ounce) package beef-flavored instant ramen noodles
- 1 (16 ounce) package frozen vegetable mix (such as broccoli, cauliflower and carrots)
- ⅔ cup sweet-and-sour sauce
- Salt and pepper to taste

1. Cook beef in oil over medium heat until cooked through. Drain and set aside.
2. In separate saucepan, cook noodles and vegetables in boiling water for 3 minutes, stirring occasionally. Drain.
3. Combine beef, noodle mixture, contents of seasoning packet from ramen noodles, sweet-and-sour sauce, and salt and pepper to taste. Toss to blend.Warm if necessary.

{SERVES 6}

Who Knew? Light Switch

Save money by using our Sweet-and-Sour Stir-Fry Sauce rather than buying a bottle at the store.

201 French Fry Supper

- 1 (28 ounce) package frozen shoestring French fries
- 1½ pound ground beef
- 1 (16 ounce) jar spaghetti sauce
- ½ teaspoon salt
- ¼ teaspoon black pepper

1. Preheat oven to 425°.
2. Spread French fries on baking sheet and cook according to package directions.
3. In skillet, cook beef over medium heat, stirring occasionally, until cooked through, about 8 minutes.

   Drain fat.
4. Add spaghetti sauce and stir to mix. Cook until heated through, about 5 minutes.
5. Transfer to an 8-inch square baking dish and top with French fries. Sprinkle with salt and pepper.

{SERVES 5}

Who Knew? Light Switch

To save money and make this recipe lower in fat, substitute 1¾ cups of our Homemade Spaghetti Sauce for the jar of sauce.

202 Bachelor's Beef Skillet

1½ pounds lean ground beef
2⅓ cups water
⅔ cup stir-fry sauce
1 (16 ounce) package frozen stir-fry vegetables
2 (3 ounce) packages ramen noodles

1. Cook beef, stirring frequently, in large skillet over medium-high heat. When browned, drain.
2. Add water, stir-fry sauce, vegetables, and seasoning packets from ramen package. Cook and stir on medium heat until heated through, about 8 minutes.
3. Break up noodles, add to beef-vegetable mixture, and cook until noodles are tender, about 6 minutes.

   Stir to separate noodles as they soften.
4. Serve hot.

{SERVES 4-6}

Who Knew? Light Switch

Don't forget to use our Sweet-and-Sour Stir-Fry Sauce rather than the store-bought variety! It tastes great and will save you money.

203 Cheesy Beefy Gnocchi

Gnocchi are tiny potato dumplings from Italy that are often easy to find in your frozen foods section. If you don't have gnocchi, you can also use macaroni or small shell pasta.

1 pound lean ground beef
1 (10 ounce) can Cheddar cheese soup
1 (10 ounce) can tomato bisque soup
1½ cups water
2 cups frozen gnocchi, thawed

1. Cook beef, stirring frequently, in large skillet over medium-high heat. When browned, drain.
2. Add soups and water. Bring mixture to a boil, then add gnocchi.
3. Cover and cook over medium heat, stirring occasionally, until gnocchi is tender, about 10 minutes.

{SERVES 6}

204 Hot Tamale Cheese Fiesta

- 2 (13 ounce) jars beef tamales with sauce
- ¾ of 1 (8 ounce) package shredded Mexican 4-cheese blend, divided
- 1 (10 ounce) can cream of mushroom soup
- 2 teaspoons taco seasoning

1. Preheat oven to 350°.
2. Drain sauce from tamales into cup and set aside. Remove wrappers from tamales.
3. Place tamales side by side in baking dish. Sprinkle one-third of cheese over top of tamales.
4. Combine ½ cup sauce from tamales, mushroom soup, and taco seasoning in bowl and mix well.
5. Pour sauce mixture over tamales and cheese.
6. Bake, covered, until tamales are heated through, about 5–10 minutes.
7. Remove from oven and sprinkle remaining cheese over top. Continue to bake, uncovered, until cheese melts.

{SERVES 8}

Who Knew? Light Switch

To make this recipe low-fat, use 1½ cups of our Low-Fat Four-Cheese Blend for the cheese, and substitute 1¼ cups of our Low-Fat Cream of Mushroom Soup Base for the can of soup.

205 Stroganoff Made Easy

- 1 pound beef sirloin, cut into 1-inch squares
- ½ teaspoon black pepper
- 2 tablespoons olive oil
- 1 onion, chopped
- 1 (10 ounce) can cream of mushroom soup
- 1 tablespoon tomato paste
- ½ cup water
- ¼ cup sour cream
- 1 (12 ounce) package fettuccini pasta, cooked, drained

1. Sprinkle beef with black pepper and place in large skillet with oil. Cook on medium-high heat, stirring often, until beef browns. Remove beef with slotted spoon and set aside.
2. Reduce heat to medium and sauté onion until it begins to turn translucent, about 5 minutes.
3. Stir in soup, tomato paste, and water; bring to a boil.
4. Return beef to skillet, mix well, and cook on high until mixture is heated through. Stir in sour cream and spoon over hot, cooked noodles.

{SERVES 4}

206 Thai Beef, Noodles, and Veggies

Transform prepared foods into something more. Start with Thai sesame noodles and end with a meal!

2 (4½ ounce) packages Thai sesame noodles
1 pound sirloin steak, cut in strips
¼ teaspoon salt
⅛ teaspoon black pepper
1 tablespoon vegetable or canola oil
1 (16 ounce) package frozen stir-fry vegetables, thawed
½ cup water
½ cup chopped peanuts

1. Cook noodles according to package directions, remove from heat. Place in serving bowl, cover, and keep warm.
2. Sprinkle salt and pepper over sirloin strips, then brown in oil for 2 minutes on each side. Remove from skillet and drain. (If skillet isn't large enough, you may need to brown in two separate batches.)
3. In same skillet, place vegetables and water, cover and cook for 5 minutes or until vegetables are tender-crisp.
4. Remove from heat, add steak strips, and toss to mix.
5. Spoon over warm noodles and sprinkle with peanuts before serving.

{SERVES 6}

207 Steak with Creamy Horseradish Sauce

1 (2 pound) sirloin steak
2 teaspoons salt
1 teaspoon black pepper
1 (8 ounce) carton sour cream
¼ cup prepared horseradish

1. Preheat broiler. Pat steak dry and sprinkle liberally with salt and pepper.
2. Broil steak on rack, 3 inches from heat, for 5 minutes on each side. Let stand for 5 minutes before slicing.
3. Combine sour cream and horseradish in bowl and mix well. Serve with steaks.

{SERVES 4}

208 Skillet Steak and Veggies

1 pound boneless sirloin steak, cut in strips
1 tablespoon vegetable or canola oil
2 (15 ounce) cans Italian stewed tomatoes with juice
1 (16 ounce) package frozen Italian green beans, thawed
1 (8 ounce) carton sour cream
Noodles, cooked

1. Place sirloin strips in large skillet with oil. Cook on high heat for about 3 minutes, stirring occasionally.
2. Add stewed tomatoes and green beans and bring to a boil. Lower heat and cook for 10 minutes.
3. Just before serving, fold in sour cream. Serve over noodles.

{SERVES 6}

209 Savory Steak with Rosemary Root Vegetables

4 (8 ounce) New York, strip, or sirloin steaks, each 1-inch thick
1 teaspoon salt
½ teaspoon black pepper
3 tablespoons olive oil, divided
3 carrots, peeled and thinly sliced
3 parsnips, peeled and thinly sliced
1 tablespoon fresh rosemary
Salt and pepper to taste

1. Sprinkle both sides of steaks with salt and pepper.
2. Heat 1 tablespoon of oil in large skillet over mediumhigh heat. When hot, add steaks as space permits and cook, flipping halfway through, until desired doneness, about 5 minutes for medium. Keep warm and repeat with remaining steaks until all are cooked.
3. In separate skillet, heat remaining oil over mediumlow heat. When hot, add carrots and parsnips and cook until tender, about 5–7 minutes. Season with rosemary and salt and pepper to taste.
4. Serve together on individual plates.

{SERVES 4}

Who Knew?

How do you know when your steak is done if you don't have a thermometer? Just give it a poke! Press your thumb into the center of the steak—if it's soft, it's rare; firmer but still with some give, it's medium-rare; and if it's hard and springy, consider it well-done.

210 Grilled Steak with Garlic-Mustard Sauce

⅓ cup apple juice
2 tablespoons dijon-style mustard
1 tablespoon minced garlic
1 teaspoon black pepper
4 (1 inch) thick boneless beef top strip steaks

1. Combine apple juice, mustard, garlic, and pepper in bowl, and mix well. Brush steaks with sauce, reserving ¼ cup for basting.
2. Grill steaks on grill over medium-hot heat, turning occasionally, until desired doneness, about 15–18 minutes.
3. During last 8–10 minutes of grilling, baste steaks with remaining sauce.

{SERVES 4}

Who Knew?

Remove the strong smell of garlic from your hands with this neat trick! Rub your hands under cold, running water while holding a stainless steel spoon in the same way as soap. Then rinse with soap and water.

211 London-in-Asia Broil

½ cup low-sodium soy sauce
¼ cup light brown sugar, firmly packed
1 clove garlic, chopped
1 ½ pounds top round London broil, about 1½-inch thick
8 scallions, chopped
1 tablespoon sesame seeds (optional)

1. Preheat broiler.
2. In large bowl, combine soy sauce, brown sugar, and garlic. Mix well until sugar is dissolved. Add meat and turn to coat. Let sit for 5 minutes (can be left in refrigerator for up to 8 hours to intensify soy flavor).
3. Line baking dish with foil and place meat in it. Broil to desired doneness, flipping halfway through, about 7 minutes per side for medium. Let sit for 5 minutes before slicing.
4. Transfer remaining soy sauce mixture to saucepan and heat over medium-high heat until boiling. Reduce heat to low, then add scallions and let simmer 2 minutes.
5. Slice meat and serve with rice. Pour soy sauce mixture over top and sprinkle with sesame seeds if desired.

{SERVES 4}

212 All-the-Trimmings Corned Beef

- **1 (4–5 pound) corned beef brisket**
  Water
- **4 large potatoes, peeled, chopped**
- **6 carrots, peeled, chopped**
- **4 medium onions, chopped**
- **1 head cabbage**
  Salt and pepper to taste

1. Place corned beef in roasting pan and add water until just covered. Bring to a boil over high heat, then reduce heat and simmer for 3 hours. Add more water if necessary.
2. Add potatoes, carrots, and onions. Cut cabbage into eighths and lay over top of other vegetables.
3. Bring to a boil, then reduce heat and cook until vegetables are done, about 30–40 minutes.
4. Let sit 10–15 minutes, then slice across grain to serve.
   Add salt and pepper to taste.

{SERVES 8-10}

213 Ravioli and More

- **1 pound lean ground beef**
- **1 teaspoon garlic powder**
- **½ teaspoon salt**
- **½ teaspoon black pepper**
- **1 large onion, chopped**
- **2 zucchini squash, grated**
- **¼ cup (½ stick) butter**
- **1 (28 ounce) jar spaghetti sauce**
- **1 (25 ounce) package ravioli with portobello mushrooms, cooked**
- **1 (12 ounce) package shredded mozzarella cheese**

1. Preheat oven to 350°.
2. Brown ground beef in large skillet over medium heat until no longer pink; drain.Add garlic powder, salt, and pepper. Set aside.
3. Cook onion and zucchini in butter in skillet over medium-high heat just until tender-crisp, about 4 minutes.
   Stir in spaghetti sauce.
4. Spread ½ cup sauce in sprayed, 9 x 13-inch baking dish.
5. Layer half of ravioli, half of remaining sauce, half of beef, and half of cheese. Repeat with remaining ravioli, sauce, and beef.
6. Cover and bake for 35 minutes.
7. Sprinkle remaining cheese on top. Let stand for
10 minutes before serving.

{SERVES 6-8}

Who Knew? Light Switch

To make this recipe lower in fat, substitute 2¾ cups of our Homemade Spaghetti Sauce for the jar of spaghetti sauce.

214 Cheesy Stuffed Bell Peppers

This is one of the rare occasions in which bell peppers are the star attractions at the dinner table—and they're so delicious, you'll want to stuff 'em all the time!

6 red, green, yellow, or orange bell peppers

1 ½ pounds ground beef

½ cup chopped onion

¾ cup cooked rice

1 egg

2 (15 ounce) cans petite tomatoes, divided

½ teaspoon garlic powder

1 tablespoon Worcestershire sauce

½ teaspoon salt

½ teaspoon black pepper

1 (8 ounce) package shredded Cheddar cheese, divided

1. Preheat oven to 350º.
2. Cut off tops of bell peppers and remove seeds and membranes. Place in roasting pan with salted water and boil for 10 minutes. (They will be only partially cooked.)

   Drain and set aside to cool.
3. Cook ground beef and onion in skillet over medium heat, stirring occasionally, until beef is browned and onions are tender, about 7 minutes. Drain.
4. Add rice, egg, 1 can tomatoes, garlic powder,

   Worcestershire sauce, salt, and pepper. Simmer for 5 minutes. Remove from heat and add 1 cup cheese; mix well.
5. Stuff peppers with meat mixture and set upright in sprayed baking dish.
6. Pour remaining can of tomatoes over and around peppers.
7. Bake for 25 minutes.
8. Remove from oven, sprinkle remaining cheese on top, and return to oven until cheese melts, about 10 minutes.

{SERVES 6}

Who Knew?

If you can't get the pepper to stand upright, trim the bottoms, a small sliver at a time, until they have a more even base..

215 Best Pot Roast Dinner

1 (4 pound) boneless rump roast

3 tablespoons plus ½ teaspoon salt, divided

2 tablespoons plus ½ teaspoon black pepper, divided

2 tablespoons garlic powder

2¼ cups water, divided, plus more if needed

6 potatoes, peeled, quartered

8 carrots, peeled, quartered

3 onions, peeled, quartered

3 tablespoons cornstarch

1. Preheat oven to 375°.
2. Set roast in roasting pan with lid and sprinkle with 3 tablespoons salt, 2 tablespoons pepper, and garlic powder. Add 1½ cups water.
3. Cover and bake for 30 minutes.
4. Turn heat down to 325° and bake until roast is fork tender, about 2 hours–2 hours 30 minutes. Add water if needed.
5. Add potatoes, carrots, and onions. Cook for additional 35–40 minutes.
6. Lift roast out of roasting pan and place on serving platter.
7. Place potatoes, carrots, and onions around roast.
8. Combine cornstarch and ¾ cup water in bowl. Add to juices left in roasting pan. Add ½ teaspoon each of salt and pepper and stir to make gravy.
9. Place pan on stove and cook on high, stirring constantly, until gravy thickens. Serve in gravy boat with roast and vegetables.

{SERVES 8-10}

216 Seasoned-Beef Tenderloin

1 tablespoons Dijon-style mustard

4 tablespoons horseradish

6 (3 pound) center-cut beef tenderloin

4 cup seasoned breadcrumbs

1. Combine mustard and horseradish in bowl and spread over beef tenderloin.
2. Spread breadcrumbs onto mustard-horseradish mixture and wrap beef in foil. Refrigerate for at least 12 hours.
3. When ready to bake, preheat oven to 375°.
4. Remove wrap and place beef on sprayed broiler pan.
   Bake for 30 minutes.
5. Let tenderloin stand for 15 minutes before slicing.

{SERVES 8-10}

217 Skillet Sirloin

This is one of the easiest-and most delicious-ways to prepare beef sirloin.

2 teaspoons vegetable or canola oil
2 teaspoons minced garlic
½ teaspoon cayenne pepper
2 tablespoons soy sauce
2 tablespoons honey
1 pound beef sirloin, thinly sliced

1. Combine oil, garlic, cayenne pepper, soy sauce, and honey. Place in resealable plastic bag.
2. Add sliced beef, seal bag, and shake. Refrigerate for 30 minutes.
3. Place beef mixture in large sprayed skillet over medium-high heat. Cook until beef reaches desired doneness without overcooking, about 5–6 minutes. If desired, serve with vegetables over rice.

{SERVES 6}

Who Knew?

It's easier to thinly slice meat if it's partially frozen. Leave the beef for this recipe in the freezer for about 10 minutes before you slice it.

218 Steak and Potatoes

2 pounds round steak
⅓ cup flour
⅓ cup vegetable or canola oil
5 peeled potatoes, diced
¼ teaspoon salt
⅛ teaspoon black pepper
¼ cup chopped onions
½ cup water
1 (10 ounce) can cream of mushroom soup

1. Preheat oven to 350°.
2. Cut steak into serving-size pieces and coat in flour.
   Brown with oil in heavy skillet; drain. Place steak in sprayed, 9 x 13-inch baking dish.
3. Sprinkle potatoes with salt and pepper. Place over steak. Cover potatoes with onions.
4. Add water to mushroom soup and pour over top of dish.
5. Cover and bake for 1 hour 30 minutes.

{SERVES 8}

219 Italian Steak Extraordinary

1 ½ pounds beef round steak
¼ teaspoon salt
1 teaspoon black pepper
½ cup flour
2 tablespoons vegetable or canola oil
1 (14 ounce) jar spaghetti sauce
1 (10 ounce) can chopped tomatoes and green chilies
1 (10 ounce) package frozen Italian green beans, thawed
1 bunch fresh scallions, thinly sliced

1. Preheat oven to 350°.
2. Cut steak into 6 serving-size pieces, and sprinkle with salt and pepper.
3. Pour flour into resealable plastic bag. Add steak pieces and shake until steak is covered with flour.
4. Brown steak pieces in canola oil in large skillet over medium-high heat, turning over once, about 2 minutes per side.
5. Place steak pieces in sprayed, 9 x 13-inch glass baking dish. Pour spaghetti sauce and tomatoes and green chilies over steak.
6. Cover and bake for 45 minutes.
7. Place green beans in sauce around beef. Cover and continue baking until beef is cooked through, about 30 minutes.
8. Before serving, sprinkle fresh scallions over steak.

{SERVES 6-8}

220 Marinated and Grilled London Broil

1 (12 ounce) can cola
1 (10 ounce) bottle teriyaki sauce
1 teaspoon black pepper
1 (3 pound) London broil (top round roast)

1. Combine cola, teriyaki sauce, and black pepper in large resealable plastic bag.
2. Add London broil, seal, and marinate in refrigerator for 24 hours, turning occasionally.
3. Remove London broil from marinade and discard marinade. Grill covered for 14 minutes on each side.
4. Let stand for 10 minutes before slicing diagonally across grain to serve.

{SERVES 8}

Who Knew?

To make your grill even hotter, place a large sheet of aluminum foil on top of it for 10 minutes before you start grilling. This is a great way to achieve those impressive grill marks on your meat!

CHAPTER 5

Pork and Lamb Dinners

221 Rosemary Lamb Chops

Lamb chops are such a rare, delicious treat that we like to prepare them simply to allow the taste of the lamb to come through. This recipe is as simple as it is scrumptious!

8 lamb chops
⅓ cup lemon juice
3 tablespoons chopped fresh rosemary
1 teaspoon minced garlic
¼ teaspoon salt
¼ teaspoon black pepper

1. Preheat broiler.
2. Mix together lemon juice, rosemary, pressed garlic, salt, and pepper. Rub lamb chops with mixture. Set aside on plate.
3. Broil steak on rack, 5 inches from heat, for 4–5 minutes on each side. Let stand for 5 minutes before slicing.

{SERVES 4}

222 Spicy Lamb Chops with Chickpeas

1 (15 ounce) can chickpeas, drained, rinsed
5 tablespoons olive oil, divided
¼ cup lemon juice
1 small red onion, chopped
3 medium tomatoes, chopped
1 cup fresh mint leaves, chopped
1 teaspoon salt, divided
½ teaspoon black pepper, divided
1 ½ tablespoons ground cumin
½ tablespoon paprika
8 lamb loin chops

1. In large bowl, combine chickpeas, 3 tablespoons of olive oil, lemon juice, red onion, tomatoes, mint, ½ teaspoon of salt, and ¼ teaspoon of pepper. Toss well to mix; set aside.
2. In separate bowl, combine remaining salt and pepper, cumin, and paprika. Lightly coat each lamb chop.
3. Heat 1 tablespoon of oil in skillet over medium-high heat. Add half of lamb chops to skillet, making sure they do not touch. Cook until desired doneness, about 4 minutes for medium. Remove and repeat with remaining oil and lamb chops.
4. Place chickpea mixture on plates and top with 1–2 chops.

{SERVES 5-6}

Who Knew?

Mint is easy to grow and naturally repels pests. Put some in your garden, then use it to make this delicious recipe!

223 Pork Chop Supper

- 1 (18 ounce) package smoked pork chops (or 5–6 fresh chops)
- 1 tablespoon vegetable or canola oil
- 1 (12 ounce) jar pork gravy
- ¼ cup milk
- 1 pound new (red) potatoes, quartered

1. Cook pork chops with oil in large skillet over medium-high heat.
2. When browned, pour gravy and milk into skillet and stir mixture around chops until mixed well.
3. Add new potatoes around chops and gravy. Place lid on skillet and simmer on medium-low heat until potatoes are tender, about 15 minutes.

{SERVES 6}

224 Parmesan Covered Pork Chops

- ½ cup grated Parmesan cheese
- ⅔ cup Italian seasoned breadcrumbs
- 1 egg
- 4-5 thin-cut pork chops
- Canola oil

1. Combine cheese and breadcrumbs in shallow bowl.
   Beat egg with 1 teaspoon water in separate shallow bowl or plate.
2. Dip each pork chop in beaten egg then into breadcrumb mixture.
3. Cook over medium-high heat in skillet with a little oil for about 5 minutes on each side or until golden brown.

{SERVES 4-5}

225 Pork Chops with Black Bean Salsa

- 2 teaspoons chili powder
- ½ teaspoon salt
- 2 tablespoons vegetable or canola oil
- 6 boneless thin-cut pork chops
- 1 (15 ounce) can black beans, rinsed, drained
- 1 (24 ounce) jar salsa
- 1 ripe avocado, pitted, skinned, and sliced

1. Combine chili powder and salt in bowl.
2. Rub oil over pork chops, then rub chili powder mixture over chops.
3. Place in skillet over medium heat and cook pork chops until juices run clear, about 5 minutes on each side.
4. Combine beans and salsa in bowl.
5. Place pork chops in serving dish and top with salsa mixture and avocado slices.

{SERVES 6}

Who Knew? Light Switch

For a healthier version of this recipe, substitute olive oil for the vegetable oil and use 2¾ cups of our Super Healthy Salsa instead of the jar of salsa.

226 Peppered Tenderloin

- 1 pork tenderloin, thinly sliced
- 2 tablespoons olive oil, divided
- 1 green bell pepper, seeded, thinly sliced
- 1 red bell pepper, seeded, thinly sliced
- ½ pound fresh mushrooms, quartered
- 1 onion, coarsely chopped
- 1 teaspoon minced garlic
- ½ cup beef broth
- 2 tablespoons ketchup
- 1 teaspoon lemon juice
- 1 teaspoon dried tarragon
- ½ teaspoon black pepper
- 1 tablespoon flour
- ½ cup sour cream

1. Preheat oven to 325°.
2. Brown pork slices in 1 tablespoon olive oil in skillet.
   Remove and keep warm.
3. In same skillet, sauté bell peppers, mushrooms, onion, and garlic in rest of olive oil.
4. Add broth, ketchup, lemon juice, tarragon, and pepper. Simmer for 3 minutes. Return pork to skillet.
5. Combine flour with sour cream and stir into pork mixture. Spoon into sprayed, 7 x 11-inch baking dish.
6. Cover and bake for 20 minutes. Serve over noodles.

{SERVES 6}

Who Knew?

Before thinly slicing the pork for this recipe, partially freeze it by placing in the freezer for an hour or two beforehand. It will be much easier to slice.

227 Ham, Corn, and Goat Cheese Omelets

The French often eat omelets for meals other than breakfast, and with this delicate-tasting omelet, you'll see why!

- 6 eggs
- ½ teaspoon salt
- ¼ teaspoon black pepper
- 1 cup fresh chopped spinach
- ¾ cup chopped ham
- 2 tablespoons unsalted butter, divided
- 2 ounces goat cheese, crumbled

1. In bowl, whisk together eggs, salt, and pepper.
   Add spinach and ham; mix well.
2. In skillet, melt 1 tablespoon of butter over medium heat. Add half of egg mixture.
3. Cook, without stirring, until the eggs just begin to set, about 1 minute. Using a spatula, lift the edge of the omelet so the uncooked egg flows underneath. Then cook until top is almost set, about 2 minutes.
4. Sprinkle half of cheese over half of omelet, then fold over and cook until set. Remove from heat and repeat with remaining butter, egg mixture, and cheese.
   Serve immediately.

{SERVES 2}

228 Italian Sausage and Ravioli

1 pound sweet Italian pork sausage

1 (26 ounce) jar extra chunky mushroom and green pepper spaghetti sauce

1 (20 ounce) package frozen cheese filled ravioli

Grated Parmesan cheese for garnish

1. Remove casing from sausage and cook, stirring frequently, in large skillet over medium heat until brown.

   Drain.
2. Stir in spaghetti sauce and heat until bubbling.

   Reduce heat to low and simmer for 10 minutes.
3. Cook ravioli according to package directions and add to spaghetti and sausage.
4. Serve with Parmesan cheese for garnish.

{SERVES 6-8}

229 Colorful Sausage Supper

- ½ pound cooked Polish sausage, cut into ¼-inch slices
- ⅔ red bell pepper, seeded and cut into strips
- 1 small zucchini, sliced
- 4-5 small yellow squash, sliced
- 4 tablespoons olive oil, divided
- 1 (16 ounce) package penne (tube) pasta
- 1 (26 ounce) jar spaghetti sauce, heated

1. Sauté sausage, bell pepper, zucchini, and squash with 2 tablespoons olive oil in large skillet until vegetables are tender-crisp. Keep warm.
2. Cook pasta in saucepan according to package directions, drain, and stir in remaining oil.
3. Spoon into large serving bowl and spread hot spaghetti sauce over pasta.
4. Use slotted spoon to top with sausage-vegetable mixture and serve immediately.

{SERVES 8}

Who Knew? Light Switch

To save money and make this recipe lower in fat, substitute 3¾ cups of our Homemade Spaghetti Sauce for the jar of sauce.

230 Grilled Garlic-Herb Tenderloin

Charcoal grills may be a little more work, but they sure make food taste good! This home-style pork dish requires a charcoal grill and marinade brush.

2 (1 pound) pork tenderloins

1 (12 ounce) bottle roasted garlic-herb marinade, divided

1 (8 ounce) package medium egg noodles

¼ cup (½ stick) butter

1. Butterfly pork lengthwise, being careful not to cut all the way through. Press open to flatten. Place in large resealable plastic bag.
2. Pour ¾ cup marinade into bag and close top securely. Marinate for 25 minutes, turning several times.
3. Grill for 8 minutes, with pork 4–5 inches from hot coals.
4. Turn pork over and brush with additional marinade. Cook for another 8 minutes.
5. Cook noodles according to package directions. Drain. Add butter and coat well. When ready to serve, place pork chops over noodles.

{SERVES 8}

231 Praiseworthy Pork Tenderloin

3 cup ketchup

¼ cup packed brown sugar

1 tablespoon dry white wine

1 tablespoon soy sauce

¼ teaspoon ground mustard

1 teaspoon minced garlic

2 (1 pound) pork tenderloins

1. Combine ketchup, brown sugar, wine, soy sauce, mustard, and garlic in bowl. Mix well. Pour in shallow bowl or plastic dish.
2. Place tenderloins in ketchup–brown sugar mixture and turn to coat. Cover and refrigerate for at least 1 hour, but no longer than 8 hours.
3. When ready to bake, preheat oven to 425°.
4. Using slotted spoon, place pork in shallow roasting pan and roast uncovered for 29–30 minutes. Discard marinade.
5. Slice tenderloins and serve over pasta or rice.

{SERVES 6}

Who Knew?

The best place to store your brown sugar is in the freezer. The lower temperature will ensure it won't clump up.

232 Sweet Peach Pork Tenderloin

- **3 cup ketchup**
- **¼ cup packed brown sugar**
- **1 tablespoon dry white wine**
- **1 tablespoon soy sauce**
- **¼ teaspoon ground mustard**
- **1 teaspoon minced garlic**
- **2 (1 pound) pork tenderloins**

1. Preheat oven to 325°.
2. Combine mustard, soy sauce, and peach preserves in saucepan. Heat and stir just until mixture blends.
3. Place tenderloins in sprayed baking pan and spoon peach mixture over top.
4. Sprinkle salt and pepper over tenderloins.
5. Cover pan with foil and bake for 1 hour.
6. Remove from oven and let stand for 10 minutes before slicing.

{SERVES 8}

233 Orange Pork Chops

- **1 teaspoon salt**
- **½ teaspoon black pepper**
- **6 (½ inch) boneless pork chops**
- **2 tablespoons vegetable or canola oil**
- **1⅓ cups instant rice**
- **1 cup orange juice**
- **¼ teaspoon ground ginger**
- **1 (10 ounce) can chicken with rice soup**
- **½ cup chopped walnuts**

1. Preheat oven to 350°.
2. Sprinkle salt and pepper over pork chops. Brown with oil in skillet over medium-high heat, about 2–3 minutes on each side.
3. Sprinkle rice into sprayed, 7 x 11-inch baking dish.
4. Add orange juice. Then arrange pork chops over rice.
5. Add ginger to soup can, stirring right in can.
   Pour soup over pork chops.
6. Sprinkle walnuts on top.
7. Cover and bake for 25 minutes.
8. Uncover and bake until rice is tender, about
10. minutes.

{SERVES 6}

Who Knew?

Never use quick-cooking rice in a dish that will be frozen, as it becomes mushy when reheated. Make sure to only refrigerate this one (not freeze!) for later.

234 Italian-Style Pork Chops

6 (¾-inch thick) bone-in pork chops
½ teaspoon salt, divided
1 teaspoon black pepper, divided
1 tablespoon vegetable or canola oil
2 green bell peppers
1 (15 ounce) can tomato sauce
1 (15 ounce) can Italian stewed tomatoes with liquid
1 cup water
½ of 1 onion, chopped
1 teaspoon Italian seasoning
1 clove garlic, minced
2 tablespoon Worcestershire sauce
½ cup brown rice

1. Preheat oven to 350°.
2. Sprinkle pork chops with 1 teaspoon salt and ½ teaspoon pepper. In hot oil, brown chops on both sides over medium-high heat, about 2–3 minutes per side. Remove chops from skillet, drain, and set aside.
3. Cut top off 1 bell pepper and remove seeds.

   Cut 6 thick rings and set aside. Seed remaining bell pepper and roughly chop.
4. Combine chopped bell pepper, tomato sauce, stewed tomatoes, water, onion, Italian seasoning, garlic,Worcestershire sauce, and remaining salt and pepper in bowl. Mix well.
5. Spread rice evenly in lightly sprayed, 9 x 13-inch baking dish. Slowly pour tomato mixture over rice.
6. Arrange pork chops over rice mixture and top each with 1 bell pepper ring.
7. Cover and bake until rice is tender, about 1 hour.

{SERVES 6}

235 Onion-Smothered Pork Chops

6 (½-inch thick) pork chops
1 tablespoon vegetable or canola oil
2 tablespoons butter
1 medium onion, chopped
1 (10 ounce) can cream of onion soup
½ cup water

1. Preheat oven to 325°.
2. Cook pork chops on each side with oil in skillet over medium-high heat until brown, about 4 minutes per side.

   Reduce heat to low and simmer for 5 minutes per side.

   Place chops in shallow baking pan.
3. Add butter to skillet and cook onion, stirring, until onion is tender. (Pan juices will turn onion brown.)
4. Add onion soup and water and stir well. Pour mixture over pork chops.
5. Cover and bake for 40 minutes. Serve over rice.

{SERVES 6}

236 Pork Chops and Apples

Apples are a traditional accompaniment to pork chops, and we've added raisins and pecans to this recipe for a touch of even more sweetness.

6 (¾ inch thick) bone-in pork chops
¼ cup (½ stick) butter, divided
6 cups croutons
1 cup green apples, peeled, chopped
½ cup chopped celery
½ cup golden raisins
½ cup chopped pecans
½ cup water
2 teaspoons crushed, dried sage
1 teaspoon salt
1 tablespoon Dijon-style mustard

1. Preheat oven to 325°.
2. Brown pork chops on both sides with 2 tablespoons butter in large skillet over medium-high heat, about 2 minutes per side. Set aside.
3. In same skillet, melt remaining butter and stir in croutons, apples, celery, raisins, pecans, water, sage, and salt. Mix well.
4. Place crouton mixture into sprayed, 7 x 11-inch baking dish. Top with pork chops.
5. Spread thin layer of mustard over each pork chop.
6. Cover and bake for 40 minutes. Uncover and bake for additional 10 minutes.

{SERVES 6}

Who Knew?

To crush the sage for this recipe, simply rub the dried sage between your fingers until it turns into a powder.

237 Apricot Pork Chops

1 (15 ounce) can apricot halves with juice
8 (½ inch thick) boneless pork chops
3 tablespoons butter
⅓ cup chopped celery
1 yellow bell pepper, seeded, chopped
2½ cups instant rice
¾ cup water
1 teaspoon chicken bouillon granules
⅓ cup golden raisins
½ teaspoon ground ginger
½ teaspoon salt
½ cup slivered almonds

1. Preheat oven to 350°.
2. Place apricots in food processor, cover, and process until smooth. Set aside.
3. Brown pork chops on both sides with butter in large skillet over medium-high heat, about 3–5 minutes per side. Reduce heat to low and simmer, covered, for 10 minutes. Remove pork chops to heated plate.
4. In same skillet, sauté celery and bell pepper. Add rice, water, bouillon granules, raisins, ginger, salt, and apricot puree; bring to a boil.
5. Remove from heat and stir in almonds. Spoon into 9 x 13-inch baking dish.
6. Place pork chops on top of rice mixture.
7. Cover and bake for 20 minutes.

{SERVES 8}

238 German-Style Ribs and Kraut

3-4 pounds baby back pork ribs or country-style pork ribs, trimmed
½ teaspoon black pepper
1 cup water
3 potatoes, peeled, cubed or sliced
1 (32 ounce) jar refrigerated sauerkraut, drained
¼ cup pine nuts, toasted

1. In large, sprayed pan, cook ribs over medium-high heat until browned on all sides, about 2 minutes per side.
2. Add pepper and water. Bring to a boil, then reduce heat to low and simmer until ribs are very tender, about 2 hours.
3. Add potatoes and continue to cook on low heat for 20 minutes. Add sauerkraut and continue cooking until potatoes are tender.
4. Sprinkle pine nuts on ribs and kraut just before serving.

{SERVES 6-8}

Who Knew?

To toast pine nuts, place them in skillet on medium heat, stirring constantly until golden brown. You can also put them on a baking sheet and cook at 300° for 5–10 minutes.

239 Oven-Roasted Baby Backs

⅓ cup orange juice
⅓ cup soy sauce
1 teaspoon ground cumin
½ cup packed brown sugar
2-3 pounds baby back pork ribs

1. Combine orange juice, soy sauce, cumin, and brown sugar in large, resealable plastic bag. Shake or mash bag to blend thoroughly and to dissolve brown sugar.
2. Cut ribs into individual ribs, add to bag, and marinate for 1–2 hours.
3. When ready to bake, preheat oven to 325°.
4. Transfer ribs and marinade to shallow baking pan and arrange in one layer. Ribs should not touch.
5. Bake for 45 minutes. Remove from oven, turn ribs with tongs, and continue roasting for an additional 1 hour.

{SERVES 5-7}

Who Knew?

When picking out the best rack of ribs, go for some that have an even dispersal of fat throughout the rack. This will ensure even cooking.

240 Italian Stuffed Peppers

4 large bell peppers
1 pound bulk Italian pork sausage
1 onion, chopped
1 teaspoon dried basil
1 (4 ounce) can chopped green chilies
2 tablespoons seasoned breadcrumbs
1 ½ cups shredded mozzarella cheese, divided
1 egg
1 (16 ounce) jar spaghetti sauce

1. Preheat oven to 375°.
2. Cut off top of each pepper and cut pepper in half lengthwise. Discard seeds and white membranes.

   Place pepper shells in sprayed, 9 x 13-inch baking dish and set aside.
3. Cook sausage and onion in large skillet on medium heat for 5 minutes, stirring to break up sausage; drain.
4. Stir in basil, green chilies, breadcrumbs, 1 cup cheese, and egg. Mix well.
5. Spoon sausage mixture into each green pepper shell.
6. Pour spaghetti sauce over peppers.
7. Cover and bake for 45 minutes. Sprinkle remaining cheese over peppers.

{SERVES 6-8}

Who Knew? Light Switch

To make this recipe lower in fat, substitute 1¾ cups of our Homemade Spaghetti Sauce for the jar of spaghetti sauce.

Who Knew?

A great way to save money on peppers is to grow your own! Peppers are perennials and can be grown year-round in 2- to 5-gallon containers of potting soil. Just bring the plants in when the nights drop below 50°, and let them live indoors until the nights are consistently above 50°.

CHAPTER 6

Fish and Seafood

241 Creamy Noodle Tuna

- **1 (8 ounce) package pappardelle pasta**
- **2 (6 ounce) cans white tuna, drained**
- **1 (10 ounce) can cream of chicken soup**
- **¾ cup milk**
- **¾ cup chopped black olives**

1. Preheat oven to 300°.
2. Cook pasta according to package directions, then place half of pasta in sprayed, 2-quart baking dish.
3. Combine tuna, soup, milk, and olives in saucepan.
   Heat through and mix well.
4. Pour half soup mixture over pasta, then add rest of pasta and top with rest of soup mixture.
5. Cover and bake for 20 minutes.

{SERVES 6}

Who Knew? Light Switch

To lower the fat content of this dish, substitute 1¼ cups of our Low-Fat Cream of Chicken Soup Base for the can of soup.

242 Salmon and Green Beans

We love this simple, delicious way to prepare salmon! You can substitute regular soy sauce for the low-sodium variety, but we find the dish is a little salty when using regular soy sauce.

- **1½ tablespoons olive oil**
- **4 (6 ounce) salmon steaks**
- **¼ cup low-sodium (light) soy sauce**
- **2 tablespoon lemon juice**
- **1 (10 ounce) package frozen whole green beans**
- **2 tablespoons water**
- **Salt and pepper to taste**

1. Place oil in skillet over medium-high heat and add salmon steaks.
2. Combine soy sauce and lemon juice in bowl and pour over steaks.
3. Cover and cook for about 5 minutes. Turn over salmon and place green beans over salmon with water.
4. Cover and steam for 5 minutes or until beans are tender-crisp. Season green beans with a little salt and pepper and serve over rice.

{SERVES 4}

Who Knew?

Always keep salt on hand, not only to flavor your dishes, but to prevent stains! If you spill something on the carpet, quickly cover with salt before the liquid can be absorbed.

243 Alfredo Salmon and Noodles

This recipe uses canned salmon, but you may be able to find fresh, cooked salmon in the salad bar or deli section of your grocery store.

3 cups medium egg noodles

1 (16 ounce) package frozen broccoli florets, thawed

1 cup alfredo sauce

1 (15 ounce) can salmon, drained, boned

1. Cook noodles in large saucepan according to package directions. During last 5 minutes of cooking, add broccoli. Drain.
2. Stir in alfredo sauce and salmon and cook on low heat, stirring occasionally, until mixture heats through.

   Pour into serving bowl.

{SERVES 6}

Who Knew? Light Switch

To make this recipe low-fat, use our Low-Fat Alfredo Sauce

244 Red Snapper with Fresh Salsa

½ cup chopped fresh cilantro

1 (15 ounce) can great northern beans, drained

1 (15 ounce) can Italian stewed tomatoes, drained

⅓ cup chopped green olives

1 teaspoon minced garlic

1 tablespoon fresh lime juice

6 (6 ounce) red snapper fillets

2 tablespoons vegetable or canola oil

1 teaspoon ground cumin

½ teaspoon cayenne pepper

½ teaspoon salt

1. Combine cilantro, beans, tomatoes, olives, garlic, and lime juice in bowl and mix well. Set aside.
2. Dry snapper with paper towels and rub oil on both sides. Sprinkle with cumin, cayenne pepper, and salt.
3. Grill snapper for about 5 minutes on each side or until fish flakes easily when tested with fork.
4. Serve snapper with salsa.

{SERVES 6}

245 Orange Roughy with Peppers

In this recipe, you'll be steaming fish over onions and peppers, which will add enough moisture to a covered pan to allow it to cook right on your stove.

1 pound orange roughy fillets
1 tablespoon olive oil
1 teaspoon dried thyme leaves
¼ teaspoon salt
¼ teaspoon black pepper
1 onion, sliced
2 red bell peppers, cut into strips

1. Cut fish into serving-sized pieces.
2. Mix thyme, salt, and pepper in bowl.
3. Add oil, onion, and bell peppers to large skillet and sprinkle with half of thyme mixture.
4. Place fish on top peppers and sprinkle with remaining thyme mixture.
5. Turn burner on high until fish is hot enough to cook, about 3 minutes. Lower heat to low, cover, and cook for 15–20 minutes or until fish flakes easily.

{SERVES 6}

246 Halibut With Orzo

½ cup extra-virgin olive oil, divided
¼ cup fresh lemon juice
4 (6 ounce) halibut fillets
½ teaspoon salt
½ teaspoon black pepper
1 (16 ounce) package orzo
2 teaspoons minced garlic
1 (9 ounce) package baby spinach
1½ cups halved cherry tomatoes

1. Preheat oven to 400°.
2. Whisk ½ cup olive oil with lemon juice in bowl.
3. Place halibut on sprayed baking pan and sprinkle with salt and pepper. Drizzle on olive oil mixture and bake for about 12 minutes or just until translucent in center.
4. Cook orzo in saucepan according to package directions and drain. Add remaining olive oil and garlic to same saucepan and sauté over medium heat for 1 minute.
5. Stir in drained pasta, spinach, and tomatoes and stir to coat.
6. Remove from heat, cover and let stand for 1–2 minutes (spinach will wilt).
7. Place orzo mixture on serving platter and top with halibut fillets and remaining dressing.

{SERVES 4}

Who Knew?

To test fish for doneness, insert a thin-bladed knife into the flesh at the thickest part. If it's done, it will be just barely translucent in the center. Even though it might look not quite done, the fish will continue to cook after you remove it from the heat, so make sure not to overcook it.

247 Pan-Fried Flounder

½ tablespoon plus 1 teaspoon seafood seasoning, divided
¼ teaspoon cayenne pepper
⅔ cup flour
¼ teaspoon black pepper
½ teaspoon salt
¼ cup olive oil
6 small flounder fillets
¾ cup tartar sauce
⅓ cup ketchup

1. Combine 1 tablespoon seafood seasoning, cayenne pepper, flour, pepper, and salt in bowl.
2. Heat oil over high heat in large skillet. Dredge each fillet in flour-seasoning mixture and place in skillet (in batches).
3. Fry each fillet for about 3 minutes on each side (depending on thickness of fillet), or until cooked through. Drain on paper towels.
4. Combine tartar sauce, ketchup, and 1 teaspoon seafood seasoning in bowl and serve with fried flounder.

{SERVES 6}

248 Seasoned Fried Fish

Serve this fish with French fries for an authentic "fish and chips" experience.

1 (16 ounce) package cooked, frozen batter-dipped fish
1 cup spaghetti sauce
2 teaspoons Italian seasoning
1 cup shredded mozzarella cheese

1. Heat fish according to package directions. While fish is heating, combine spaghetti sauce and Italian seasoning in bowl.
2. When fish heats thoroughly, place each piece on serving plate and spoon spaghetti mixture over fish.

   Sprinkle cheese on top and serve.

{SERVES 6}

Who Knew?

When cooking on a gas stove, the flame should extend no farther than two-thirds up the pan. (If it does, opt for a bigger pan.) Never leave an empty pan on a hot stove for more than a couple of minutes, and keep an eye out for shiny rainbow-colored marks on the pan. These are signs that you've been cooking at too high a heat.

249 Broiled Red Snapper

2 tablespoons dijon-style mustard
¼ cup Italian salad dressing
4 (6 ounce) red snapper fillets

1. Preheat broiler.
2. Combine mustard and Italian dressing in bowl.
3. Place snapper, skin-side down, on sprayed, foil-lined baking pan.
4. Brush mustard-dressing mixture over fillets and broil for about 8 minutes or until snapper flakes easily when tested with fork.

{SERVES 4}

Who Knew?

Before handling snapper fillets, rub your hands with lemon juice and you won't smell of fish for the rest of the day!

250 Grilled Swordfish with Pepper Sauce

You won't often find them cheap, but since swordfish is one of our favorites, we had to include this recipe!

4 (1 inch) swordfish steaks
3 tablespoons olive oil
¾ teaspoon seasoned salt
½ teaspoon lemon pepper
½ of 1 (12 ounce) jar roasted red peppers, drained and chopped
1 tablespoon dijon-style mustard
3 tablespoons mayonnaise
½ teaspoon black pepper

1. Rub swordfish with olive oil and sprinkle with seasoned salt and lemon pepper.
2. Place red peppers, mustard, mayonnaise, and pepper in blender and process until well blended.
3. Grill swordfish over medium-high heat, turning once, for 10 minutes, or until fish cooks thoroughly. (Do not overcook, as it will dry out the fish.)
4. Pour sauce over fish and serve.

{SERVES 4}

Who Knew?

Pining for fresh fish but stuck with frozen? Try this: Cover the frozen fish in milk until it thaws, then cook. It will taste fresher and your family will never know it was frozen.

251 Spicy Baked Fish

- 1 (16 ounce) package cooked, frozen batter-dipped fried fish
- ¾ cup chili sauce
- 1 bunch fresh scallions, chopped
- 1 cup shredded Cheddar cheese

1. Preheat oven to 325°.
2. Arrange fish in sprayed, 9 x 13-inch glass baking dish and bake until fish is heated through, about 20 minutes.
3. Heat chili sauce in saucepan or microwave and spoon over each piece of fish. Top with scallions and Cheddar cheese. Serve right from baking dish.

{SERVES 6}

252 Sea Scallop Stir-Fry

- 2 tablespoons lemon juice
- ¼ cup low-sodium soy sauce
- ¼ teaspoon garlic powder
- 1 tablespoon sugar
- 3 tablespoons chopped fresh cilantro
- 1 teaspoon dried oregano
- 1 pound sea scallops
- 2½ tablespoons olive oil, divided
- ½ of 1 (10 ounce) package frozen spinach, thawed
- 1 (8 ounce) package frozen sugar snap peas, thawed

1. In small bowl, combine lemon juice, soy sauce, garlic powder, and sugar. Mix until sugar dissolves. Add cilantro and oregano and set aside.
2. Rinse scallops and pat dry.
3. Heat 2 tablespoons oil in large skillet over mediumhigh heat. When hot, add scallops. Cook until browned on pan side, about 3 minutes, then flip and cook until consistent color throughout, about 1–2 minutes. Remove from skillet.
4. In separate or cleaned skillet, add remaining oil and heat on medium-high. Add spinach, peas, and lemon juice mixture to saucepan and cook, stirring occasionally, for 4 minutes.
5. Add scallops and cook, stirring occasionally, until heated through, about 1 minute.
6. Serve with rice.

{SERVES 5}

253 Supper-Ready Shrimp Salad

- 1 (14 ounce) package frozen tortellini
- ½ of 1 (2 pound) package frozen, shelled shrimp
- ½ cup sliced ripe olives
- ½ cup chopped celery
- ½ cup zesty Italian salad dressing

1. Prepare tortellini and shrimp according to package directions.
2. Combine tortellini, shrimp, olives and celery in salad bowl.
3. Pour salad dressing over salad and toss. Serve immediately or refrigerate until ready to serve.

{SERVES 8}

254 Skillet Shrimp

- 2 teaspoons olive oil
- 2 2 pounds fresh shrimp, peeled, veined
- ⅔ cup herb-garlic marinade with lemon
- ¼ cup finely chopped scallion with tops

1. Heat oil in large non-stick skillet. Add shrimp and marinade and cook, stirring often, until shrimp turn pink.
2. Stir in scallions. Serve over rice or pasta.

{SERVES 6}

255 Thai Shrimp-Peanut Noodles

- 3 cups water
- 1 (5.5 ounce) box Thai stir-fry noodles with seasoning packet
- 1 pound fresh, peeled, veined shrimp
- 1 (10 ounce) package frozen broccoli florets, thawed
- 2 tablespoons vegetable or canola oil
- ½ cup chopped peanuts

1. Boil water in saucepan and stir in noodles. Turn heat off and soak noodles for about 5 minutes. Drain and rinse in cold water.
2. Sauté shrimp and broccoli in skillet with oil for about 8 minutes or just until shrimp turns pink.
3. Add noodles, seasoning packet, and peanuts.

{SERVES 6}

256 Shrimp Newburg

Legend has it that the term "Newburg" for a sauce was invented at the Delmonico restaurant in New York City. The sauce was originally named after a frequent diner named "Wenburg," but the name was changed after he had an argument with the chef.

- 1 (10 ounce) can cream of shrimp soup
- ¼ cup water
- 1 teaspoon seafood seasoning
- 1 (1 pound) package cooked, frozen salad shrimp, thawed

1. Combine soup, water, and seafood seasoning in saucepan. Bring to a boil, reduce heat, and stir in shrimp.
2. Heat thoroughly and serve over rice.

{SERVES 6}

257 Celebration Clams and Linguine

- **1 (12 ounce) package linguine (thin egg noodles) pasta**
- **1½ cups chicken broth, divided**
- **½ onion, finely chopped**
- **2 teaspoons minced garlic**
- **2 (6 ounce) cans chopped clams with liquid**
- **1 tablespoon dried parsley**
- **2 teaspoons lemon juice**
- **¼ teaspoon salt**
- **⅛ teaspoon black pepper**

1. Cook linguine in saucepan according to package directions.
2. While pasta cooks, place ½ cup chicken broth, onion, and garlic in large saucepan on high heat and bring to a boil. Reduce heat to medium-low and cook for about 5 minutes or until onion is soft.
3. Add clam liquid and remaining broth and bring to a boil. Reduce heat to medium and simmer for 4 minutes.

   Stir in clams and cook until mixture is heated through.
4. Drain pasta and return to pot; add clam sauce, parsley, lemon juice, salt, and pepper. Toss to mix well and pour into serving bowl.

{SERVES 6-8}

Who Knew?

To make this recipe even healthier, use our Healthy Chicken Broth.

258 Red Clam Sauce Over Vermicelli

- **1 tablespoon olive oil**
- **1 teaspoon minced garlic**
- **2 (7 ounce) cans chopped clams with liquid**
- **1 (8 ounce) can tomato sauce**
- **1 teaspoon dried parsley**
- **3 tablespoons grated Parmesan cheese, divided**
- **½ teaspoon dried basil**
- **½ teaspoon dried oregano**
- **Dash of cayenne pepper**
- **1 (8 ounce) package vermicelli noodles**
- **1 cup bean sprouts**

1. Place oil in skillet over medium-high heat and sauté garlic for 1 minute.
2. Drain clams, saving liquid from one can. Set clams aside.
3. Add saved clam liquid, tomato sauce, parsley, 1 tablespoon cheese, basil, oregano, and cayenne pepper to skillet. Cover and simmer on low heat for 20 minutes.

   Stir in clams and cook until warmed through.
4. Cook vermicelli in saucepan according to package directions, drain, and place in serving bowl. Add bean sprouts and toss.
5. Pour clam sauce over pasta and sprouts and sprinkle with remaining cheese.

{SERVES 3-4}

259 Shrimp Scampi

Shrimp Scampi is just a fancy way to say "shrimp in garlic butter sauce." It's a uniquely American term—*scampi* in England refers to deep fried lobster tail!

½ cup (1 stick) butter
3 cloves garlic, minced
¼ cup lemon juice
1-3 dashes hot sauce
2 pounds shrimp, peeled

1. Melt butter in skillet, then sauté garlic until tender. Add lemon juice and hot sauce and heat through.
2. Arrange shrimp in single layer in shallow pan. Pour butter mixture over shrimp, reserving some for dipping.
3. Broil shrimp for 2 minutes, turn shrimp over, and broil for additional 2 minutes.
4. Serve with reserved garlic butter.

{SERVES 6}

Who Knew?

Before heating the butter in step 1, try heating your pan up alone for a couple of minutes. It will ensure nothing sticks and that everything heats evenly.

260 Florentine Shrimp and Pasta

2 (9 ounce) frozen, boil-in-bag creamed spinach
1 (12 ounce) package penne (tube) pasta
¼ cup whipping cream
1 teaspoon Cajun seasoning
1 pound fresh peeled, medium shrimp
2 tablespoons olive oil

1. Bring large pot of water to boil and add spinach pouches. Cook according to package directions.
2. In separate, large saucepan, cook pasta according to package directions. Drain, add cream and Cajun seasoning, and mix until blended well.
3. Cook shrimp in skillet with olive oil until shrimp turn pink, about 3 minutes.
4. Cut open spinach pouches and add to pasta. Stir in shrimp and transfer to serving dish.

{SERVES 6}

CHAPTER 7

Casseroles

261 Carbonara Skillet Pie

- **1 (8 ounce) package spaghetti pasta**
- **8 slices bacon**
- **3 eggs**
- **1 (16 ounce) jar alfredo sauce, divided**
- **½ cup grated Parmesan cheese**
- **1 (8 ounce) can green peas, drained**

1. Cook spaghetti in saucepan according to package directions and drain.
2. Cook bacon in skillet on medium-high heat until crisp; drain. Cut or crumble into small pieces.
3. Whisk eggs, 1 cup alfredo sauce, and cheese in large bowl. Stir in spaghetti, peas, and bacon, and place in same skillet used to cook bacon. Cook over medium heat until bottom is slightly crisp, about 5 minutes.
4. Spoon remaining sauce over top, cover, and cook for 7–8 minutes. Cut in wedges to serve.

{SERVES 5-6}

Who Knew? Light Switch

To make this recipe low-fat, substitute fat-trimmed ham for the bacon and 1¾ cups of our Low-Fat Alfredo Sauce for the jar of alfredo sauce.

262 Sensational Spaghetti

Forget the tomato sauce. This is spaghetti to love!

- **½ cup (1 stick) butter**
- **1 ½ 1½ teaspoons minced garlic**
- **1 1 (12 ounce) package vermicelli pasta**
- **1 cup grated Parmesan cheese**
- **1 (1 pint) carton whipping cream**
- **1 teaspoon dried parsley flakes**
- **½ teaspoon salt**
- **½ teaspoon black pepper**
- **5-6 slices crisp bacon, crumbled**

1. Preheat oven to 325°.
2. Melt butter in large skillet and sauté garlic until slightly brown.
3. Cook spaghetti in saucepan according to package directions and drain.
4. Combine garlic mixture, spaghetti, Parmesan cheese, cream, parsley flakes, salt, and pepper in bowl and mix well.
5. Spoon into sprayed, 2-quart baking dish. Cover and bake just until warm, about 15 minutes.
6. Uncover and sprinkle crumbled bacon over casserole.

{SERVES 6-8}

Who Knew?

Always rinse bacon under cold water before frying—it will reduce the amount the bacon shrinks when you cook it.

263 Quick Chili Dog Supper

2 (15 ounce) cans chili without beans
1 (16 ounce) package hot dogs, cut in half
1 (8 ounce) package Velveeta cheese, cubed
1 (4 ounce) can chopped green chilies
1 small onion, finely chopped
1 cup chunky salsa
1 (12 ounce) can refrigerated pastry twists
½ teaspoon chili powder
½ teaspoon ground cumin

1. Preheat oven to 350°.
2. Combine chili, hot dogs, cheese, green chilies, onion, and salsa in large saucepan. Cook, stirring constantly, over medium heat until mixture is bubbly. Spoon mixture into sprayed, 9 x 13-inch baking dish.
3. Separate dough into 16 strips. Gently twist each strip and arrange over chili mixture.
4. Combine chili powder and cumin in bowl and sprinkle over cornbread twists.
5. Bake until cornbread twists are golden brown, about 20–25 minutes.

{SERVES 6-8}

Who Knew? Light Switch

To make this recipe lower in fat, use our Super Healthy Salsa and substitute 1½ cups of our Melty Cheese Sauce for the package of Velveeta cheese.

264 Chicken Tetrazzini

½ cup (1 stick) butter
6 tablespoons flour
½ teaspoon salt
¼ teaspoon black pepper
2 (14 ounce) cans chicken broth
1 (8 ounce) carton whipping cream
1 (16 ounce) package linguine, cooked, drained
5-6 boneless, skinless chicken breast halves, cooked, cubed
1 cup sliced fresh mushrooms
2 ribs celery, chopped
1 green bell pepper, seeded, chopped
1 (4 ounce) jar diced pimentos, drained
4-5 drops hot sauce
½ cup grated Parmesan cheese

1. Preheat oven to 350°.
2. Melt butter in saucepan over medium heat, add flour, salt, and pepper and stir until smooth. Gradually add broth and bring to boil. Cook, stirring constantly, until mixture thickens.
3. Remove from heat and stir in cream. If sauce seems too thick, add a little milk.
4. Mix 2 cups sauce with cooked linguine, and spread into sprayed, 9 x 13-inch baking dish.
5. In separate container, combine chicken, mushrooms,celery, bell pepper, pimentos, and hot sauce and mix well.
   Pour over linguine.
6. Sprinkle with Parmesan cheese.
7. Cover and bake until bubbling, about 45 minutes.
   Uncover and bake for additional 10 minutes.

{SERVES 10}

265 Garden Chicken

This colorful, scrumptious casserole is not only packed with flavor, it also looks great on the table. You can't beat this bountiful dish when you have company for dinner!

- **1 teaspoon minced garlic**
- **1 tablespoon olive oil**
- **1 small yellow squash, thinly sliced**
- **1 small zucchini, thinly sliced**
- **1 red bell pepper, seeded, thinly sliced**
- **1 3 tablespoons butter**
- **¼ ¼ cup flour**
- **2 teaspoons pesto sauce**
- **½ ½ teaspoon salt**
- **½ ½ teaspoon black pepper**
- **1 1 (14 ounce) can chicken broth**
- **1 1 cup half-and-half**
- **4 4 chicken breast halves, cooked, cut into strips**
- **1 1 (8 ounce) package angel hair pasta, cooked, drained**
- **⅓ 1/3 cup grated Parmesan cheese**

1. Preheat oven to 350°.
2. In large skillet, heat olive oil over medium-high heat.
   When hot, add garlic, squash, zucchini, and bell pepper.
   Cook, stirring frequently, until vegetables are tendercrisp.
   Remove vegetables from skillet.
3. Add butter to skillet and melt over medium-high heat. Add flour, pesto sauce, salt, and pepper. Stir to form smooth paste.
4. Gradually add broth and stir constantly until mixture begins to thicken. Stir in half-and-half and cook, stirring, until mixture further thickens, about 5 minutes.
5. In large bowl, combine chicken, vegetables, brothcream mixture, and pasta. Transfer to sprayed, 9 x 13- inch baking dish.
6. Cover and bake for 30 minutes. Sprinkle Parmesan cheese over top of casserole and bake, uncovered, for additional 5 minutes.

{SERVES 6-8}

266 Creamy Chicken Enchiladas

- **2 (10 ounce) cans cream of chicken soup, divided**
- **½ cup finely chopped onion**
- **1 teaspoon minced garlic**
- **1 (4 ounce) can chopped green chilies**
- **1 ½ cups cooked, shredded chicken**
- **1 cup shredded Monterey Jack cheese, divided**
- **8 (6 inch) corn tortillas**
- **½ cup milk**

1. Preheat oven to 375°.
2. Combine ½ can of chicken soup, onion, garlic, green chilies, chicken, and half of cheese in medium bowl.
3. Spoon about 1/3 cup chicken mixture down center of each tortilla. Roll tortillas and place seam-side down in sprayed, 9 x 13-inch baking dish.
4. Mix remaining 1½ cans soup and milk in saucepan and stir until blended well. Pour over enchiladas.
5. Bake until enchiladas are hot and bubbly, about 20 minutes. Remove from oven and sprinkle with remaining cheese.

{SERVES 4}

267 Discover Green Enchiladas

1 (8 ounce) carton sour cream
1 (16 ounce) jar green salsa
8 flour tortillas
2½3 cups cooked, shredded chicken
1 small (or ½ of 1 large) onion, finely chopped
1 (4 ounce) can chopped green chilies
1½ cups shredded mozzarella cheese
Extra sour cream for garnish

1. Preheat oven to 350°.
2. Combine sour cream and salsa in bowl; mix well.
   Dip each tortilla into sauce to coat both sides.
3. Evenly divide chicken, onion, and green chilies among each tortilla. Spoon onto tortilla and roll.
4. Place seam-side down in sprayed, 9 x 13-inch baking dish. Pour remaining sauce over enchiladas.
5. Bake, uncovered, for 15 minutes; remove from oven and sprinkle mozzarella cheese over top. Return to oven for 5 minutes. Serve with extra sour cream.

{SERVES 4}

Who Knew?

If you're using half of 1 large onion, use the top half first, because the root half will store longer in the refrigerator (it won't sprout).

268 Quick Chicken Divan

1 (10 ounce) package frozen broccoli florets, thawed
2 cups cooked, chopped chicken
1 (10 ounce) can broccoli cheese soup
½ cup milk
2 tablespoons mayonnaise
½ cup shredded Cheddar cheese
2 teaspoons lemon juice
¼ cup seasoned breadcrumbs
2 tablespoons butter, melted

1. Preheat oven to 375°.
2. Cook broccoli in microwave according to package directions; drain well.
3. Layer broccoli and chicken in sprayed, 2-quart glass baking dish.
4. In medium bowl, combine soup, milk, mayonnaise, cheese, and lemon juice. Mix with wire whisk until blended well. Pour over broccoli-chicken mixture.
5. Combine breadcrumbs and melted butter in bowl and sprinkle over casserole.
6. Bake, uncovered, until breadcrumbs are light brown, about 30 minutes.

{SERVES 4}

269 Confetti Orzo

- **8 ounces orzo pasta**
- **½ cup (1 stick) butter**
- **3 cups broccoli florets, stems chopped off**
- **1 bunch scallions with tops, chopped**
- **1 red bell pepper, seeded, chopped**
- **2 cups chopped celery**
- **1 clove garlic, minced**
- **½ teaspoon cumin**
- **2 teaspoons chicken bouillon granules**
- **1 (8 ounce) carton sour cream**
- **1 (16 ounce) jar alfredo sauce**
- **3-4 cups cooked, chopped chicken or turkey**
- **1 teaspoon salt**
- **1 teaspoon black pepper**

1. Preheat oven to 325°.
2. Cook orzo according to package directions, stirring several times during cooking time.
3. While orzo is cooking, melt butter in large saucepan and sauté broccoli, onions, bell pepper, celery, garlic, cumin, and chicken bouillon and cook just until tendercrisp.
4. Fold in sour cream, alfredo sauce, chicken or turkey, salt, pepper, and orzo.
5. Spoon into sprayed, 9 x 13-inch baking dish.
6. Cover and bake for 30 minutes.

{SERVES 8-10}

270 Chicken Taco Casserole

- **1 (10 ounce) cream of mushroom soup**
- **1 (10 ounce) can cream of chicken soup**
- **1 cup milk**
- **1 (1 ounce) packet taco seasoning**
- **1 onion, chopped**
- **1 (4 ounce) can chopped green chilies, drained**
- **5-6 boneless, skinless chicken breast halves, cooked**
- **1 (16 ounce) bag tortilla chips, divided**
- **1 (16 ounce) package four-cheese blend, divided**

1. Preheat oven to 325°.
2. Combine soups, milk, taco seasoning, onion, and green chilies in bowl. Cut chicken breasts into bite-size pieces.
3. Place half of chips in bottom of sprayed, 9 x 13-inch glass dish. Top with half of chicken, half of soup mixture, and half of cheese, then remaining chips, chicken, soup mixture, and cheese.
4. Bake covered, for 45 minutes. Remove cover and bake for additional 15 minutes.

{SERVES 8}

271 Divine Chicken Casserole

- 5 cups cooked broccoli spears
- ½ teaspoon salt
- 3 cups cooked, diced chicken
- 1 (10 ounce) can cream of chicken soup
- 2 tablespoons milk
- ½ cup mayonnaise
- 2 teaspoons lemon juice
- 1 cup shredded Cheddar cheese
- ¼ teaspoon black pepper
- 1½ cups cracker crumbs
- 3 tablespoons butter, melted

1. Preheat oven to 350°.
2. Cook broccoli according to package directions; drain. Cut off stems if desired.
3. Place in sprayed, 9 x 13-inch baking dish and sprinkle with salt. Cover with chicken.
4. Combine soup, milk, mayonnaise, lemon juice, cheese, and pepper in saucepan. Heat over medium heat until cheese melts and mixture is blended, about 5–7 minutes. Pour over chicken and broccoli.
5. Combine cracker crumbs and butter in bowl and sprinkle over casserole.
6. Bake until bubbling and heated through, about 35–40 minutes.

{SERVES 6-8}

Who Knew?

If you don't have leftover broccoli to use for this recipe, you can use 2 (10 ounce) packages of frozen broccoli spears. Thaw before using.

272 Speedy Chicken Pie

This dinner is so quick to make, it will allow you extra minutes to create an out-of-sight dessert… or get the kids to bed at a decent hour.

- 1 (12 ounce) package shredded Cheddar cheese, divided
- 1 (10 ounce) package frozen chopped broccoli, thawed, drained
- 2 cups cooked, chopped chicken
- ½ cup finely chopped onion
- ½ cup finely chopped red bell pepper
- 1⅓ cups half-and-half
- 3 eggs
- ¾ cup biscuit mix
- 1 teaspoon salt
- ½ teaspoon black pepper

1. Preheat oven to 375°.
2. Combine 2 cups Cheddar cheese, broccoli, chicken, onion, and bell pepper in bowl. Spread into sprayed, 10-inch, deep-dish pie pan.
3. Beat half-and-half, eggs, biscuit mix, salt, and pepper in bowl and mix well. Slowly pour over broccoli-chicken mixture, but do not stir.
4. Cover and bake until center is firm, about 35 minutes.
5. Sprinkle remaining cheese over top. Bake uncovered until cheese melts, about 5 minutes.

{SERVES 4-6}

273 Chicken Pot Pie

This version of pot pie uses cream of chicken soup for the perfect filling.

- **2 refrigerated piecrusts**
- **2 (10 ounce) cans cream of chicken soup**
- **2 cups cooked, chopped chicken**
- **2½ cups cooked, chopped vegetables or 1 (10 ounce) package frozen mixed vegetables, thawed**

1. Preheat oven to 325°.
2. Place 1 piecrust in 9-inch pie pan. Fill with chicken soup, chicken, and vegetables.
3. Cover with second piecrust; fold edges under and crimp. With knife, cut 4 slits in center of piecrust.
4. Bake until crust is golden brown, about 1 hour 15 minutes

{SERVES 6}

Who Knew? Light Switch

To make this recipe lower in fat, substitute 2½ cups of our Low-Fat Cream of Chicken Soup Base for the cans of soup.

274 Gourmet Couscous Salad

- **1 tablespoon lemon juice**
- **¼ cup olive oil**
- **½ teaspoon dried basil**
- **½ teaspoon black pepper**
- **1 (10 ounce) box chicken-flavored couscous**
- **2 tomatoes, coarsely chopped**
- **2 zucchini, coarsely chopped**
- **4 fresh scallions, sliced**
- **1 cup chopped turkey**
- **1 cup crumbled feta cheese**

1. Combine lemon juice, olive oil, basil, and pepper and mix well. Set aside in refrigerator.
2. Cook couscous according to package directions, but omit butter.
3. Combine couscous, tomatoes, zucchini, scallions, and turkey in salad bowl.
4. When ready to serve, add feta cheese, pour dressing over salad, and toss..

{SERVES 6}

Who Knew?

To quickly and easily "grate" Feta or other soft cheeses, just push the cheese through a colander with a potato masher.

275 Turkey-Stuffed Peppers

1 red, yellow, or orange bell peppers
1 (15 ounce) can Italian stewed tomatoes
½ cup orzo pasta
1 teaspoon dried oregano
1 teaspoon dried basil
½ teaspoon ground allspice
½ teaspoon salt
½ cup water
1 pound ground turkey, cooked
¾ cup grated Parmesan cheese, divided

1. Preheat oven to 375°.
2. Cut off tops of bell peppers and remove seeds and membranes. Immerse in large pot of boiling water for 3 minutes.
3. Remove peppers with slotted spoon and invert on paper towels to drain.
4. Combine tomatoes, orzo, oregano, basil, allspice, salt and water. Stir, then cover and cook on medium-low heat until orzo is tender and water is mostly absorbed, about 10 minutes.
5. Add ground turkey and half of Parmesan cheese.

   Stir, and continue to cook until heated through.
6. Fill peppers with turkey mixture and place in sprayed, 3-quart baking dish. Place any remaining meat mixture around peppers.
7. Bake for 15 minutes, then sprinkle with remaining cheese.

{SERVES 4-6}

Who Knew?

Don't have allspice? Substitute 1 part ground cinnamon and 2 parts ground cloves instead.

276 Beefy Mushroom Ravioli

1 large onion, chopped
2 zucchini squash, grated
½ teaspoon minced garlic
¼ cup (½ stick) butter
3¼ cups prepared spaghetti sauce, or 1 (28 ounce) jar spaghetti sauce
1 pound ground beef, cooked
2 (13 ounce) packages mushroomfilled ravioli, cooked
1 (12 ounce) package shredded mozzarella cheese
Salt and pepper to taste

1. Preheat oven to 350°.
2. Melt butter over medium-high heat in saucepan. Add onion, zucchini, and garlic and cook, stirring frequently, until onions are tender-crisp, about 3 minutes. Add spaghetti sauce and mix well. Cook until heated through, about 5 minutes.
3. Spread ½ cup spaghetti sauce mixture in sprayed, 9 x 13-inch baking dish. Top with half of ravioli, half of remaining spaghetti sauce, half of beef, and half of cheese, then remaining ravioli, remaining spaghetti sauce, remaining beef, and remaining cheese.
4. Cover and bake for 35 minutes. Uncover and bake until cheese is bubbling, about 10 more minutes. Let stand for several minutes before serving.

{SERVES 8}

277 Cornbread-Beef Bake

This recipe calls for both cooked ground beef and a cooked onion. But if you have leftover beef with onions, peppers, or any other veggies mixed in, just use that and omit the cooked onion.

- **1 pound lean ground beef, cooked**
- **1 small onion, finely chopped, cooked**
- **1 (4 ounce) can chopped green chilies**
- **2 large eggs, beaten**
- **1 (8 ounce) package corn muffin mix**
- **¼ cup milk**
- **1 (15 ounce) can cream-style corn**
- **1 (8 ounce) package Velveeta cheese, cubed**

1. Preheat oven to 400°.
2. Combine green chilies, eggs, corn muffin mix, milk, and cream-style corn; mix until well blended.
3. Pour half of mixture into sprayed, 9-inch square baking pan.
4. Mix beef and onions and pour over corn muffin batter mixture. Top with cheese and remaining corn muffin batter mixture.
5. Bake, uncovered, until batter is light brown, about 30 minutes.

{SERVES 6}

Who Knew? Light Switch

To make this recipe lower in fat, substitute 1½ cups of our Melty Cheese Sauce for the package of Velveeta cheese.

278 Tasty Taco Squares

- **½ cup finely chopped onion**
- **1 1 tablespoon olive oil**
- **1 1 pound ground beef, cooked**
- **(1 ounce) packet taco seasoning mix**
- **½ ½ cup + 1/3 cup water**
- **1 1 (10 ounce) can chopped tomatoes and green chilies with liquid**
- **1 cup biscuit mix**
- **Sour cream as garnish**
- **1 large tomato, chopped, as garnish**

1. Preheat oven to 425°.
2. Cook onion in hot olive oil over medium-high heat until tender-crisp, about 3–5 minutes.
3. Add beef, taco seasoning, ½ cup water, and tomatoes and green chilies. Bring to a boil, then reduce heat to low and simmer for 5 minutes; drain.
4. Combine biscuit mix and 1/3 cup cold water in bowl and stir until mixture is smooth. Spread into sprayed, 9 x 9-inch glass baking dish. Spread beef mixture over dough.
5. Bake, uncovered, until edges are golden brown, about 30 minutes.
6. Cut into squares and serve with sour cream and tomatoes as garnish.

{SERVES 4}

279 Italian Chicken and Rice

- 1 tablespoon olive oil
- 3 boneless, skinless chicken breast halves, cut into strips
- 1 (14 ounce) can chicken broth
- 1 teaspoon Italian seasoning
- ¾ ¾ cup rice
  Water, as necessary
- ¼ cup grated Parmesan cheese

1. Heat oil over medium heat in large skillet. When hot, add chicken strips. Cook, stirring, until chicken is cooked through, about 10 minutes. Set aside chicken.
2. Add broth and rice to skillet, and heat to boil. Cover and simmer over low heat for 25 minutes. (Add water if necessary.)
3. Stir in cheese, and return chicken to pan. Cover and cook until done, about 5 minutes..

{SERVES 6}

280 Dijon Skillet Chicken

- ¼ cup ranch salad dressing
- 1 tablespoon Dijon-style mustard
- 2 tablespoons butter
- 4 boneless, skinless chicken breast halves
- 3 3 tablespoons white wine or chicken broth

1. Combine salad dressing and mustard in salad bowl and set aside.
2. Melt butter in large skillet over medium heat. Add chicken and cook, flipping occasionally, until chicken is brown on both sides, about 10–15 minutes.
3. Add wine or broth and simmer for additional 20 minutes, flipping once.
4. Whisk in mustard mixture and cook, stirring constantly, until it blends and is heated through.
5. Serve over rice or egg noodles.

{SERVES 4}

Who Knew?

Have leftover rice after eating this dish? Rice can be stored in fridge for a longer amount of time if you store a slice of toast on top of it. The toast will absorb excess moisture and keep the rice fluffy and fresh.

281 Spinach Enchiladas

2 (10 ounce) packages frozen chopped spinach, thawed, drained

1 (1 ounce) packet onion soup mix

3 cups shredded Cheddar cheese, divided

3 cups shredded Monterey Jack cheese or mozzarella cheese, divided

12 flour tortillas

1 (1 pint) carton whipping cream

1. Preheat oven to 350°.
2. Squeeze spinach between paper towels to completely remove excess moisture. Combine spinach and onion soup mix in medium bowl.
3. Blend in half of Cheddar cheese and half of Jack cheese.
4. Spread out 12 tortillas. Place about 3 heaping tablespoons spinach mixture down middle of each tortilla. Roll into enchiladas.
5. Place each filled tortilla, seam-side down, into sprayed, 10 x 15-inch baking dish.
6. Pour whipping cream over enchiladas and sprinkle with remaining cheeses. (If freezing for later, place in freezer without whipping cream and remaining cheeses and add just before baking.)
7. Cover and bake for 20 minutes. Uncover and bake for additional 10 minutes.

{SERVES 10-12}

Who Knew? Light Switch

To make this recipe lower in fat, use our Low-Fat Four-Cheese Blend instead of the Cheddar and Monterey Jack cheeses, and use half-and-half rather than whipping cream.

282 Spicy Vegetable Couscous

- **1 (6 ounce) package herbed-chicken couscous**
- **3 tablespoons butter**
- **3 tablespoons vegetable or canola oil**
- **1 small yellow squash, diced**
- **1 small zucchini, diced**
- **½ red onion, diced**
- **1 red bell pepper, diced**
- **1 (10 ounce) package frozen green peas, thawed**
- **½ teaspoon garlic powder**
- **½ teaspoon ground cumin**
- **½ teaspoon curry powder**
- **¼ teaspoon cayenne pepper**
- **½ teaspoon salt**
- **3-4 tablespoons water, as needed (optional)**
- **1½ cups shredded mozzarella cheese**

1. Preheat oven to 350°.
2. Cook couscous according to package directions, but add 3 tablespoons butter instead of amount specified.
3. Heat oil in skillet and sauté squash, zucchini, onion, and bell pepper for 10 minutes. Do not brown.
4. Add peas, garlic powder, cumin, curry powder, cayenne pepper, and salt. Toss.
5. Combine vegetables and couscous. If it seems a little dry, add water.
6. Pour into sprayed, 2½-quart baking dish and sprinkle with mozzarella cheese.
7. Cover and bake for 25 minutes.

{SERVES 6-8}

Who Knew?

If you prefer a milder spice, use only 1/8 teaspoon cayenne pepper.

283 Spinach-Cheese Manicotti

This recipe will give you enough yummy enchiladas for two meals!

1 onion, minced

2 teaspoons minced garlic

1 tablespoon vegetable or canola oil

1 (15 ounce) container ricotta cheese

1 (3 ounce) package cream cheese, softened

1 (8 ounce) package shredded mozzarella cheese, divided

1 (3 ounce) package grated Parmesan cheese, divided

2 teaspoons Italian seasoning

½ teaspoon salt

½ teaspoon black pepper

1 (10 ounce) box frozen chopped spinach, thawed, drained

9 manicotti shells, cooked

1 (28 ounce) jar spaghetti sauce

1. Preheat oven to 350°.
2. Sauté onion and garlic with oil in skillet and set aside.
3. Combine ricotta, cream cheese, half of mozzarella, half of Parmesan, Italian seasoning, salt, and pepper in bowl. Beat until they are mixed well.
4. Squeeze spinach between paper towels to completely remove excess moisture.
5. Add spinach and onion-garlic mixture to cheese mixture, and mix well.
6. Spoon mixture into manicotti shells, 1 teaspoon at a time. (Be careful not to tear shells.)
7. Pour half of spaghetti sauce into sprayed, 9 x 13-inch baking dish. Arrange shells over sauce and top with remaining sauce.
8. Cover and bake for 30 minutes. Sprinkle remaining cheeses over top. Bake uncovered until cheese melts.

{SERVES 8-10}

284 Pasta Frittata

1 onion, chopped

1 green bell pepper, seeded, chopped

1 red bell pepper, seeded, chopped

2 tablespoons butter

1 (7 ounce) box thin spaghetti, slightly broken, cooked

1 (8 ounce) package shredded mozzarella cheese

5 eggs

1 cup milk

⅓ cup shredded Parmesan cheese

1 tablespoon dried basil

1 teaspoon oregano

½ teaspoon salt

½ teaspoon black pepper

1. Preheat oven to 375°.
2. Sauté onion and bell peppers with butter in skillet over medium heat for 5 minutes. Do not brown.
3. Combine onion-pepper mixture and spaghetti in large bowl and toss. Add mozzarella cheese and toss.
4. In separate bowl, beat eggs, milk, Parmesan cheese, basil, oregano, salt, and pepper. Add spaghetti mixture and pour into sprayed, 9 x 13-inch baking dish.
5. Cover and bake for 15–20 minutes. Uncover and make sure eggs are set. If not, bake for additional 2–3 minutes. Cut into squares to serve.

{SERVES 8-10}

285 Quick Chicken Casserole

¼ cup (½ stick) butter
4 boneless, skinless chicken breast halves, chopped
8 ounces fresh mushrooms, sliced
1 (14 ounce) jar artichoke hearts, drained
2 tablespoons flour
1 (14 ounce) can chicken broth

1. Preheat oven to 350°.
2. Melt butter in skillet over medium heat. Add chicken pieces and cook, stirring, for 5 minutes. Add mushrooms and continue to cook, stirring, until chicken is cooked through and mushrooms and tender.
3. Keeping melted butter in skillet, transfer chicken and mushrooms to sprayed, 3 quart baking dish. Top with artichoke hearts.
4. Add flour to remaining butter and juices in skillet.

   Stir to blend. Add broth and cook over medium-high heat until thickened, about 6–10 minutes. Pour over chicken.
5. Baked, covered, for 45 minutes. Let sit for 5–10 minutes before serving.

{SERVES 4}

286 Creamy, Cheesy Chicken

¼ cups cooked rice (2 cups uncooked)
6 tablespoons (¾ stick) butter, divided
¼ cup flour
2 cups milk
2 teaspoons chicken bouillon granules
1 teaspoon parsley flakes
½ teaspoon celery salt
½ teaspoon salt
4 cups cooked, cubed chicken
2 (8 ounce) packages Velveeta cheese, cubed
1 (8 ounce) carton sour cream
1½ cups crushed round buttery crackers

1. Preheat oven to 325°.
2. Spread cooked rice into sprayed, 9 x 13-inch baking dish and set aside.
3. Melt 4 tablespoons butter in large saucepan. Stir in flour and mix until smooth. Gradually stir in milk, bouillon, parsley flakes, celery salt, and salt.
4. Cook over medium heat, stirring constantly, until sauce thickens, about 2 minutes.
5. Reduce heat and add chicken, cheese, and sour cream. Stir until cheese melts.
6. Spoon chicken mixture over rice in baking dish.
7. Melt remaining 2 tablespoons butter and toss with cracker crumbs. Sprinkle over casserole.
8. Bake until hot, about 35 minutes.

{SERVES 8}

Who Knew? Light Switch

To make this recipe lower in fat, substitute 3 cups of our Melty Cheese Sauce for the 2 packages of Velveeta cheese, and 1 cup of our Low-Fat Sour Cream Substitute for the carton of sour cream.

287 Award-Winning Casserole

- **1 tablespoons olive oil**
- **2 boneless, skinless chicken breasts, chopped into cubes**
- **1 bell pepper, seeded, chopped**
- **1 medium onion, chopped**
- **½ cup chicken broth or water**
- **½ teaspoon garlic powder**
- **½ teaspoon salt**
- **½ teaspoon black pepper**
- **1 (7 ounce) can whole green chilies, drained**
- **1½ cups shredded Monterey Jack cheese**
- **1½ cups shredded sharp Cheddar cheese**
- **3 large eggs**
- **1 tablespoon flour**
- **1 cup cream**

1. Preheat oven to 350°.
2. Heat oil over medium heat in skillet. When hot, add chicken, bell pepper, and onion. Cook, stirring, until onion and bell pepper is tender-crisp, about 5 minutes. Add broth, garlic powder, salt, and pepper and mix well. Cook, stirring occasionally, until chicken is cooked through, about 10–15 minutes.
3. Seed whole chilies and spread into sprayed, 9 x 13-inch baking dish. Cover with meat mixture and sprinkle with cheeses.
4. Combine eggs and flour in bowl and beat with fork until fluffy. Add cream, mix well, and pour over top of meat in baking dish.
5. Bake until light brown, about 30–35 minutes.

{SERVES 8}

288 Broccoli Chicken

- **4 boneless, skinless chicken breast halves, cubed**
- **1 tablespoon olive oil**
- **2 (10 ounce) packages frozen broccoli**
- **2 (10 ounce) cans cream of chicken soup**
- **1 cup mayonnaise**
- **1 teaspoon lemon juice**
- **½ teaspoon curry powder**
- **1½ cups shredded sharp Cheddar cheese, divided**
- **½ cup seasoned breadcrumbs**
- **1 teaspoon butter, melted**

1. Preheat oven to 350°.
2. Cook chicken cubes in large skillet with oil, stirring occasionally, for 10 minutes.
3. Add broccoli and cook, stirring occasionally, until chicken is cooked through and broccoli is tender.

   Place chicken-broccoli mixture in sprayed, 9 x 13-inch baking dish.
4. Combine soup, mayonnaise, lemon juice, curry powder, and ¾ cup cheese in bowl. Spread mixture over chicken.
5. In separate bowl, combine breadcrumbs and butter.

   Layer breadcrumb mixture over chicken.
6. Sprinkle remaining cheese over top, and bake for 25–30 minutes.

{SERVES 8}

289 Bob's Chicken Bake

This satisfying meat-and-potato dish is Bruce's brother's favorite. Chop up three vegetables and the rest is easy!

- 4 cup (½ stick) butter
- 1 red bell pepper, seeded, chopped
- 2 medium onion, chopped
- 2 ribs celery, chopped
- 1 (8 ounce) carton sour cream
- 1 ½ cups cream
- 1 (7 ounce) can chopped green chilies, drained
- 1 teaspoon chicken bouillon granules
- 1 teaspoon salt
- ½ teaspoon black pepper
- 3-4 cups chopped rotisserie chicken
- 1 (16 ounce) package shredded Cheddar cheese, divided
- 1 (2 pound) package frozen hash-brown potatoes, thawed

1. Preheat oven to 350°.
2. Melt butter in large saucepan over medium-high heat and sauté bell pepper, onion, and celery until tender, about 5–10 minutes. Remove from heat.
3. Stir in sour cream, cream, green chilies, bouillon granules, salt, pepper, chicken, and half cheese. Fold in hash-brown potatoes.
4. Spoon into sprayed, 9 x 13-inch baking dish.
5. Bake until casserole is bubbly, about 45 minutes.
6. Remove from oven and sprinkle remaining cheese over top of casserole. Return to oven until cheese melts, about 5 minutes.

{SERVES 12-14}

290 Chicken-Noodle Delight

The red and green bell peppers in this dish make it as colorful as it is delicious!

- 2 ribs celery, chopped
- ½ onion, chopped
- ½ green bell pepper, seeded, chopped
- ½ red bell pepper, seeded, chopped
- 6 tablespoons (¾ stick) butter, divided
- 5 boneless, skinless chicken breasts, cubed
- 3 cups cooked, cubed chicken breasts
- 1 (4 ounce) can sliced mushrooms, drained
- 1 (16 ounce) jar sun-dried tomato alfredo sauce
- 1½ teaspoons chicken bouillon granules
- 1 (8 ounce) package medium egg noodles, cooked, drained
- 1 cup bread crumbs
- ½ cup grated Parmesan cheese

1. Preheat oven to 325°.
2. Combine celery, onion, bell peppers, and 4 tablespoons butter in skillet or large saucepan over medium-high heat. Cook, stirring, for 5 minutes.
3. Reduce heat to medium and add chicken cubes.
   Continue to cook and stir until chicken is cooked through, about 8 minutes.
4. Remove from heat and add mushrooms, alfredo sauce, chicken bouillon, and noodles. Mix well. Pour into sprayed, 3-quart baking dish.
5. Combine bread crumbs and cheese in bowl, and sprinkle over top.
6. Bake until bubbly around edges, about 20 minutes.

{SERVES 10}

291 Chicken and Dumplings Casserole

- ¼ cup (1/2 stick) butter or margarine
- 4 boneless, skinless chicken breasts, chopped
- 2 garlic cloves, minced
- ½ cup chopped onion
- ½ cup chopped celery
- ½ cup all-purpose flour
- 1 teaspoon salt
- ¾ teaspoon pepper
- 1 (10 ounce) package frozen
- 1 green peas
- 2 (14 ounce) cans chicken broth
- 2 teaspoons dried thyme
- 2 cups buttermilk biscuit mix
- ⅔ cup milk, warmed

1. Preheat oven to 350°.
2. Melt butter in skillet over medium-high heat. Add chopped chicken and cook, stirring, for 3 minutes. Add garlic, onion, and celery, and garlic, and cook until onion and celery are tender, about 5 minutes more.
3. Add flour and mix into melted butter and juices. Add salt, pepper, peas, and broth. Bring to a boil, then reduce heat to low and cook, stirring constantly until thickened.
4. Pour into sprayed, 9 x 13-inch baking dish and set aside.
5. Combine biscuit mix and thyme in bowl and stir in milk until dough is moist. Dollop onto chicken mixture by the spoonful.
6. Bake, uncovered, for 30 minutes. Cover and bake until dumplings are completely baked, about 10 minutes more.

{SERVES 8-10}

292 Chicken-Broccoli Deluxe

- ¼ tablespoons olive oil
- 5 boneless, skinless chicken breast halves, sliced
- ¼ cup (1 stick) butter
- ½ cup flour
- 1 (14 ounce) can chicken broth
- 1 (1 pint) carton cream
- 1 (16 ounce) package shredded Cheddar cheese, divided
- 1 (5 ounce) package grated Parmesan cheese
- 2 tablespoons lemon juice
- 2 tablespoons dried parsley
- 1 teaspoon salt
- ½ teaspoon black pepper
- ¾ cup mayonnaise
- 2 (10 ounce) boxes frozen broccoli florets
- 1 (12 ounce) box vermicelli

1. Preheat oven to 325°.
2. Heat oil in very large saucepan over medium heat.
   When hot, add chicken slices and cook, stirring, until chicken is cooked through, about 8–12 minutes. Remove chicken from pan and reduce heat to medium-low.
   Add butter.
3. When butter is melted, add flour and mix until smooth.
4. Gradually add chicken broth and cream, stirring constantly until mixture thickens.
5. Add half Cheddar cheese, Parmesan cheese, lemon juice, dried parsley, salt, and pepper. Heat on low until cheeses melt.
6. Remove from heat and add mayonnaise.
7. Punch small holes in broccoli boxes and microwave for 4 minutes. Gently add broccoli and chicken slices to sauce.
8. Cook vermicelli according to package directions; drain and pour into sprayed, 10 x 15-inch baking dish. Spoon sauce-and-chicken mixture over vermicelli.
9. Cover and bake for 40 minutes. Uncover and sprinkle remaining cheese over top of casserole. Return to oven for additional 5 minutes.

{SERVES 12}

293 Chili Casserole

- 1 40 ounce) can chili with beans
- 4 (4 ounce) can chopped green chilies
- 1 (2 ounce) can sliced ripe olives, drained
- 1 (8 ounce) package shredded Cheddar cheese
- 2 cups ranch-flavored tortilla chips, crushed

1. Preheat oven to 350°.
2. Combine all ingredients in bowl and transfer to sprayed, 3-quart baking dish.
3. Bake until bubbly, about 35 minutes.

{SERVES 8}

Who Knew? Light Switch

To make this recipe lower in fat, substitute 2 cups of our Low-Fat Four-Cheese Blend for the package of Cheddar cheese.

294 Reuben Casserole

- 1 (18 ounce) package frozen hash-brown potatoes, thawed
- ¼ teaspoon salt
- ⅛ teaspoon black pepper
- 2 pounds deli corned beef, sliced ¼-inch thick
- 1 (8 ounce) bottle Russian salad dressing, divided
- 1 (15 ounce) can sauerkraut, drained
- 8 slices Swiss cheese

1. Preheat oven to 425°.
2. Place hash-brown potatoes in sprayed, 9 x 13-inch baking dish and sprinkle with salt and pepper. Bake for 25 minutes.
3. Place overlapping corned beef slices on top of potatoes.
4. Spoon half bottle of dressing over top of beef. Arrange sauerkraut on top. Cover with slices of cheese.
5. Reduce oven to 375° and bake for 20 minutes. Serve remaining Russian dressing on the side.

{SERVES 8}

Who Knew?

Never pay for aerosol cooking sprays. Instead, buy a giant jug of vegetable oil and add it to a clean spray bottle as needed. It's the same thing, and will cost you a fraction of the price.

295 Taco Pie

1 pound lean ground beef
½ of 1 bell pepper, chopped
2 jalapeño peppers, seeded, finely chopped
1 tablespoon vegetable or canola oil
½ teaspoon salt
1 (15 ounce) can Mexican stewed tomatoes
1 cup water
1 tablespoon chili powder
1 (8 ounce) package shredded sharp Cheddar cheese
1 1 (6 ounce) package corn muffin mix
1 1 egg
⅓ cup milk

1. Cook ground beef, bell pepper, and jalapeño peppers with oil in large skillet over medium heat, stirring occasionally, until beef is brown and peppers are tender; drain well.
2. Add salt, tomatoes, water, and chili powder. Cook on medium heat for 10 minutes.
3. Pour into sprayed, 9 x 13-inch glass baking dish.

   Sprinkle cheese on top.
4. When ready for baking, preheat oven to 375°.
5. In mixing bowl, combine corn muffin mix, egg, and milk. Beat well. Pour over top of cheese.
6. Bake until corn muffin mix is light brown, about 25 minutes. Remove from oven and set aside for 10 minutes before serving.

{SERVES 8}

Who Knew? Light Switch

To make this recipe lower in fat, substitute 2 cups of our Low-Fat Four-Cheese Blend for the package of Cheddar cheese.

296 Family-Favorite Casserole

1½ pounds lean ground beef
1 (15 ounce) can stewed tomatoes
1 (10 ounce) can tomatoes and green chilies
1 (12 ounce) package tagliatelle pasta (thin egg noodles)
1 (8 ounce) package cream cheese, softened
1 (8 ounce) carton sour cream
1 (16 ounce) package shredded mozzarella cheese, divided

1. Preheat oven to 350°.
2. Brown beef in large saucepan over medium heat, stirring to break up. Drain fat.
3. Add stewed tomatoes and tomatoes and green chilies. Reduce heat and simmer 20 minutes.
4. Cook pasta in saucepan according to package directions; drain.
5. Beat cream cheese in bowl until smooth; add sour cream and mix until they blend well.
6. Spread half pasta into sprayed, 9 x 13-inch baking pan. Cover with half cream cheese mixture, then half mozzarella cheese.
7. Spread meat-tomato mixture over cheese.
8. Layer remaining pasta, cream cheese mixture, and cheese.
9. Cover and bake for 35 minutes. Let stand for
10 minutes before serving.

{SERVES 12}

297 Tator Tot Dinner

When our kids were little, they never got sick of tator tots. Here's a way to use them other than just as a side.

2 pounds lean ground beef
¼ teaspoon salt
⅛ teaspoon black pepper
1 medium onion, chopped
1 (2 pound) package frozen tator tots
1 (8 ounce) package shredded Cheddar cheese
2 (10 ounce) cans cream of mushroom soup
1 soup canful milk

1. Preheat oven to 350°.
2. Crumble ground beef into sprayed, 9 x 13-inch glass baking dish. Sprinkle with salt and pepper.
3. Cover with onion. Top with tator tots and shredded cheese.
4. Combine soup and milk in saucepan. Heat and stir just enough to mix in milk. Pour over casserole.
5. Bake covered for 1 hour. Uncover and bake for additional 15 minutes.

{SERVES 8}

Who Knew? Light Switch

To make this recipe lower in fat, substitute 2 cups of our Low-Fat Four-Cheese Blend for the package of Cheddar cheese.

298 Enchilada Lasagna

1½ pounds lean ground beef
1 medium onion, chopped
1 teaspoon minced garlic
1 (15 ounce) can enchilada sauce
1 (15 ounce) can stewed tomatoes
1 teaspoon ground cumin
½ teaspoon salt
1 egg
1½ cups small curd cottage cheese
1 (12 ounce) package shredded fourcheese blend, divided
8 (8 inch) corn tortillas, torn into strips
1 cup shredded Cheddar cheese

1. Preheat oven to 325°.
2. Cook beef, onion, and garlic in large skillet over medium heat until meat is no longer pink. Drain.
3. Stir in enchilada sauce, tomatoes, cumin, and salt.

   Bring mixture to a boil over medium-high heat, then reduce heat to low and simmer for 20 minutes.
4. Combine egg and cottage cheese in small bowl.
5. Spread one-third of meat mixture into sprayed, 9 x 13-inch baking dish. Top with half four-cheese blend, half tortillas, and half cottage cheese mixture. Repeat layers.
6. Top with remaining meat mixture and sprinkle with Cheddar cheese.
7. Cover and bake for 25 minutes. Uncover and bake for additional 10 minutes.

{SERVES 8}

Who Knew? Light Switch

To make this recipe lower in fat, substitute 3 cups of our Low-Fat Four-Cheese Blend for the package of four-cheese blend.

299 Barbecued Beef Casserole

1½ pounds ground beef
1 large onion, diced
1 red bell pepper, seeded and diced
1 (10 ounce) can whole kernel corn, drained
1 1 (15 ounce) can diced tomatoes, drained
½ cup barbecue sauce
1 teaspoon garlic powder
3 (8.5 ounce) packages cornbread mix

1. Preheat oven to 400°.
2. Cook ground beef, onion, and bell pepper in skillet over medium heat until vegetables are tender and beef is no longer pink, about 8–12 minutes. Drain.
3. Add corn, tomatoes, barbecue sauce, and garlic powder and stir to mix well. Pour into 9 x 13-inch baking dish.
4. Prepare cornbread batter according to package directions. Spread batter over beef mixture.
5. Bake, uncovered, until top is golden brown, about 20–25 minutes.

{SERVES 8-10}

300 Potato-Beef Casserole

½ tablespoon vegetable or canola oil
1¼ pounds lean ground beef
4 medium potatoes, peeled, sliced
1 (10 ounce) can cream of mushroom soup
1 (10 ounce) can vegetable beef soup
¼ teaspoon salt
⅛ teaspoon black pepper

1. Preheat oven to 350°.
2. Heat oil over medium heat in skillet. When hot, add beef and cook until beef is browned, about 8–10 minutes. Stir to break up beef throughout cooking time. Drain.
3. Combine beef with remaining ingredients in large bowl.
4. Transfer to sprayed, 3-quart baking dish. Cover and bake until potatoes are tender, about 1 hour 30 minutes.

{SERVES 4-6}

301 Beef and Broccoli Bake

1 cup rice, uncooked
1½ 1½ pounds lean ground beef
1 1 (16 ounce) package frozen broccoli florets, thawed
2 (10 ounce) cans broccoli cheese soup
¾ cup milk
1 teaspoon seasoned salt
⅛ teaspoon black pepper
1 cup crushed cheese crackers
2 tablespoon butter, melted

1. Preheat oven to 350º.
2. Cook rice according to package directions. While rice is cooking, place beef in large skillet and cook on medium heat, stirring occasionally until beef is no longer pink in color. Drain.
3. Stir in rice, broccoli, soup, milk, seasoned salt, and pepper. Spoon into 2½-quart glass baking dish.
4. Cover and bake for 25 minutes.
5. Combine cheese crackers and melted butter in bowl; sprinkle over casserole.
6. Bake uncovered until cheese crackers are light brown, about 15 minutes.

{SERVES 6}

Who Knew?

After finishing a stick of unsalted butter, hold on to the wrapper. It'll come in handy when you need to grease a pan: Simply wipe the pan with it. But don't use wrappers from salted butter, since they may cause foods to stick.

302 Pinto Bean Pie

Even though it's called "Pinto Bean Pie," you can really use black, kidney, or whatever kind of beans you find on sale.

½ tablespoon olive oil

1 pound lean ground beef

1 medium onion, chopped

2 (15 ounce) cans pinto beans with liquid, divided

1 (10 ounce) can tomatoes and green chilies with liquid, divided

1 (3 ounce) can French-fried onion rings

1. Preheat oven to 350°.
2. Heat oil over medium heat in skillet. When hot, add beef and onion. Cook, stirring, until beef is brown and onion is tender, about 10 minutes. Drain.
3. Spread 1 can beans into 2-quart baking dish. Layer half of beef-onion mixture on top, then half of tomatoes and green chilies. Repeat layers with remaining beans, remaining beef-onion mixture, and remaining tomatoes and green chilies.
4. Top with onion rings and bake for 30 minutes.

{SERVES 6}

303 Hamburger Heaven

1 (8 ounce) package medium egg noodles

1 pounds lean ground beef

1 (8 ounce) package fresh mushrooms, halved

2 ribs celery, sliced

1 teaspoon minced garlic

2 (1 ounce) packets beef gravy mix

2½ cups water

1 (8 ounce) carton sour cream

1 (3 ounce) package fried onion rings

1. Preheat oven to 375°.
2. Cook noodles according to package directions; drain. Cover to keep warm.
3. Cook beef, mushrooms, celery, and garlic in sprayed skillet over medium heat, stirring often, until beef is cooked through, about 6 minutes. Drain and remove from skillet.
4. In same skillet, combine gravy mix and water; cook over medium heat, stirring constantly, until thickened, about 5 minutes. Remove from heat and stir in sour cream.
5. Add cooked noodles and beef mixture to gravy and mix well. Spoon mixture into sprayed, 3-quart baking dish.
6. Cover and bake for 25 minutes. Remove from oven and sprinkle onion rings over casserole. Return to oven and bake uncovered for additional 15 minutes.

{SERVES 6}

Who Knew? Light Switch

To make this recipe lower in fat, substitute 1 cup of our Low-Fat Sour Cream Substitute for the carton of sour cream.

304 Cabbage Casserole

1½ pounds lean ground beef
½ cup chopped onion
½ cup chopped green bell pepper
1 can (15 ounces) diced tomatoes
1 teaspoon garlic powder
2 teaspoon salt
½ teaspoon black pepper
1 cabbage
1 cup four-cheese blend

1. Preheat oven to 350º.
2. Cook ground beef, onion, and pepper in skillet over medium heat until vegetables are tender and meat is no longer pink, about 8–12 minutes. Drain.
3. Stir in tomatoes, garlic powder, salt, and pepper.

   Reduce heat to low and simmer, uncovered, for 10 minutes, stirring ocassionaly.
4. Cut cabbage into 6 wedges. Cook in boiling water, covered, until cooked through, about 10 minutes. Drain.

   Line bottom and sides of sprayed, 9-inch square baking dish with cabbage leaves. Top with ground beef mixture.
5. Bake, uncovered, 25 minutes. Top with cheese and bake for additional 5 minutes.

{SERVES 6}

Who Knew? Light Switch

To make this recipe lower in fat, use our Low-Fat Four-Cheese Blend.

305 Meatballs and Orzo Casserole

10 (10 ounce) package frozen onions and bell peppers
2 ribs celery, sliced
2 tablespoons Italian salad dressing
1 (14 ounce) can beef broth
1 cup orzo (tiny pasta)
18 cooked, frozen Italian meatballs, thawed
2 tomatoes, chopped, drained
1 1 teaspoon dried parsley
⅓ cup grated Parmesan cheese

1. Stir-fry onions and bell peppers, celery, and dressing in large sprayed skillet over medium-high heat for 2 minutes.
2. Add broth and bring to a boil. Stir in orzo and meatballs and bring to a boil. Cover and cook for 10 minutes, stirring occasionally.
3. Stir in tomatoes and parsley. Cover and cook until most of liquid absorbs and orzo is tender, about 5 minutes.
4. Spoon into serving bowl and top with

   Parmesan cheese.

{SERVES 6}

306 Pizza Topping Pie

If your family loves meaty pizza, they'll love this versatile pasta casserole that features both pepperoni and sausage.

2 cups tomato-spinach macaroni (spiral pasta)
1 pound bulk Italian sausage
1 onion, chopped
1 green bell pepper, seeded, chopped
1 (15 ounce) can pizza sauce
1 (8 ounce) can tomato sauce
⅓ cup milk
1 (3 ounce) package sliced pepperoni, halved
1 (4 ounce) jar sliced mushrooms, drained
1 (2 ounce) can sliced ripe olives, drained
1 (8 ounce) package shredded mozzarella cheese, divided

1. Preheat oven to 350°.
2. Cook macaroni in saucepan according to package directions; drain.
3. Cook sausage, onion, and bell pepper in skillet over medium heat until sausage is no longer pink, about 10–12 minutes. Drain
4. Combine pizza sauce, tomato sauce, and milk in large bowl. Stir in sausage mixture, macaroni, pepperoni, mushrooms, olives, and half cheese. Mix well.
5. Spoon into sprayed, 9 x 13-inch baking dish.
   Cover and bake for 30 minutes.
6. Remove from oven and sprinkle remaining cheese over top of casserole. Return to oven and bake until cheese is melted, about 5–10 minutes.

{SERVES 8}

307 Penne Pizzazz

1 (8 ounce) package penne pasta
1 pound bulk Italian sausage
1 teaspoon minced garlic
1 (4 ounce) can sliced mushrooms, drained
1 (10 ounce) can chopped tomatoes and green chilies
1 (28 ounce) jar spaghetti sauce
¼ teaspoon hot sauce (optional)
1 (8 ounce) package shredded mozzarella cheese, divided

1. Preheat oven to 350°.
2. Cook pasta according to package directions and drain.
3. Place sausage and garlic in skillet over medium-high heat and cook, stirring occasionally, until sausage is no longer pink; drain.
4. Combine pasta, sausage, mushrooms, tomatoes and green chilies, spaghetti sauce, hot sauce (if desired), and ½ cup cheese in large bowl; toss to mix well. Spoon into sprayed, 9 x 13-inch glass baking dish.
5. Cover and bake for 35 minutes. Uncover and sprinkle remaining cheese over casserole; return to oven for 5 minutes.

{SERVES 6-8}

Who Knew? Light Switch

To make this recipe lower in fat, substitute 2¾ cups of our Homemade Spaghetti Sauce for the jar of spaghetti sauce.

308 Hot Cheese Squares

This is a great way to use refrigerated crescent rolls when you have one of those buy-one-get-one-free coupons.

1 (8 ounce) can refrigerated crescent rolls

1 (16 ounce) package refrigerated cocktail sausage links, halved

1 (10 ounce) package frozen

1 chopped bell peppers and onions, thawed

1 (4 ounce) can pimentos, drained

1 (8 ounce) package shredded mozzarella cheese, divided

1 (10 ounce) can cream of celery soup

2 tablespoons cream

4 large eggs, slightly beaten

1. Preheat oven to 350°.
2. Unroll crescent rolls and place dough in sprayed, 7 x 11-inch glass baking dish. Press seams closed and push dough 1 inch up sides of pan.
3. Arrange sausage links evenly over dough and sprinkle with bell pepper–onion mixture, pimentos, and half cheese.
4. Combine soup, cream, and eggs in bowl. Beat with wire whisk and spoon over bell pepper–cheese mixture.

   Sprinkle with remaining cheese.
5. Bake uncovered until knife inserted in center comes out clean, about 35 minutes. Let stand for 5 minutes before cutting into squares to serve.

{SERVES 8}

Who Knew? Light Switch

To make this recipe lower in fat, substitute 1¼ cup of our Low-Fat Cream of Celery Soup Base for the cans of cream of celery soup, and 2% milk for the cream.

309 Bacon-Potato Casserole

2 pounds new (red) potatoes with peels

2 teaspoons salt, divided

1 pound sliced bacon, cooked, drained, crumbled, divided

1 (8 ounce) package shredded Monterey Jack cheese, divided

1 (12 ounce) package Velveeta cheese, cubed

1 teaspoon black pepper

2 onions, chopped

1 (4 ounce) jar chopped pimentos, drained

1 cup mayonnaise

1 (8 ounce) carton sour cream

1 teaspoon basil

1. Preheat oven to 325°.
2. Cut potatoes in half and cook in boiling water with
3. Combine potatoes, half crumbled bacon, half Jack cheese, and all other ingredients in large bowl; mix well.
4. Spoon into sprayed, 2 smaller dishes. (You may freeze one.)
5. Bake until edges bubble, about 40 minutes.
6. Remove from oven and sprinkle remaining Jack cheese over top of casserole. Return to oven and bake just until cheese melts, about 5 minutes.
7. Before serving, sprinkle remaining crumbled bacon over top of casserole. 10 x 15-inch baking dish or 1 teaspoon salt in saucepan until tender, about 20-25 minutes

{SERVES 8-10}

310 Spinach Casserole

This vegetarian creation is a casserole Popeye would be proud of!

2 (10 ounce) packages chopped spinach

½ cup (1 stick) plus 2 tablespoons butter, divided

1 (8 ounce) package cream cheese

1 (8 ounce) can sliced water chestnuts, drained

1 (4 ounce) can sliced pimentos

1 (14 ounce) can water-packed

1 artichoke hearts, drained, quartered

¾ cup seasoned breadcrumbs

1. Preheat oven to 375°.
2. Cook spinach according to package directions. Drain and place in large bowl.
3. Combine ½ cup butter and cream cheese in saucepan; cook on medium heat, stirring constantly, until butter and cheese melt and blend together.
4. Stir mixture into spinach and add water chestnuts and pimentos.
5. Line sprayed, 7 x 11-inch glass baking dish with artichoke hearts and cover with spinach mixture.
6. Melt 2 tablespoons butter and combine with breadcrumbs in bowl. Sprinkle over casserole.
7. Bake uncovered for 25 minutes.

{SERVES 6-8}

311 Serious Squash Casserole

This casserole is vegetarian, but it's also filling. Eating vegetarian one night a week is a great way to save money and calories!

1 cup biscuit mix

¾ cup shredded mozzarella cheese

1 tablespoon dried dill weed

¼ teaspoon salt

⅛ 1/8 teaspoon black pepper

4 4 large eggs, beaten

½ ½ cup (1 stick) butter, melted

2 cups finely chopped zucchini, drained

2 cups finely chopped yellow squash

1 (10 ounce) package frozen chopped bell peppers and onions, thawed

1. Preheat oven to 350°.
2. Combine biscuit mix, cheese, dill weed, salt, and pepper in large bowl. Add eggs and melted butter; mix well.
3. Stir in zucchini, yellow squash, and bell pepper–onion mixture.
4. Pour into sprayed, 7 x 11-inch glass baking dish.
5. Bake uncovered until golden brown, about 30–35 minutes.

{SERVES 6-8}

312 Awesome Butternut Casserole

2 large butternut squash
½ cup (1 stick) butter, melted
¾ cup sugar
3 tablespoons brown sugar
3 eggs, beaten
1 (5 ounce) can evaporated milk
1 teaspoon vanilla
½ teaspoon ground cinnamon
1 cup crushed corn flakes
½ cup packed light brown sugar
½ cup chopped pecans

1. Preheat oven to 350°.
2. Cut the butternut squash in half and scoop out seeds and membranes.
3. Place cut-side down on plate and microwave on HIGH for 1–2 minutes.
4. Let stand in microwave for several minutes. If squash is not tender, microwave for additional 1 minute intervals until soft, letting sit for 1–2 minutes between microwaving.
5. Scoop out squash and place in bowl. Beat until fairly smooth.
6. Add butter, sugar, brown sugar, eggs, evaporated milk, vanilla, and cinnamon;mix well. (Mixture will be thin.)
7. Pour into sprayed, 3-quart baking dish.
8. Bake until almost set, about 45 minutes.
9. Combine corn flakes, light brown sugar, and pecans in bowl. Sprinkle over hot casserole and return to oven until top is crunchy, about 10–15 minutes.

{SERVES 6-8}

Who Knew? Light Switch

To make this recipe lower in fat, substitute 1¼ cup of our Low-Fat Cream of Celery Soup Base for the cans of cream of celery soup, and 2% milk for the cream.

313 Early-Morning Vegetable Lasagna

1 (14 ounce) can Italian stewed tomatoes
1½ cups pasta sauce
2 cups cottage cheese, drained
1 cup grated Parmesan cheese
¼ teaspoon salt
¼ teaspoon black pepper
9 lasagna noodles, divided
4 zucchini, shredded, divided
7 (1 ounce) slices provolone cheese, cut into strips, divided

1. Combine stewed tomatoes and pasta sauce in bowl and set aside.
2. In separate bowl, combine cottage cheese, Parmesan cheese, salt, and pepper.
3. In sprayed, 9 x 13-inch baking dish, layer one-third tomato mixture, 3 lasagna noodles, one-third zucchini, one-third cheese mixture, and one-third provolone cheese strips. Repeat layers twice more.
4. Cover and refrigerate for at least 8 hours.
5. When ready to bake, remove from refrigerator and let stand for 30 minutes. Preheat oven to 350º.
6. Cover and bake for 45 minutes.
7. Uncover and bake for additional 20 minutes. Let stand for 15 minutes before serving.

{SERVES 8-10}

314 Vegetarian Pasta Bake

- **1 (12 ounce) package rotini (spirals) pasta**
- **½ cup bottled balsamic vinaigrette salad dressing**
- **1 (15 ounce) can cannellini beans, rinsed and drained**
- **2 (15 ounce) cans diced tomatoes with garlic, drained**
- **1 (8 ounce) package feta cheese, crumbled**
- **1 cup coarsely chopped pitted Greek black olives**
- **⅓ cup bread crumbs with Italian seasonings**
- **1 (8 ounce) carton plain, low-fat yogurt**
- **¾ cup milk**
- **⅓ cup grated Parmesan cheese**
- **1 tablespoon all-purpose flour**

1. Preheat oven to 375°.
2. Cook pasta according to package directions. Drain. In sprayed, 3-quart baking dish, combine pasta, vinaigrette dressing, beans, tomatoes, feta cheese, and olives.
3. In bowl, combine milk, yogurt, Parmesan cheese, and flour and mix well. Pour evenly over pasta mixture. Sprinkle with bread crumbs. (If you don't have breadcrumbs with Italian seasonings, just use regular breadcrumbs and add a few pinches of garlic powder, black pepper, and dried oregano, basil, and/or thyme.)
4. Bake, covered, for 25 minutes. Uncover and bake 10–15 minutes more until heated through and top is lightly browned. Let stand 5 minutes before serving.

{SERVES 4-5}

315 Green Bean Casserole

- **¼ cup (½ stick) butter, divided**
- **½ cup chopped onion**
- **½ cup chopped celery**
- **1 tablespoon flour**
- **1 teaspoon sugar**
- **½ teaspoon salt**
- **½ teaspoon black pepper**
- **1 cup cream**
- **3 (15 ounce) cans French-style green beans, drained**
- **¾ cup crushed corn flakes**
- **1 cup shredded Swiss cheese**

1. Preheat oven to 325°.
2. Melt half butter in skillet over medium-high heat and sauté onion and celery until tender, about 6–8 minutes.

   Stir in flour, sugar, salt, and pepper. Cook, stirring constantly, for 1 minute over medium heat.
3. Reduce heat to low, slowly add cream, and stir until smooth. Cook, stirring constantly, until mixture thickens, about 2 minutes; do not boil.
4. Fold in green beans. Spread into sprayed, 9 x 13-inch baking dish.
5. Melt remaining butter in saucepan and toss with corn flake crumbs. Mix in cheese, then sprinkle over top of casserole.
6. Bake until hot, about 25 minutes.

{SERVES 8-10}

316 Zucchini Bake

- 3 cups grated zucchini
- 1½ cups shredded Cheddar cheese
- 4 eggs, beaten
- ¼ teaspoon garlic powder
- ½ teaspoon salt
- ½ teaspoon black pepper
- 2 cups cheese cracker crumbs

1. Preheat oven to 350°.
2. Combine zucchini, cheese, eggs, garlic powder, salt, and pepper and mix well. Spoon into sprayed, 2-quart baking dish.
3. Sprinkle cracker crumbs over top.
4. Bake for 35–40 minutes.

{SERVES 4-6}

Who Knew? Light Switch

To make this recipe lower in fat, use our Low-Fat Four-Cheese Blend instead of the Cheddar cheese.

317 Vegetable Frittata

This makes an elegant dish that works just as well for brunch as it does dinner.

- ¼ cup light olive oil
- 1 onion, chopped
- ¾ cup chopped green bell pepper
- ¾ cup chopped red bell pepper
- 2 cups chopped zucchini
- 2 cups chopped yellow squash
- ¼ cup cream
- 1 (8 ounce) package cream cheese, softened
- 6 eggs
- 1 cup shredded mozzarella cheese
- ¾ teaspoon garlic powder
- 2 teaspoons marinade for chicken
- ½ teaspoon salt
- ½ teaspoon black pepper
- 1 cup seasoned breadcrumbs
- 3 tablespoons butter, melted

1. Preheat oven to 350°.
2. Heat oil in large skillet. Sauté onion, bell peppers, zucchini, and squash just until tender-crisp. Remove from heat and set aside to cool.
3. Beat cream and cream cheese in bowl until creamy.
   Add eggs and beat until mixed well, about 4 minutes.
4. Add mozzarella cheese, garlic powder, marinade for chicken, salt, and pepper; mix with spoon.
5. Fold in breadcrumbs, butter, and vegetables. Pour into sprayed, 9-inch springform pan.
6. Bake until light brown and set in center, about 55–60 minutes.
7. Set aside for 10 minutes before slicing. Be sure to use a thin, sharp knife to cut around the edge of the springform pan before you open the pan.

{SERVES 6-8}

CHAPTER 8

Slow Cooker Favorites

318 Oregano Chicken

½ cup (1 stick) butter, melted
1 (1 ounce) packet Italian salad dressing
1 tablespoon lemon juice
4-5 boneless, skinless chicken breast halves
2 tablespoons dried oregano

1. Combine butter, salad dressing, and lemon juice in bowl and mix well.
2. Place chicken breasts in sprayed, large slow cooker.
   Spoon butter mixture over chicken.
3. Cover and cook on low heat for 5–6 hours.
4. One hour before serving, baste chicken with pan juices and sprinkle oregano over top.

{**SERVES 4-6**}

Who Knew? Light Switch

Try our Italian Salad Dressing Mix for this recipe!

319 Sweet-and-Spicy Chicken

2 pounds chicken thighs
¾ cup chili sauce
¾ cup packed brown sugar
1 (1 ounce) packet onion soup mix
⅛ teaspoon cayenne pepper
¼ cup water

1. Arrange chicken pieces in bottom of sprayed, 5-quart slow cooker.
2. Combine chili sauce, brown sugar, onion soup mix, cayenne pepper, and water in bowl and spoon over chicken.
3. Cover and cook on low heat for 6–7 hours. Serve over rice.

{**SERVES 6**}

Who Knew?

Here's an important safety tip when using slow cookers: Make sure that the slow cooker is at least half to two-thirds full or the food may not absorb enough heat to kill all of the bacteria from the meat.

320 Easy Chunky Chili

This recipe works great with beef, pork, and even chicken, so buy whatever is on sale!

4 pounds cubed stew meat

2 tablespoons olive oil

2 (10 ounce) cans beef broth

2 medium onions, chopped

4 (15 ounce) cans diced tomatoes

2 (10 ounce) cans tomatoes with green chilies

2 (15 ounce) cans pinto beans with liquid

2 (15 ounce) cans kidney beans with liquid

2 tablespoons chili powder

1 tablespoon ground cumin

2 teaspoons oregano

1. If stew meat is in large chunks, cut each chunk in half.
2. Add oil to large skillet. When hot, add meat and cook, stirring, over medium-high heat until meat is browned on all sides, about 8–10 minutes.
3. Add all remaining ingredients. Bring to a boil, then reduce heat and cook on low heat for 1 hour.

{SERVES 12}

321 Chicken Delicious

Dig that old bottle of sherry out of your cabinet for this dish that's so delicious we had to include the word in its name!

5-6 boneless, skinless chicken breast halves

1 tablespoon olive oil

1 (16 ounce) package frozen broccoli florets, thawed

1 red bell pepper, seeded, julienned

1 (16 ounce) jar alfredo sauce

3 tablespoons sherry

1. Place chicken breast halves in skillet with oil and cook over medium-high heat until brown on both sides, about 3 minutes per side. Then place in sprayed, 5- or 6-quart oval slow cooker.
2. Place broccoli florets on plate, remove much of stems, and discard.
3. Combine broccoli florets, bell pepper, cheese sauce, and sherry in bowl and mix well. Spoon over chicken breasts.
4. Cover and cook on low heat for 4–5 hours. Serve over noodles.

{SERVES 4-6}

Who Knew? Light Switch

To make this recipe lower in fat, substitute 1¾ cups of our Low-Fat Alfredo Sauce for the jar of Alfredo sauce.

322 Slow Cooker Cordon Bleu

4 boneless, skinless chicken breast halves

4 slices cooked ham

4 slices Swiss cheese, softened

1 (10 ounce) can cream of chicken soup

¼ cup milk

4 cups noodles, cooked

1. Place chicken breasts on cutting board and pound until breast halves are thin.
2. Place ham and cheese slices on chicken breasts; roll and secure with toothpicks.
3. Arrange chicken rolls in sprayed, 4-quart slow cooker.
4. Pour chicken soup and milk into saucepan, heat just enough to mix well, and pour over chicken rolls.
5. Cover and cook on low heat for 4–5 hours.
6. Serve over noodles and cover with sauce from soup.

{SERVES 4}

Who Knew? Light Switch

To make this recipe lower in fat, substitute 1¼ cup of our Low-Fat Cream of Chicken Soup Base for the can of cream of chicken soup.

323 Chicken 'n' Stuffing Supper

1 tablespoon olive oil
3 boneless, skinless chicken breast halves, chopped
1 (6 ounce) package stuffing mix
3 cups chopped chicken breasts
1 (16 ounce) package frozen whole green beans, thawed
2 (12 ounce) jars chicken gravy

1. Heat oil in skillet over medium-high heat. When hot, add chicken pieces and cook, stirring, until brown on all sides, about 8–10 minutes.
2. Prepare stuffing mix according to package directions and place in sprayed, oval slow cooker.
3. Follow with layer of chopped chicken, then layer of green beans. Pour chicken gravy over green beans.
4. Cover and cook on low heat for 3 hours 30 minutes–4 hours.

{SERVES 4-6}

Who Knew?

Take a bit of that olive oil and rub it into your cuticles! Olive oil will help them stay moisturized at a fraction of the cost of cuticle creams.

324 Chicken Marseilles

4-5 boneless, skinless chicken breast halves
2 tablespoons butter
1 (2 ounce) packet leek soup and dip mix
½ teaspoon dill weed
1 cup milk
½ cup water
4 cups brown rice, cooked
¾ cup sour cream

1. Place chicken breasts in sprayed, large slow cooker.
2. Combine butter, leek soup mix, dill weed, milk, and water in saucepan and heat just enough for butter to melt and ingredients to mix well. Pour over chicken.
3. Cover and cook on low heat for 3–5 hours.
4. When ready to serve, remove chicken breasts to platter with hot, cooked brown rice. Cover to keep warm.
5. Add sour cream to cooker liquid and stir well. Pour sauce over chicken and rice.

{SERVES 4-5}

Who Knew? Light Switch

To make this recipe lower in fat, use our Low-Fat Sour Cream Substitute.

325 Chicken Breast Deluxe

- **4 slices bacon**
- **5-6 boneless, skinless chicken breast halves**
- **1 cup sliced celery**
- **1 cup sliced red bell pepper**
- **1 (10 ounce) can cream of chicken soup**
- **2 tablespoons white wine or cooking wine**
- **6 slices Swiss cheese**
- **2 tablespoons dried parsley**

1. Cook bacon in large skillet; drain, crumble, and reserve drippings.
2. Place chicken in skillet with bacon drippings and lightly brown on both sides, about 3 minutes per side.
3. Transfer chicken to sprayed oval slow cooker and place celery and bell pepper over chicken.
4. In same skillet, combine soup and wine; stir. Spoon over vegetables and chicken.
5. Cover and cook on low heat for 3–4 hours.
6. Place 1 slice of cheese over each chicken breast and sprinkle parsley on top. Cook for additional 10 minutes.
7. Sprinkle with crumbled bacon.

{SERVES 4-6}

Who Knew? Light Switch

To make this recipe lower in fat, substitute 1¼ cup of our Low-Fat Cream of Chicken Soup Base for the can of cream of chicken soup.

326 Southwestern Chicken Pot

- **6 boneless, skinless chicken breast halves**
- **1 teaspoon ground cumin**
- **1 1 teaspoon chili powder**
- **¼ teaspoon salt**
- **⅛ teaspoon black pepper**
- **1 (10 ounce) can cream of chicken soup**
- **1 (10 ounce) can fiesta nacho cheese soup**
- **1 cup salsa**

1. Sprinkle chicken breasts with cumin, chili powder, salt, and pepper and place in sprayed, oval slow cooker.
2. Combine soups and salsa in saucepan and heat just enough to mix; pour over chicken breasts.
3. Cover and cook on low heat for 6–7 hours. Serve over rice or with warmed flour tortillas.

{SERVES 4-6}

327 Honey-Baked Chicken

2 small fryer chickens, quartered
¼ teaspoon salt
½ cup (1 stick) butter, melted
¾ cup honey
¼ cup Dijon-style mustard
1 teaspoon curry powder

1. Place chicken pieces in sprayed, large slow cooker, skin-side up, and sprinkle salt over chicken.
2. Combine butter, honey, mustard, and curry powder in bowl and mix well.
3. Pour butter-honey mixture over chicken quarters.
4. Cover and cook on low heat for 6–8 hours. Baste chicken once during cooking.

{SERVES 6-8}

Who Knew?

While you have the salt out, throw a handful down your garbage disposal, turn on a small stream of hot water, and run it for 10 seconds. The salt will get rid of any buildup in your drain and help your disposal run more smoothly.

328 White Wine Chicken

4-5 carrots
6 medium new (red) potatoes with peels, cleaned, quartered
4-5 boneless, skinless chicken breast halves
1 tablespoon poultry seasoning
2 (10 ounce) cans cream of chicken soup
⅓ cup white wine
¼ cup water

1. Cut carrots into ½-inch pieces. Place potatoes and carrots in sprayed slow cooker.
2. Sprinkle chicken breasts with poultry seasoning and place chicken over vegetables.
3. Heat soup, wine, and water in saucepan just to mix, and pour over chicken and vegetables.
4. Cover and cook on low heat for 5–6 hours.

{SERVES 4-5}

Who Knew? Light Switch

To make this recipe lower in fat, substitute 2½ cups of our Low-Fat Cream of Chicken Soup Base for the cans of cream of chicken soup.

329 Lemon Chicken

1 (2½–3 pound) chicken, quartered
1 teaspoon salt
½ teaspoon black pepper
1 teaspoon dried oregano
2 2 teaspoons minced garlic
2 2 tablespoons butter
⅓ 1/3 cup water
¼ cup lemon juice

1. Sprinkle chicken quarters with salt, pepper, and oregano. Rub garlic on chicken.
2. Place butter in skillet and melt over medium-high heat. Add chicken quarters and cook until browned, about 3 minutes per side. Transfer to sprayed, oval slow cooker.
3. Add water to skillet, scrape bottom, and pour over chicken.
4. Cover and cook on low heat for 6–7 hours.
5. Pour lemon juice over chicken, then cook for additional 1 hour.

{SERVES 4-6}

330 Alfredo's Chicken

5 (2½–3 pound) chicken, quartered
1 teaspoon salt
½ teaspoon black pepper
1 teaspoon dried oregano
2 2 teaspoons minced garlic
2 2 tablespoons butter
⅓ 1/3 cup water
¼ cup lemon juice

1. Sprinkle chicken quarters with salt, pepper, and oregano. Rub garlic on chicken.
2. Place butter in skillet and melt over medium-high heat. Add chicken quarters and cook until browned, about 3 minutes per side. Transfer to sprayed, oval slow cooker.
3. Add water to skillet, scrape bottom, and pour over chicken.
4. Cover and cook on low heat for 6–7 hours.
5. Pour lemon juice over chicken, then cook for additional 1 hour.

{SERVES 4-5}

Who Knew? Light Switch

To make this recipe lower in fat, substitute 2½ cups of our Low-Fat Cream of Chicken Soup Base for the cans of cream of chicken soup.

331 Imperial Chicken

2 (6 ounce) box long-grain and wild rice mix
2½ cups water
2 teaspoons minced garlic
1 (16 ounce) jar Alfredo sauce
6 boneless, skinless chicken breast halves
1 (16 ounce) box frozen French-style green beans, thawed
½ cup slivered almonds, toasted

1. Combine rice, seasoning packet, water, and garlic in sprayed, oval slow cooker and stir well.
2. Spoon in Alfredo sauce and mix well.
3. Place chicken breasts in slow cooker and cover with green beans.
4. Cover and cook on low heat for 3–5 hours. When ready to serve, sprinkle with slivered almonds.

{SERVES 4-6}

Who Knew? Light Switch

To make this recipe lower in fat, substitute 1¾ cups of our Low-Fat Alfredo Sauce for the jar of Alfredo sauce.

332 Chicken Fajitas

2 pounds boneless, skinless chicken breast halves
1 onion, thinly sliced
1 red bell pepper, cored, seeded, julienned
1 teaspoon ground cumin
1½ teaspoons chili powder
1 tablespoon lime juice
½ cup chicken broth
8-10 flour tortillas
Lettuce and tomatoes, chopped, for garnish

1. Cut chicken into diagonal strips and place in sprayed slow cooker. Top with onion and bell pepper.
2. Combine cumin, chili powder, lime juice, and chicken broth in bowl and pour over chicken and vegetables.
3. Cover and cook on low heat for 5–7 hours.
4. Warm tortillas by placing in microwave one at a time for 10 seconds.
5. Place several slices of chicken mixture with sauce in center of each warm tortilla; fold.
6. Garnish with lettuce and tomatoes and serve with guacamole or sour cream, if desired.

{SERVES 4-6}

333 Arroz Con Pollo

- 3 pounds chicken thighs
- 2 (15 ounce) cans Italian stewed tomatoes
- 1 (16 ounce) package frozen green peas, thawed
- 2 cups long-grain rice (uncooked)
- 1 teaspoon poultry seasoning
- 2 (14 ounce) cans chicken broth
- 1 heaping teaspoon minced garlic
- 1 teaspoon dried oregano
- ¾ cup water

1. Combine all ingredients in sprayed large slow cooker and stir well.
2. Cover and cook on low heat for 7–8 hours or on high heat for 3 hours 30 minutes–4 hours.

{**SERVES 6-8**}

Who Knew?

Don't have any poultry seasoning on hand? Use some sage and a blend of any of these spices: thyme, marjoram, savory, black pepper, and rosemary.

334 Chicken Coq au Vin

- 1 large fryer chicken, quartered, skinned
- 1 tablespoon vegetable or canola oil
- 10-12 small white onions, peeled
- ½ pound whole mushrooms
- 1 teaspoon minced garlic
- ½ teaspoon dried thyme leaves
- 10-12 small new (red) potatoes with peels
- 1 (10 ounce) can chicken broth
- ¼ teaspoon salt
- ⅛ teaspoon black pepper
- 1 cup Burgundy wine
- 6 bacon slices, cooked, crumbled

1. Place quarters in skillet with oil and cook over medium-high heat until brown on all sides, about 3 minutes per side.
2. Place white onions, whole mushrooms, garlic, and thyme in sprayed, oval slow cooker.
3. Add chicken quarters, potatoes, chicken broth, salt, and pepper.
4. Cover and cook on low heat for 8–10 hours or on high heat for 3–4 hours.
5. During last hour, turn heat to high, add wine, and continue cooking.
6. Sprinkle crumbled bacon over chicken before serving.

{**SERVES 4-6**}

335 Maple-Plum Glazed Turkey Breast

- 1 cup red plum jam
- 1 cup maple syrup
- 1 teaspoon dry mustard
- ¼ cup lemon juice
- 1 (3–5 pound) boneless turkey breast

1. Combine jam, syrup, mustard, and lemon juice in saucepan. Bring to a boil, reduce heat, and simmer until slightly thick, about 20 minutes. Reserve 1 cup.
2. Place turkey breast in sprayed slow cooker and pour remaining glaze over turkey.
3. Cover and cook on low heat for 5–7 hours.
4. When ready to serve, slice turkey and serve with heated reserved glaze. remaining glaze over turkey.

3. Cover and cook on low heat for 5–7 hours.
4. When ready to serve, slice turkey and serve with heated reserved glaze.

{SERVES 6-8}

336 Turkey Bake

- 1½ pounds turkey tenderloins
- 1 tablespoon olive oil
- 1 (6 ounce) package Asian rice and vermicelli
- 1 (10 ounce) package frozen green peas, thawed
- 1 cup sliced celery
- ¼ cup (½ stick) butter, melted
- 1 1 (14 ounce) can chicken broth
- 1 1 cup water
- 1½ cups fresh broccoli florets

1. Cut tenderloins into strips. Cook in skillet with oil over medium heat, stirring occasionally, until turkey is cooked through.
2. Combine turkey strips, rice-vermicelli mix plus seasoning packet, peas, celery, butter, chicken broth, and water in sprayed, large slow cooker; mix well.
3. Cover and cook on low heat for 4–5 hours. Turn heat to high, add broccoli, and cook for additional 20 minutes.

{SERVES 4-8}

337 Turkey Cassoulet

This version of the French classic is great for leftover turkey.

½ pound smoked turkey sausage
2 cups cooked, cubed turkey
3 carrots, sliced
1 onion, halved, sliced
1 (15 ounce) can navy beans
1 (15 ounce) can white lima beans
1 (8 ounce) can tomato sauce
1 teaspoon dried thyme
¼ teaspoon ground allspice

1. Cut turkey sausage into ½-inch pieces.
2. Combine all ingredients in sprayed slow cooker.
3. Cover and cook on low heat for 4–5 hours.

{SERVES 6}

338 Sausage and Rice

1 pound turkey sausage
1 (6 ounce) box flavored rice mix
1 cup water
2 (14 ounce) cans chicken broth
2 cups sliced celery
1 red bell pepper, cored, seeded, julienned
1 (15 ounce) can cut green beans, drained
⅓ 1/3 cup slivered almonds, toasted

1. Break up turkey sausage and brown in skillet.
2. Place turkey in sprayed, 4- or 5-quart slow cooker.
3. Add rice, water, chicken broth, celery, bell pepper, and green beans and stir to mix.
4. Cover and cook on low heat for 3–4 hours.
5. When ready to serve, sprinkle almonds over top.

{SERVES 4}

Who Knew?

To easily remove the skin of almonds, soak them in hot water for 15–20 minutes.

339 Turkey Loaf

2 pounds ground turkey
1 1 onion, very finely chopped
½ red bell pepper, very finely chopped
2 teaspoons minced garlic
½ cup chili sauce
2 large eggs, beaten
⅓ cup Italian seasoned breadcrumbs
1 teaspoon salt
½ teaspoon black pepper

1. Make foil handles by cutting 3 strips of heavy foil; place in bottom of slow cooker in crisscross strips (resembling spokes on a wheel) up and over sides.
2. Combine all ingredients in large bowl and mix well.
3. Shape into round loaf and place on top of foil. Fold extended strips over turkey loaf.
4. Cover and cook on low heat for 5–6 hours. Lift loaf out by handles.

{SERVES 4-6}

Who Knew?

If your plastic storage containers smell like garlic, onions, or another potent food, wash them thoroughly, then stuff crumpled newspaper inside before snapping on the lids. In a few days, the smell will be gone.

340 Mac 'n' Cheese Supper

2 ½ pounds lean ground beef
1 teaspoon salt
2 (7 ounce) packages macaroni-and cheese dinners
1 (15 ounce) can whole kernel corn, drained
1½ cups shredded Monterey Jack cheese

1. Place ground beef in large skillet and sprinkle with salt. Heat, stirring, over medium heat until brown, about 8–10 minutes. Drain.
2. Prepare macaroni and cheese in saucepan according to package directions.
3. Spoon beef, macaroni, and corn into sprayed, 5-quart slow cooker; mix well.
4. Cover and cook on low heat for 4–5 hours.
5. When ready to serve, sprinkle Jack cheese over top and leave in cooker until cheese melts.

{SERVES 4-6}

Who Knew?

To make this recipe lower in fat, use our Low-Fat Four-Cheese Blend instead of the Monterey Jack cheese.

341 Enchilada Soup

1 pound lean ground beef, browned, drained

1 (15 ounce) can Mexican stewed tomatoes

1 (15 ounce) can pinto beans with liquid

1 (15 ounce) can whole kernel corn with liquid

1 onion, chopped

2 (10 ounce) cans enchilada sauce

1 cup water

1 (8 ounce) package shredded four-cheese blend

20 tortilla chips, crushed (optional)

1. Combine beef, tomatoes, beans, corn, onion, enchilada sauce, and water in sprayed, 5- or 6-quart slow cooker and mix well.
2. Cover and cook on low heat for 6–8 hours or on high heat for 3–4 hours.
3. Stir in shredded cheese. If desired, top each serving with a few crushed tortilla chips.

{SERVES 6}

Who Knew? Light Switch

To make this recipe lower in fat, substitute 2 cups of our Low-Fat Four-Cheese Blend instead of the package of four-cheese blend.

342 Mushroom Meat and Potatoes

4 medium potatoes, peeled, sliced

1¼ pounds lean ground beef, browned

1 onion, sliced

1 (10 ounce) can cream of mushroom soup

1 (10 ounce) can vegetable beef soup

¼ teaspoon salt

⅛ teaspoon black pepper

1. Layer potatoes, beef, onion, soups, salt, and pepper in sprayed, large slow cooker.
2. Cover and cook on low heat for 5–6 hours.

{SERVES 4-6}

Who Knew?

Freezing causes russet or Idaho potatoes to fall apart; make sure to use potatoes with red skin or waxy flesh for this dish!

343 Cheeseburger Supper

- **1 (5 ounce) box bacon and Cheddar scalloped potatoes**
- **2¼ cups boiling water**
- **⅓ cup milk**
- **¼ cup (½ stick) butter, melted**
- **1½ pounds lean ground beef**
- **1 onion, coarsely chopped**
- **1 tablespoon vegetable or canola oil**
- **1 (15 ounce) can whole kernel corn with liquid**
- **1 (8 ounce) package shredded Cheddar cheese**

1. Place scalloped potatoes in sprayed slow cooker.
2. Pour boiling water, milk, and butter over potatoes.
3. Brown ground beef and onion with oil in skillet; drain and spoon over potatoes. Top with corn.
4. Cover and cook on low heat for 6–7 hours.
5. When ready to serve, sprinkle cheese over corn.

{SERVES 4-6}

Who Knew? Light Switch

To make this recipe lower in fat, substitute 2 cups of our Low-Fat Four-Cheese Blend for the package of Cheddar cheese.

344 Debra's Favorite Meat Loaf

- **2 pounds lean ground beef**
- **2 eggs**
- **½ cup chili sauce**
- **1¼ cups seasoned breadcrumbs**
- **1 (8 ounce) package shredded Monterey Jack cheese, divided**

1. Make foil handles by cutting 3 strips of heavy foil; place in bottom of slow cooker in crisscross strips (resembling spokes on a wheel) up and over sides.
2. Combine beef, eggs, chili sauce, and breadcrumbs in bowl and mix well.
3. Shape half beef mixture into flat loaf and place in sprayed slow cooker.
4. Sprinkle half cheese over meat loaf and press into meat.
5. Form remaining meat mixture into same shape. Place over cheese as top layer and seal seams.
6. Cover and cook on low heat for 6–7 hours.
7. When ready to serve, sprinkle remaining cheese over loaf and leave in cooker until cheese melts.
8. Carefully remove loaf with handles and place on serving plate.

{SERVES 4-6}

345 Southwest Spaghetti

- **1½ pounds lean ground beef**
- **2½ teaspoons chili powder**
- **1 (15 ounce) can tomato sauce**
- **1 (7 ounce) package spaghetti**
- **2⅓ 21/3 cups water**
- **1 heaping tablespoon beef seasoning**
- **1 (8 ounce) package shredded Cheddar-Jack cheese**

1. Cook ground beef in skillet over medium heat, stirring occasionally to break up, until no longer pink. Place in sprayed, 4- or 5-quart slow cooker.
2. Add chili powder, tomato sauce, spaghetti, water, and beef seasoning and mix well.
3. Cover and cook on low heat for 6–7 hours.
4. When ready to serve, cover with shredded Cheddar-Jack cheese.

{SERVES 4-6}

Who Knew? Light Switch

To make this recipe lower in fat, substitute 2 cups of our Low-Fat Four-Cheese Blend for the package of Cheddar-Jack cheese.

346 Big-Batch Sloppy Joes

- **3 pounds ground beef**
- **1 tablespoon minced garlic**
- **1 large onion, finely chopped**
- **2 ribs celery, chopped**
- **¼ cup packed brown sugar**
- **3½ tablespoons mustard**
- **1 tablespoon chili powder**
- **1½ cups ketchup**
- **3 tablespoons Worcestershire sauce**
- **16-18 hamburger buns**

1. Cook beef, garlic, and onion in large skillet over medium heat, stirring occasionally, until beef is brown and onion is tender, about 12–16 minutes. Drain.
2. Combine celery, brown sugar, mustard, chili powder, ketchup, andWorcestershire sauce in sprayed, 5-quart slow cooker. Stir in meat mixture.
3. Cover and cook on low heat for 6–7 hours.

{SERVES 9-12}

Who Knew?

Mustard isn't only great at providing a tangy kick to dinners, it's also good at removing stains from plastic! Place a dab on and leave overnight, then wipe clean.

347 Sweet-and-Sour Slow-Cooker Meatballs

These delicious meatballs are great served over rice or noodles. To make them for an appetizer, just insert toothpicks into each meatball for easy pickup.

1 (16 ounce) can whole-berry cranberry sauce
1 cup ketchup
⅔ cup packed brown sugar
½ cup beef broth
1 (18 ounce) package frozen meatballs, thawed

1. Combine cranberry sauce, ketchup, brown sugar, and broth in sprayed, large slow cooker.
2. Turn heat to high and boil for 30 minutes–1 hour. Place thawed meatballs in sauce.
3. Cover and cook on low heat for 2 hours.
4. Remove meatballs to serving dish using slotted spoon.

{SERVES 4-6}

Who Knew? Light Switch

To make this recipe lower in fat, substitute our Low-Fat Meatballs for the package of frozen meatballs.

348 Beef Tips Over Pasta

2-2½ pounds lean beef stew meat
2 cups frozen, small whole onions, thawed
1 green bell pepper, seeded
1 (6 ounce) jar pitted Greek olives or ripe olives
½ cup sun-dried tomatoes in oil,
1 drained, chopped
1 (28 ounce) jar spaghetti sauce
1 (8 ounce) package pasta twirls, cooked

1. Place beef and onions in sprayed, 4- or 5-quart slow cooker.
2. Cut bell pepper in 1-inch cubes and add to slow cooker.
3. Add olives and tomatoes and pour marinara sauce over top.
4. Cover and cook on low heat for 8–10 hours.
5. Prepare pasta twirls according to package directions. Serve beef and marinara sauce mixture over pasta.

{SERVES 4-6}

349 Pot Roast with Veggies

1 (2 pound) chuck roast
2 tablespoons olive oil, divided
4-5 medium potatoes, peeled, quartered
4 large carrots, quartered
1 onion, quartered
1 (14 ounce) can beef broth, divided
2 tablespoons cornstarch

1. Trim fat from roast and cut roast into 2 equal pieces.
2. Place each piece in skillet with 1 tablespoon oil and brown on all sides over medium-high heat, about 3–5 minutes per side.
3. Place potatoes, carrots, and onion in sprayed, 4- or 5-quart slow cooker; mix well.
4. Place browned roast halves over vegetables.
5. Pour 1½ cups broth over beef and vegetables. Save remaining broth and refrigerate.
6. Cover and cook on low heat for 8–9 hours.
7. About 5 minutes before serving, remove beef and vegetables with slotted spoon and place on serving platter. Cover to keep warm.
8. Pour liquid from slow cooker into medium saucepan.
9. Blend remaining ½ cup broth and cornstarch in bowl until smooth; add to liquid in saucepan. Boil for 1 minute and stir constantly to make gravy.
10. Serve gravy with roast and veggies; season with salt and pepper to taste, if desired.

{SERVES 4-6}

350 Sweet-and-Sour Beef

1 (2 pound) boneless chuck roast
½ cup flour
1 teaspoon salt
½ teaspoon black pepper
1 tablespoon vegetable or canola oil
1 onion, sliced
½ cup chili sauce
¾ cup packed brown sugar
¼ cup red wine vinegar
1 tablespoonWorcestershire sauce
1 cup water
1 (16 ounce) package baby carrots

1. Cut beef into 1-inch cubes and dredge in flour, salt, and pepper.
2. Heat oil in large skillet over medium-high heat. Add beef and cook, stirring, until brown on all sides, about 10–12 minutes. Place in sprayed slow cooker.
3. Add remaining ingredients, except carrots.
4. Cover and cook on low heat for 7–8 hours.
5. Add carrots and cook for additional 1 hour 30 minutes.

{SERVES 4-6}

351 Savory Steak

Make some mashed potatoes to serve with this saucy steak for a perfect meal.

1 ½ pounds lean round steak
1 teaspoon black pepper
1 onion, halved, sliced
1 (10 ounce) cans golden mushroom soup
1½ cups hot, chunky salsa

1. Trim fat from steak and cut into serving-size pieces.
2. Sprinkle with pepper and place in sprayed, 5- or 6-quart slow cooker.
3. Place onion slices on top of steak.
4. Combine mushroom soup and salsa in bowl and mix well. Spoon over steak and onions.
5. Cover and cook on low heat for 7–8 hours.

{SERVES 4-6}

Who Knew? Light Switch

To save money and make this recipe even more delicious, use our Super Healthy Salsa with a pinch of cayenne pepper added.

352 Mushroom Round Steak

1½-2 pounds round steak
1 (1 ounce) packet onion soup mix
½ cup dry red wine
1 (8 ounce) carton fresh mushrooms, sliced
1 (10 ounce) can French onion soup
½ cup water

1. Cut round steak in serving-size pieces and place in sprayed, oval slow cooker.
2. Combine soup mix, red wine, mushrooms, French onion soup, and water in bowl. Spoon over steak pieces.
3. Cover and cook on low heat for 7–8 hours.

{SERVES 4-6}

353 Beefy Onion Supper

1-1½ pounds round steak
1 medium onion
2 cups fresh sliced mushrooms
1 (10 ounce) can French onion soup
1 (6 ounce) package herb stuffing mix
½ cup (1 stick) butter, melted

1. Cut beef into 5–6 serving-size pieces.
2. Slice onion and separate into rings.
3. Place steak pieces in sprayed, oval slow cooker and top with onions and mushrooms.
4. Pour soup over ingredients in cooker.
5. Cover and cook on low heat for 7–9 hours.
6. Just before serving, combine stuffing mix with seasoning packet, butter, and ½ cup liquid from cooker and toss to mix.
7. Place stuffing mixture on top of steak and increase heat to high.
8. Cover and cook until stuffing is fluffy, about 15 minutes.

{SERVES 4-6}

354 Classic Slow-Cooker Stroganoff

2 pounds round steak
¾ cup flour, divided
½ teaspoon mustard
¼ teaspoon salt
⅛ teaspoon black pepper
2 medium onions, thinly sliced
½ pound fresh mushrooms, sliced
1 (10 ounce) can beef broth
¾ cup dry white wine or cooking wine
1 (8 ounce) carton sour cream

1. Trim excess fat from steak and cut into 3-inch strips about ½-inch wide.
2. Combine ½ cup flour, mustard, salt, and pepper in bowl and toss with steak strips.
3. Place strips in sprayed, oval slow cooker.
4. Cover with onions and mushrooms. Add beef broth and wine. Cover and cook on low heat for 8–10 hours.
5. Just before serving, combine sour cream and remaining ¼ cup flour in bowl.
6. Stir into cooker and cook until stroganoff thickens slightly, about 10–15 minutes.

{SERVES 4-6}

355 Swiss Steak

1½-2 pounds round steak
1 (1 ounce) packet onion soup mix
½ cup dry red wine
1 (8 ounce) carton fresh mushrooms, sliced
1 (10 ounce) can French onion soup
½ cup water

1. Cut steak into 6–8 serving-size pieces. Sprinkle with seasoned salt and pepper, then cook, stirring, over medium heat in skillet until browned on all sides, about 8–10 minutes.
2. Layer steak pieces, potatoes, carrots, and onion in sprayed slow cooker.
3. Combine tomatoes and beef gravy in bowl and spoon over vegetables.
4. Cover and cook on low heat for 7–8 hours.

{SERVES 6-8}

Who Knew?

Wine corks (the natural kind, not plastic) contain a chemical that, when heated, will help tenderize beef. Save one to throw into your slow cooker while making this or another beef dish!

356 Spicy Swiss Steak

1½ pounds boneless round steak
1 tablespoon olive oil
½ pound spicy bratwurst
2 small onions
2 tablespoons quick-cooking tapioca
1 teaspoon dried thyme
¼ teaspoon salt
⅛ teaspoon black pepper
2 (15 ounce) cans Mexican stewed tomatoes

1. Trim fat from steak and cut into 4 serving-size pieces.
2. Heat oil in skillet over medium-high heat. When hot, add steak and bratwurst. Cook, stirring occasionally, until browned on all sides, about 8–10 minutes. Drain and place in sprayed, 4- or 5-quart slow cooker.
3. Slice onions and separate into rings.
4. Cover meat with onions and sprinkle with tapioca, thyme, salt, and pepper. Pour stewed tomatoes over onion and seasonings.
5. Cover and cook on low heat for 5–8 hours.
6. Serve over noodles.

{SERVES 4-6}

Who Knew?

Don't spend money on store-bought breadcrumbs. Set aside a special jar and pour in the crumbs from the bottom of cracker boxes or low-sugar cereal boxes.

357 Beef Roulades

1½ pounds beef flank steak
5 slices bacon
¾ cup finely chopped onion
1 (4 ounce) can mushroom pieces
1 tablespoonWorcestershire sauce
⅓ cup Italian-seasoned breadcrumbs
1 (12 ounce) jar beef gravy

1. Cut steak into 4–6 serving-size pieces.
2. Cut bacon into small pieces and combine with onion, mushrooms,Worcestershire sauce, and breadcrumbs in bowl. Place about ½ cup onion mixture on each piece of steak.
3. Roll each steak and secure ends with toothpicks. Dry steak rolls with paper towels.
4. Place steak rolls in skillet over medium-high heat and brown on all sides, about 6–10 minutes. Transfer to sprayed slow cooker.
5. Pour gravy evenly over steaks to thoroughly moisten. Cover and cook on low heat for 7–9 hours.
6. Serve over noodles, rice, or mashed potatoes.

{SERVES 4-6}

Who Knew? Light Switch

To make this recipe lower in fat, substitute 1¼ cup of our Low-Fat Cream of Chicken Soup Base for the can of cream of chicken soup.

358 Herb-Crusted Beef Roast

1 pound) rump roast
¼ teaspoon salt
⅛ teaspoon black pepper
¼ cup chopped fresh parsley
¼ cup chopped fresh oregano leaves
½ teaspoon dried rosemary leaves
1 teaspoon minced garlic
1 tablespoon oil
6 slices thick-cut bacon

1. Rub roast with salt and pepper.
2. Combine parsley, oregano, rosemary, garlic, and oil in small bowl; press mixture on top and sides of roast.
3. Place roast in sprayed slow cooker. Place bacon over top of roast and tuck ends under bottom.
4. Cover and cook on low heat for 6–8 hours.

{SERVES 4-6}

359 Old-Time Pot Roast

1 (2–2½ pound) boneless rump roast
5 medium potatoes, peeled, quartered
1 (16 ounce) package peeled baby carrots
½ medium onions, quartered
1 (10 ounce) can golden mushroom soup
½ teaspoon dried basil
½ teaspoon salt

1. Brown roast on all sides in skillet.
2. Place potatoes, carrots, and onions in sprayed, 4- or 5-quart slow cooker.
3. Place browned roast on top of vegetables.
4. Combine soup, basil, and salt in bowl and pour mixture over meat and vegetables.
5. Cover and cook on low heat for 9–11 hours.
6. To serve, transfer roast and vegetables to serving plate. Stir juices remaining in slow cooker and spoon over roast and vegetables.

{SERVES 8}

Who Knew?

Here's a simple tip to make this dish even more tender. When your roast is ready to slice, make sure to cut it against the grain (look for slight lines on the surface). Meat cut across the grain will be more tender.

360 Smoked Brisket

1 (4–6 pound) trimmed brisket
1 (4 ounce) bottle liquid smoke
½ tablespoon garlic salt
1 teaspoon celery salt
Worcestershire sauce
1 onion, chopped
1 (6 ounce) bottle barbecue sauce

1. Place brisket in large shallow dish and pour liquid smoke over top.
2. Sprinkle with garlic salt and celery salt. Cover and refrigerate overnight.
3. Before cooking, drain liquid smoke and douse brisket withWorcestershire sauce.
4. Place chopped onion in slow cooker and place brisket on top of onion.
5. Cover and cook on low heat for 7–8 hours.
6. Pour barbecue sauce over brisket and cook for additional 1 hour.

{SERVES 6-8}

361 Shredded Brisket Sandwiches

2 teaspoons onion powder
1 teaspoon minced garlic
1 tablespoon liquid smoke
1 (3–4 pound) beef brisket
⅓ cup water
1 (16 ounce) bottle barbecue sauce
6-8 6–8 kaiser rolls or hamburger buns

1. Combine onion powder, minced garlic, and liquid smoke in bowl and rub over brisket.
2. Place brisket in sprayed, large slow cooker. Add water to cooker.
3. Cover and cook on low heat until brisket is tender, about 6–8 hours.
4. Remove brisket, cool, and reserve ½ cup cooking juices.
5. Shred brisket with 2 forks and place in large saucepan. Add ½ cup cooking juices and barbecue sauce and heat thoroughly.
6. Make sandwiches with kaiser rolls or hamburger buns.

{SERVES 6-8}

Who Knew?

If you're reheating this brisket in the microwave, place it in a casserole dish between lettuce leaves. The lettuce provides just the right amount of moisture to keep the beef from drying out.

362 Beef Ribs and Gravy

Ribs take awhile to tenderize in a slow cooker (9–11 hours), but the results are delicious and the recipe is simple!

4 pounds beef short ribs
1 onion, sliced
1 teaspoon pepper
1 (12 ounce) jar beef gravy
1 (1 ounce) packet beef gravy mix

1. Place beef ribs in sprayed, 6-quart slow cooker. Cover with onion and sprinkle with pepper.
2. Combine beef gravy and dry gravy mix in small bowl and pour over ribs and onion.
3. Cover and cook on low heat for 9–11 hours.

{SERVES 4-6}

363 Terrific Pork Tenderloin

2-3 (1 pound) pork tenderloins
1 teaspoon seasoned salt
1 teaspoon garlic powder
1 (4 ounce) can chopped green chilies
2 (10 ounce) cans cream of celery so

1. Place tenderloins in sprayed, oval slow cooker. Sprinkle with seasoned salt and garlic powder.
2. Combine green chilies and celery soup in bowl. Spoon over tenderloins, covering completely.
3. Cover and cook on low heat for 8 hours. Serve over rice.

{SERVES 4-5}

Who Knew?

To make this recipe lower in fat, substitute 2½ cups of our Low-Fat Cream of Celery Soup Base for the cans of cream of celery soup.

364 Spinach-Stuffed Pork Roast

1 (2–2½ pound) pork tenderloin
1 (10 ounce) package frozen chopped spinach, thawed
⅓ 1/3 cup seasoned breadcrumbs
⅓ 1/3 cup grated Parmesan cheese
2 tablespoons vegetable or canola oil
½ teaspoon seasoned salt

1. Cut tenderloin horizontally lengthwise about ½ inch from top to within ¾ inch of opposite end; open flat.
2. Turn pork to cut other side, from inside edge to outer edge, and open flat. If one side is thicker than other side, cover with plastic wrap and pound until both sides are ¾-inch thick.
3. Squeeze spinach between paper towels to completely remove excess moisture.
4. Combine spinach, breadcrumbs, and cheese in bowl and mix well.
5. Spread mixture on inside surfaces of pork and press down. Roll pork and tie with kitchen twine.
6. Heat oil in large skillet over medium-high heat; cook pork until browned on all sides, about 3 minutes per side.
7. Place in sprayed oval slow cooker and sprinkle with salt. Cover and cook on low heat for 6–8 hours.

{SERVES 4-6}

Who Knew?

If you don't have kitchen twine, the perfect substitute is dental floss!

365 Roasted Red Pepper Tenderloin

- 2 tablespoon olive oil
- 2 pounds pork tenderloin
- 1 (1 ounce) packet ranch dressing mix
- 1 cup roasted red bell peppers, rinsed, chopped
- ½ cup water
- 1 (8 ounce) carton sour cream

1. Heat oil in skillet over medium-high heat.
   Add tenderloins and brown on all sides, about 3–5 minutes per side. Place in sprayed, 6-quart oval slow cooker.
2. Combine ranch dressing mix, red bell peppers, and water in bowl and spoon over tenderloins.
3. Cover and cook on low heat for 4–5 hours.
4. Remove tenderloins from slow cooker and reserve sauce.
5. Stir sour cream into remaining sauce. Serve over tenderloin slices.

{SERVES 4-6}

Who Knew? Light Switch

To make this recipe lower in fat, substitute 2½ cups of our Low-Fat Cream of Celery Soup Base for the cans of cream of celery soup.

366 Western Pork Supper

- 6 (¾ inch thick) pork loin chops
- 1 (15 ounce) can pinto beans with jalapeños
- 1½ cups salsa
- 1 (16 ounce) package frozen seasoned corn with black beans, tomatoes, bell peppers, and onions, thawed
- (4 ounce) can sliced ripe olives
- 1½-2 cups instant brown rice
- 2 tablespoons butter, melted

1. Arrange pork chops in sprayed, oval slow cooker and cover with chili beans and salsa.
2. Cover and cook on low heat for 5 hours or on high heat for 2 hours 30 minutes. Increase heat to high (if cooking on low) and stir in seasoned corn and olives. Cover and cook for additional 30 minutes.
3. Cook brown rice according to package directions and stir in melted butter.
4. Place on serving platter. Spoon pork chops and vegetables over rice.

{SERVES 4-6}

Who Knew? Light Switch

To make this recipe even healthier, use our Super Healthy Salsa instead of jarred salsa.

367 Tender Pork Loin

It might be hard to find a small (3–4 pound) pork loin, but they are commonly available in larger (8–9 pound) sizes. Because pork loin is such a good cut of pork—no bones, no fat—you can buy a whole loin, cut it into 2 or 3 pieces, and freeze the pieces not used for later.

- **1 (3–4 pound) pork loin**
- **2 teaspoons minced garlic**
- **½ teaspoon rosemary**
- **1 teaspoon sage**
- **1½ teaspoons marjoram**
- **¼ cup water**

1. Place pork loin in sprayed slow cooker, rub with minced garlic, and sprinkle with rosemary, sage, and marjoram. Add water to slow cooker.
2. Cover and cook on low heat for 4–5

{SERVES 6-8}

Who Knew?

Want to wake up the flavor of dried herbs before using them in a recipe? Just toast them in a pan for a minute or two, and their flavors will be revived.

368 Good-Time Chops, Tators, and Peas

- **1 (10 ounce) can cream of mushroom soup**
- **1 (4 ounce) can sliced mushrooms**
- **¼ cup water**
- **5-6 boneless pork chops**
- **1 tablespoon lemon pepper**
- **2 (15 ounce) cans whole new potatoes, drained**
- **1 (10 ounce) package frozen green peas, thawed**

1. Spoon soup and mushrooms into sprayed slow cooker and stir in water to thin soup slightly.
2. Sprinkle each pork chop with lemon pepper and place in slow cooker.
3. Cover and cook on low heat for 6–8 hours.
4. Remove lid and place potatoes and peas around pork chops. Turn heat to high and cook for additional 1 hour 30 minutes.

{SERVES 5}

369 Ranch Pork Chops

- 6 (¾ inch thick) bone-in pork chops
- 1 (1 ounce) packet ranch dressing mix
- ½ teaspoon pepper
- 2 pounds new (red) potatoes, cleaned, quartered
- 1 (10 ounce) can French onion soup
- ½ cup water

1. Place pork chops in sprayed, 6-quart oval slow cooker.
2. Sprinkle pork chops with ranch dressing mix and pepper.
3. Place potatoes around pork chops and pour French onion soup and water around potatoes and chops.
4. Cover and cook on low heat for 4–5 hours.

{SERVES 4-6}

370 Pork Chops and Gravy

- 6 (½-inch thick) pork chops
- 1 tablespoon salt
- 1 tablespoon black pepper
- 1 tablespoon olive oil
- 1 8–10 new (red) potatoes with peels, quartered
- 1 (16 ounce) package baby carrots
- 2 (10 ounce) cans cream of mushroom soup with roasted garlic
- ½ cup water

1. Sprinkle pork chops with salt and pepper.
2. Heat oil over medium-high heat in skillet. When hot, add pork chops and brown on each side, about 3–5 minutes per side.
3. Place pork chops in 5- or 6-quart slow cooker. Place potatoes and carrots around pork chops.
4. Heat mushroom soup with water in saucepan and pour over chops and vegetables.
5. Cover and cook on low heat for 6–7 hours.

{SERVES 6}

Who Knew?

Whether you're pan frying or deep-frying, it's important to heat the oil above 350° before tossing in your ingredients. Otherwise, your food can absorb too much oil and become heavy and greasy. A good test is to toss a hunk of bread in the oil, and if it browns in 10 seconds or less, you're ready to cook!

371 Honey-Mustard Pork Chops

1 (10 ounce) can golden mushroom soup
⅓ cup white wine
¼ cup honey mustard
1 teaspoon minced garlic
1 teaspoon salt
4-5 (¾ inch thick) pork chops
⅛ teaspoon black pepper

1. Combine soup, wine, honey mustard, minced garlic, and salt in large bowl and mix well.
2. Sprinkle pork chops with pepper and place in sprayed, 5-quart slow cooker. Spoon soup mixture over chops.
3. Cover and cook on low heat for 5–6 hours.
4. When ready to serve, lift pork chops out of sauce and place on serving plate. Stir sauce to mix well and serve with chops.

{SERVES 4-5}

Who Knew?

For a "meat-and-potatoes meal," just slice 3 potatoes and place in slow cooker before adding pork chops.

372 Easy Slow Cooker Pork Chops

1¾ cups flour
2 2 tablespoons dry mustard
8 8 boneless, thick pork chops
1 tablespoon vegetable or canola oil
1 (10 ounce) can chicken-and-rice soup
¼ cup water

1. Place flour and mustard in shallow bowl. Dredge pork chops in flour-mustard mixture.
2. Heat oil over medium-high heat in skillet. When hot, add pork chops and brown on each side, about 3–5 minutes per side. Place all chops in sprayed, 6-quart oval slow cooker.
3. Pour soup over pork and add water. Cover and cook on low heat for 6–8 hours.

{SERVES 6-8}

373 Country Pork Chops

- 7-8 new (red) potatoes with peels, sliced
- 2 onions, sliced
- 1 (10 ounce) can cream of celery soup
- ⅓ 1/3 cup chicken broth
- 3 tablespoons Dijon-style mustard
- 1 (4 ounce) can sliced mushrooms, drained
- 1 teaspoon minced garlic
- ¾ teaspoon dried basil
- 8 boneless pork chops
- ¼ teaspoon salt
- ⅛ teaspoon black pepper
- 1 tablespoon vegetable or canola oil

1. Place potatoes and onions in sprayed, large slow cooker.
2. Combine soup, broth, mustard, mushrooms, garlic, and basil in bowl; mix well and pour over potatoes and onions. Stir to coat vegetables.
3. Sprinkle pork chops with salt and pepper. Heat oil over medium-high heat in skillet. When hot, add pork chops and brown on each side, about 3–5 minutes per side.
4. Place chops over vegetables.
5. Cover and cook on low heat for 6–7 hours.

{SERVES 6-8}

Who Knew? Light Switch

To make this recipe lower in fat, substitute 1¼ cup of our Low-Fat Cream of Celery Soup Base for the can of cream of celery soup.

374 Deconstructed Pork Chop Pizza

This recipe came about after one of our kids requested pizza on slow-cooker night. The pizza sauce gives it the taste of pizza without the shape!

- 6 (1 inch thick) boneless pork chops
- ¼ teaspoon salt
- ⅛ teaspoon black pepper
- 1 medium onion, finely chopped
- 1 green bell pepper, seeded, finely chopped
- 1 (8 ounce) jar pizza sauce
- 1 (10 ounce) box plain couscous
- 2 tablespoons butter
- 1 cup shredded mozzarella cheese

1. Trim fat from pork chops and sprinkle with salt and pepper. Place in skillet and cook over medium-high heat until browned, about 3 minutes per side. Transfer chops to sprayed, oval slow cooker.
2. Spoon onion and bell pepper over chops and pour pizza sauce over top.
3. Cover and cook on low heat for 4–6 hours.
4. Cook couscous according to package directions, except add 2 tablespoons butter instead of 1 tablespoon.
5. Place couscous on serving platter. Spoon chops and sauce over couscous and sprinkle cheese over chops.

{SERVES 4-6}

375 Cranberry-Glazed Pork

- **2 tablespoons vegetable or canola oil**
- **1 (3–4 pound) pork shoulder roast**
- **1 (16 ounce) package frozen stew vegetables, thawed**
- **1 (16 ounce) can whole cranberry sauce**
- **1 (4 ounce) can chopped green chilies**
- **¼ cup chili sauce**
- **1 teaspoon Dijon-style mustard**
- **1 tablespoons brown sugar**

1. Heat oil in large skillet over medium heat. Add roast and brown on all sides, about 5–8 minutes per side.
2. Place roast in sprayed slow cooker and top with stew vegetables.
3. Combine cranberry sauce, green chilies, chili sauce, mustard, and brown sugar in saucepan; heat just enough to blend ingredients. Pour mixture over roast and vegetables.
4. Cover and cook on low heat for 8–9 hours or on high heat for 4 hours–4 hours 30 minutes. Transfer roast and vegetables to serving platter and keep warm.
5. Strain cooking juices and skim off fat. Bring juices to a boil in medium saucepan; reduce heat and simmer until mixture thickens, about 25 minutes.
6. Serve sauce with sliced pork roast.

{SERVES 6-8}

376 Barbecue Pork Roast

Recycle any leftovers for tasty next-day pork sandwiches. Just shred the pork and place in slow cooker until heated through and it's ready for buns!

- **1 onion, thinly sliced**
- **2 tablespoons flour**
- **1 (2–3 pound) pork shoulder roast**
- **1 (8 ounce) bottle barbecue sauce**
- **1 tablespoon chili powder**
- **1 teaspoon ground cumin**

1. Separate onion slices into rings and place in sprayed, 4- or 5-quart slow cooker. Sprinkle flour over onions.
2. If necessary, cut roast to fit cooker; place roast over onions.
3. Combine barbecue sauce, chili powder, and cumin in bowl and pour over roast.
4. Cover and cook on low heat for 8–10 hours.
5. Remove roast from cooker and slice. Serve remaining sauce over sliced roast.

{SERVES 6-8}

377 Pork and Cabbage Supper

- 2 (16 ounce) package baby carrots
- 1 cup chicken broth
- 1 cup water
- 1 (1 ounce) packet golden onion soup mix
- ½ tablespoon black pepper
- 1 (3–4 pound) pork shoulder roast
- 1 medium head cabbage

1. Place carrots in sprayed, 5-quart slow cooker.
2. Add chicken broth and water. Sprinkle dry soup mix and pepper over carrots.
3. If roast is too large to fit in cooker, cut it in half. Place over carrot mixture.
4. Cover and cook on low heat for 6–7 hours.
5. Cut cabbage in small-size chunks and place over roast. Cover and cook until cabbage cooks through, about 1–2 hours.

{SERVES 6-8}

Who Knew? Light Switch

Try using our Healthy Chicken Broth in this recipe!

378 Home-Style Ribs

- 4-6 pounds boneless pork spareribs
- 1 tablespoon salt
- 1 tablespoon black pepper
- ½ cup water
- 1 cup chili sauce
- 1 cup packed brown sugar
- 2 tablespoons vinegar
- 2 tablespoonsWorcestershire sauce

1. Sprinkle ribs liberally with salt and pepper. Place ribs in sprayed slow cooker.
2. Combine water, chili sauce, brown sugar, vinegar, and Worcestershire sauce in bowl. Pour over ribs.
3. Cover and cook on low heat for 5–6 hours.

{SERVES 6-8}

Who Knew?

Wet some washcloths and place them in bowls next to each plate for easy cleaning of messy fingers!

379 Mushroom Ham and Rice

- 1 (6.7 ounce) box Uncle Ben's Brown and Wild Rice Mushroom Recipe rice
- 3-4 cups cooked, chopped or cubed ham
- 1 (4 ounce) can sliced mushrooms, drained
- 1 (10 ounce) package frozen green peas
- 2 cups chopped celery
- 2⅔ cups water

1. Combine rice, seasoning packet, ham, mushrooms, peas, celery, and water in sprayed, 4- or 5-quart slow cooker. Stir to mix well.
2. Cover and cook on low heat for 2–4 hours.

{SERVES 4-6}

Who Knew?

Keep celery lasting even longer in your refrigerator by wrapping it in aluminum foil!

380 Black Bean Soup

- 2 (14 ounce) cans chicken broth
- 3 (15 ounce) cans black beans, rinsed and drained
- 2 (10 ounce) cans tomatoes and green chilies
- 1 onion, chopped
- 1 teaspoon ground cumin
- ½ teaspoon dried thyme
- ½ teaspoon dried oregano
- 2-3 cups cooked, finely diced ham
- ¾ cup water

1. Combine chicken broth and black beans in slow cooker and cook on high heat just long enough for ingredients to get hot, about 20–30 minutes.
2. With potato masher, mash about half beans in slow cooker.
3. Reduce heat to low and add tomatoes and green chilies, onion, cumin, thyme, oregano, ham, and water.
4. Cover and cook for 5–6 hours.

{SERVES 4-6}

381 Corn-Ham Chowder

In this ingenious recipe, potato flakes are used to thicken up the soup without using flour.

1 (14 ounce) can chicken broth
2 cup milk
1 (10 ounce) can cream of celery soup
1 (15 ounce) can cream-style corn
1 (15 ounce) can whole kernel corn
½ cup dry potato flakes
1 onion, chopped
2-3 cups cooked, chopped, ham
Salt and black pepper to taste

1. Combine broth, milk, soup, cream-style corn, whole kernel corn, potato flakes, onion, and ham in 6-quart slow cooker.
2. Cover and cook on low heat for 4–5 hours.
3. When ready to serve, sprinkle with salt and pepper to taste.

{SERVES 6}

Who Knew?

Make this recipe low fat by substituting 1¾ cups of our Healthy Chicken Broth for the can of chicken broth, and 1¼ cups of our Low-Fat Cream of Celery Soup Base for the can of soup.

382 Sauerkraut and Bratwurst Supper

1 (28 ounce) jar refrigerated sauerkraut
¾ cup beer
1 tablespoonWorcestershire sauce
1 (1 ounce) packet onion soup mix
2 pounds bratwurst

1. Combine sauerkraut, beer,Worcestershire sauce, and onion soup mix in sprayed, 4- or 5-quart slow cooker; mix well.
2. Cut bratwurst in diagonal slices and place on top of sauerkraut-beer mixture.
3. Cover and cook on low heat for 5–6 hours or on high heat for 2 hours 30 minutes–3 hours.

{SERVES 4-6}

383 Sausage and Beans

- 1 (1 pound) cooked link sausage
- 2 (15 ounce) cans baked beans
- 1 (15 ounce) can great northern beans, drained
- 1 (15 ounce) can pinto beans, drained
- ½ cup chili sauce
- ⅔ 2/3 cup packed brown sugar
- ⅛ teaspoon black pepper
- 1 tablespoon Worcestershire

1. Cut link sausage into 1-inch slices. Place sausage in slow cooker, then layer baked beans, great northern beans, and pinto beans on top.
2. Combine chili sauce, brown sugar, pepper, and Worcestershire sauce in bowl and pour over beans and sausage.
3. Cover and cook on low heat for 4 hours. Stir before serving.

{SERVES 8}

384 Spicy Sausage Soup

- 2 pounds hot bulk sausage
- 2 (15 ounce) cans Mexican stewed tomatoes
- 3 cups chopped celery
- 1 cup sliced carrots
- 1 (15 ounce) can cut green beans, drained
- 1 (14 ounce) can chicken broth
- 1 cup water

1. Shape spicy sausage into small balls, and place in nonstick skillet. Cook over mediumhigh heat until brown on all sides, about 2–3 minutes per side. Drain and place in large slow cooker.
2. Add remaining ingredients and stir gently, making sure to keep meatballs intact.
3. Cover and cook on low heat for 6–7 hours.

{SERVES 6}

385 Sweet-and-Sour Sausage Links

- 2 (16 ounce) packages miniature smoked sausage links
- ¾ cup chili sauce
- 1 cup packed brown sugar
- ¼ cup horseradish

1. Place sausages in sprayed, 4-quart slow cooker.
2. Combine chili sauce, brown sugar, and horseradish in bowl and pour over sausages.
3. Cover and cook on low heat for 4 hours. Serve over hot rice.

{SERVES 4-6

386 Navy Bean Soup

1 slices thick-cut bacon, divided
1 carrot
3 (15 ounce) cans navy beans with liquid
3 ribs celery, chopped
1 onion, chopped
2 (14 ounce) cans chicken broth
1 teaspoon Italian herb seasoning
1 cup water
1 (10 ounce) can cream of chicken soup

1. Cook bacon in skillet, drain, and crumble. Reserve 2 crumbled slices for garnish.
2. Cut carrot in half lengthwise and slice.
3. Combine most of crumbled bacon, carrot, beans, celery, onion, broth, seasoning, and water in 5- or 6-quart slow cooker; stir to mix.
4. Cover and cook on low heat for 5–6 hours.
5. Ladle 2 cups soup mixture into food processor or blender and process until smooth.
6. Return to cooker, add cream of chicken soup, and stir to mix.
7. Turn heat to high and cook for additional 10–15 minutes.

{SERVES 4-6}

Who Knew? Light Switch

To make this recipe lower in fat, substitute 1¼ cup of our Low-Fat Cream of Chicken Soup Base for the can of cream of chicken soup.

387 Tasty Tuna Bake

2 (6 ounce) cans white tuna, drained, flaked
1 (10 ounce) can cream of chicken soup
3 eggs, hard-boiled, chopped
3 ribs celery, thinly sliced
1 red bell pepper, seeded, chopped
½ cup coarsely chopped pecans
½ cup mayonnaise
1 teaspoon white pepper
2 cups crushed potato chips, divided
¼ teaspoon salt

1. Combine tuna, soup, eggs, celery, bell pepper, pecans, mayonnaise, white pepper, 1 cup potato chips, and salt in bowl; mix well. Transfer to sprayed slow cooker.
2. Cover and cook on low heat for 5–7 hours. When ready to serve, sprinkle remaining potato chips on top.

{SERVES 4-5}

388 Vegetarian Chili

- 1 (15 ounce) can pinto beans, drained
- 1 (15 ounce) can black beans, drained
- 1 (15 ounce) can kidney beans, drained
- 1 (15 ounce) can whole kernel corn, drained
- 2 (15 ounce) cans diced tomatoes with green chilies
- 1 (6 ounce) can tomato paste
- 1 green, red, or yellow bell pepper, seeded, chopped
- 1 medium onion, diced
- 2 garlic cloves, minced
- ½ tablespoon ground cumin
- 2 teaspoons chili powder
- Dash cayenne pepper
- ½ teaspoon salt
- ¼ teaspoon black pepper

1. Place all ingredients in slow cooker; stir to mix well. Cook on low for 5–6 hours.

{SERVES 5}

389 Cheese-Spaghetti and Spinach

- 1 (7 ounce) box spaghetti
- 2 tablespoons butter
- 1 (8 ounce) carton sour cream
- 1 cup shredded Cheddar cheese
- 1 (8 ounce) package shredded Monterey Jack cheese, divided
- 1 (12 ounce) package frozen, chopped spinach, thawed, well-drained
- 1 (6 ounce) can Cheddar French-fried onions, divided

1. Cook spaghetti according to package directions, drain, and stir in butter until it melts.
2. Combine sour cream, Cheddar cheese, half Monterey Jack cheese, spinach, and half can fried onions in large bowl.
3. Fold cheese mixture into spaghetti and spoon into sprayed slow cooker.
4. Cover and cook on low heat for 2–4 hours.
5. When ready to serve, sprinkle remaining Jack cheese and fried onions over top.

{SERVES 4}

Who Knew?

Before cooking spinach or other greens, it's important to squeeze the leaves between paper towels to remove excess moisture. The excess water on leaves in a hot pan creates steam, leaving greens that are stewed and mushy rather than bright and tender.

390 Vegetarian Coconut Curry

This Thai-inspired dish will definitely break up your normal dinner routine! Look for cans of coconut milk in the ethnic aisle of your grocery store or at Mexican and Asian markets.

- **3 cups chopped cauliflower**
- **1 (15 ounce) can garbanzo beans (chickpeas), drained**
- **1 cup frozen cut green beans, thawed**
- **1 small to medium onion, chopped**
- **½ cup chopped peanuts or cashews**
- **1 (14 ounce) can vegetable broth**
- **2½ teaspoons curry powder**
- **1 1 (14 ounce) can light coconut milk**
- **¼ cup fresh basil leaves, finely chopped**

1. Combine cauliflower, garbanzo beans, green beans, onion, and peanuts in a 3½ - or 4-quart slow cooker. Stir in broth and curry powder.
2. Cover and cook on low for 5–6 hours, or on high heat for 2½–3 hours. Stir in coconut milk and basil before serving.

{SERVES 4-6}

Who Knew?

If you're chopping nuts in a food processor, more oil is released than when you chop by hand, and you'll wind up with a sticky mess. To avoid this, simply add a bit of flour to the nuts before chopping.

391 Harvest Vegetable Casserole

- **1 medium new (red) potatoes with peels, sliced**
- **2 onions, sliced**
- **3 carrots, sliced**
- **2 cups chopped green cabbage**
- **¼ cup Italian dressing**
- **1 (1 pound) kielbasa sausage**
- **1 (15 ounce) can Italian stewed tomatoes**

1. Place potatoes, onions, carrots, cabbage, and Italian dressing in sprayed, large slow cooker.
2. Cut sausage into 1-inch pieces and place on top of vegetables.
3. Drizzle stewed tomatoes over vegetables in even layers.
4. Cover and cook on low heat until vegetables are tender, about 6–8 hours.

{SERVES 4-6}

Who Knew?

To save money, try using our Italian Salad Dressing Mix!

CHAPTER 9

Meals in Minutes

392 Parmesan and Wine Chicken

4 skinless, boneless chicken breasts
12 ounces sour cream
¼ cup grated Parmesan cheese
⅓ cup white wine
¼ cup chicken broth
¼ teaspoon salt
¼ teaspoon lemon pepper seasoning

1. Trim fat from chicken breasts and place in microwave-safe container. Add water until chicken is just covered.
2. Cover dish and microwave on HIGH for 3–5 minutes, until chicken is almost tender. Remove chicken and set aside, covered.
3. Mix remaining liquid from chicken with sour cream, Parmesan cheese, wine, salt, and lemon pepper seasoning.
4. Cut chicken into bite size pieces, and place in sauce mixture. Cover and microwave on HIGH for 10 minutes, stirring halfway through. If sauce has not thickened or chicken is not cooked through, cook on HIGH in 2-minute intervals until done. Let sit for 5 minutes before serving.

{SERVES 4–5}

393 Chicken Casserole

1 (10 oz) package frozen mixed vegetables Broiler fryer chicken (2½–4 pounds)
¼ cup (½ stick) butter or margarine, divided
2 cups cooked egg noodles (¼ of one [1 pound] package)
1 (10 ounce) can cream of celery soup
¼ cup finely chopped onion
2 tablespoons milk
1 teaspoon chicken bouillon
¼ teaspoon dry mustard
¼ teaspoon salt
⅛ teaspoon black pepper

1. Defrost vegetables in package on HIGH for 2–4 minutes. Set aside.
2. Place butter in microwave-safe dish and microwave on HIGH until melted, about 15 seconds.
3. Place chicken breast-side down in microwave-safe casserole dish and brush back with half of melted butter. Microwave, covered, on HIGH for 3 minutes.
4. Microwave, covered, on MEDIUM for 6 minutes per pound of chicken, turning halfway through if your microwave does not have a turntable.
5. Meanwhile, combine remaining ingredients.
6. Remove chicken from microwave and pour off excess fat. Add noodle mixture to bottom of dish. Turn chicken breast-side up and brush with remaining butter.
7. Microwave, covered, on MEDIUM until chicken is cooked through and legs move freely, about 6 minutes per pound of chicken.
8. Let sit for 5 minutes and stir noodle mixture before serving.

{SERVES 4–5}

394 Rush Hour Rice and Chicken

2 (5 ounce) cans premium chunk chicken breasts

2 (8.8 ounce) packages whole-grain brown ready (minute) rice

⅔ cup sun-dried tomatoes

2 ripe avocados, peeled, pitted, and diced

½ teaspoon salt

¾ cup mustard vinaigrette dressing

2 scallions, chopped (optional)

1. Prepare rice according to package directions, but substitute broth from chicken for an equal amount of water.
2. Separate chicken into chunks and combine with rice, tomatoes, avocadoes, and salt.
3. Gently stir dressing into chicken-rice mixture. Garnish with scallions before serving.

{SERVES 6}

Who Knew?

If you'd like your rice to be less sticky, add a few drops of lemon juice to it while it's cooking. The lemon juice will help keep the grains separated.

395 Chicken Couscous

Pick up an inexpensive rotisserie chicken at your local market to make this easy dinner that has a touch of sweetness.

1 (5.6 ounce) package toasted pine nut couscous

2 cups chopped rotisserie chicken

1 (15 ounce) can baby green peas, drained

⅓ cup golden raisins

1. Prepare couscous according to package directions.
2. Combine couscous, chicken, peas, and raisins in microwave-safe dish. Heat on MEDIUM until mixture is heated through, about 2 minutes.

{SERVES 6}

396 Quick Enchiladas

12 corn tortillas
1 (12 ounce) package shredded Mexican 4-cheese blend, divided
2½ pounds rotisserie chicken or deli chicken, cubed
1 small onion, chopped
2 (10 ounce) cans enchilada sauce

1. Wrap 6 tortillas in slightly damp paper towel. Place between 2 salad plates and microwave on HIGH for 30 to 40 seconds.
2. On each tortilla, place about ⅓ cup cheese, one-twelfth of the chicken, and 1 tablespoon onion.
3. Roll up each tortilla and place seam-side down on sprayed, 10 x 15-inch baking dish.
4. Repeat steps 1–3 with remaining 6 tortillas.
5. Pour enchilada sauce on top of tortillas and sprinkle with remaining cheese and onions.
6. Cover and microwave on MEDIUM for 5–6 minutes. (If microwave does not have turntable, turn tortillas once during cooking.)

{SERVES 6}

Who Knew?

To lower the fat content of this dish, substitute 3 cups of our Low-Fat Four-Cheese Blend for the package of cheese.

397 Chicken Quesadillas

This is a great recipe for using whatever ingredients you happen to have on hand. Substitute beef or pork for the chicken, and add fresh tomatoes or cooked peppers if you have some you're trying to use up.

3 cups cooked, chopped chicken
2 cups shredded Cheddar cheese
½ cup chopped scallions
10 medium-sized flour tortillas

1. Combine first three ingredients in bowl.
2. Add mixture to half of each flour tortilla, then fold over.
3. Cook on HIGH for approximately 15 seconds, or until cheese in melted. Serve with salsa.

{SERVES 5}

398 Sweet and Sour Meatballs

- ¼ cup chili sauce
- ½ cup grape jelly
- 2 teaspoons lemon juice
- 1½ pounds ground beef
- ½ cup bread crumbs
- 1 egg
- ½ cup water

1. In microwave-safe casserole dish, combine chili sauce, jelly, and lemon juice. Set aside.
2. Mix ground beef, bread crumbs, egg, and water until well blended. Shape mixture into small meatballs and place in sauce.
3. Microwave on HIGH for 6 minutes, turning halfway through if your microwave does not have a turntable. Skim off fat and stir.
4. Continue to microwave on HIGH until sauce bubbles and meatballs are cooked through, about 8 minutes.
5. Serve over rice.

{SERVES 6}

Who Knew? Light Switch

Before mixing the ingredients in step 2, slip some freezer bags over your hands to keep them clean.

399 Beef Corn Pie

- 1 pound ground beef
- 2 tablespoons chopped onion
- 1 clove garlic, minced
- 1 (8 ounce) can whole peeled tomatoes with liquid
- 1 (8 ounce) can whole kernel corn
- 2 teaspoons chili powder
- ½ teaspoon salt
- ½ cup shredded Cheddar cheese
- 1 egg
- ½ cup yellow corn meal

1. Crumble ground beef into microwave-safe casserole dish, then mix in onion and garlic.
2. Cover loosely and microwave on HIGH for 2 minutes. Stir, breaking up beef, and microwave on HIGH in 1 minute increments, stirring each time, until meat is cooked through (about 2–3 minutes). Drain excess fat.
3. Drain tomatoes, reserving ½ cup liquid. Add tomatoes, corn, chili powder, and salt to meat mixture and stir to combine.
4. Cover tightly and microwave on HIGH until mixture is hot and bubbly, about 4–6 minutes. Stir.
5. In separate bowl, beat together egg, corn meal, and reserved tomato juice. Pour over beef mixture.
6. Sprinkle cheese on top and microwave, uncovered, on HIGH until topping is no longer doughy, about 3–6 minutes.

{SERVES 6}

400 Lightning Meatloaf

- 1 pound ground chuck
- 1 egg
- 2 tablespoons quick cooking oats
- 2 tablespoons finely diced onion
- 1 (8 oz) can tomato sauce, divided
- ½ teaspoon dried thyme
- ½ teaspoon celery salt
- 1 tablespoon brown sugar
- 1 teaspoonWorcestershire sauce
- 1 teaspoon prepared mustard

1. Combine ground beef, eggs, oats, onion, half of tomato sauce, thyme, and celery salt. Shape into a microwave-safe, 9 x 5-inch loaf pan. Run a finger, knife, or chopstick around the sides so that meat doesn't touch sides of dish.
2. Cover with waxed paper and microwave on HIGH for 5 minutes. Pour off juices.
3. Stir brown sugar,Worcestershire sauce, and mustard into remaining tomato sauce. Spoon over loaf to coat top and sides.
4. Cover with waxed paper and microwave on LOW until meat thermometer inserted in the center of the loaf registers 170°, about 17–20 minutes. If your microwave does not have a turntable, turn several times during cooking.
5. Remove from microwave and cover; let stand 5 minutes. (Temperature will rise about 10° during stand time.)

{SERVES 6}

401 Microwaved Rump Roast

Yes, you can microwave a rump roast! It won't look as pretty as a rump roast you've made in the oven, but slice it before you serve it and your family won't know the difference—just that it took several hours less than usual!

- Beef rump roast (5–5½ pounds works best)
- 1 package dry onion soup mix
- 1 teaspoon garlic powder
- 1½ teaspoon black pepper
- 1 large onion, thinly sliced
- 1 cup water at room temperature

1. Pat soup mix evenly over meat, then sprinkle with garlic powder and pepper.
2. In bottom of a microwave-safe pan, spread sliced onion. Add water. Place roast in pan, fat side down.
3. Microwave 11 minutes for each pound of meat. (This will produce a roast that is medium; for well-done add 2 minutes per pound.) Microwave on 90% power for first half of cooking time, then turn roast fat-side up and cook on 70% power for the second half of cooking time.
4. Allow roast to rest for 10 minutes before slicing.

{SERVES 6–10 (depending on size of roast)}

Who Knew?

To easily turn the gravy from your roast into drippings, simply add 1 teaspoon dried thyme, rosemary, or sage along with 1–2 tablespoons flour.

402 Debra's Speedy Swiss Steak

3 tablespoons flour
1 pound beef round steak
3 tablespoons dry onion soup mix (shake to mix before measuring)
1 tablespoons brown sugar
3 tablespoons water
1 teaspoon prepared mustard
1 (8 oz.) can tomato sauce

1. Sprinkle half of flour on one side of meat; pound in with meat mallet. Turn meat over and sprinkle with remaining flour; pound until ¾-inch thick.
2. Cut into 4 equal pieces. Spread over bottom of microwave baking dish.
3. In small bowl, combine all remaining ingredients and mix well to blend. Pour over meat.
4. Microwave, covered, on MEDIUM for 12–17 minutes or until meat is almost tender. Let sit, tightly covered, for 10 additional minutes.

{SERVES 4}

Who Knew?

If you don't have a meat mallet, simply place some plastic wrap or waxed paper over the steak, then hit it with a hammer.

403 Stuffed Pork Chops

3 tablespoons butter
1 small onion, finely sliced
1 cup finely chopped button mushrooms
¼ cup rice, cooked
4 pork loin chops
½ cup shredded Cheddar cheese

1. Place butter in microwave-safe dish and microwave on HIGH until melted, about 10–15 seconds. Add onion and mushrooms and microwave on HIGH until tender, about 3 minutes. Add rice and stir to combine.
2. Make a horizontal slice in the middle of each pork chop, leaving a border on two sides to form a pocket. Spoon rice mixture into the pockets and secure with a toothpick.
3. Arrange pork chops in microwave-safe dish with thickest parts of meat at outer edge. Microwave, covered, on HIGH for 5 minutes. Flip pork chops and rearrange in dish, then microwave on MEDIUM until cooked through, about 9–10 minutes. Be aware that pork chops will continue to cook for 2–5 minutes after they have been removed from microwave.
4. Sprinkle with cheese before serving and microwave for an additional 10–15 seconds on HIGH to melt cheese.

{SERVES 4}

404 Quick Spare Ribs

2 pounds pork ribs
1 cup onion, chopped
2 tablespoon brown sugar
2 tablespoon vinegar
1 teaspoon prepared mustard
1 (15 ounce) can tomato sauce Salt and pepper to taste

1. Place ribs in 2-quart microwave-safe dish. In separate bowl, combine remaining ingredients, except salt and pepper. Pour over ribs.
2. Microwave, covered, on MEDIUM for 25–30 minutes, turning halfway through, until meat is tender and an internal temperature of 170 degrees is reached. Let sit for 10 minutes.
3. Season with salt and pepper to taste.

{SERVES 4}

405 Cornbread Casserole

If you love the taste of cornbread, you'll appreciate this easy-to-make microwave casserole.

1 (8 ounce) package cornbread stuffing mix
2 cups frozen mixed vegetables, slightly thawed
1½ cups cubed ham 3 eggs, lightly beaten
2 cups milk
¼ teaspoon salt
¼ teaspoon black pepper
½ cup shredded Cheddar cheese

1. In microwave-safe dish, combine stuffing, vegetables, and ham.
2. In separate container, mix together eggs, milk, salt, and pepper. Pour over cornbread mixture and cover with plastic wrap. Place in the refrigerator and leave for at least 2 hours, or overnight.
3. Microwave the mixture, covered, on HIGH until a knife inserted in the middle comes out clean (about 13–15 minutes), taking out to stir occasionally.
4. Sprinkle with cheese and microwave on HIGH until cheese melts, about 10–15 seconds.

{SERVES 4}

Who Knew?

The easiest way to clean a crusty casserole dish? Just fill it with hot water and place a dryer sheet on top. Then let it sit for several hours or overnight, and the baked-on food will come right off.

406 So-Easy Shrimp

½ cup (1 stick) butter or margarine

2 pounds large shrimp, peeled and de-veined

¼ cup old bay seasoning

2 tablespoons lemon juice Cocktail sauce for serving

1. Cut butter into several portions and place in microwavesafe bowl. Microwave on HIGH until melted, about 15–30 seconds.Add old bay seasoning and lemon juice and mix to combine. Pour over shrimp and toss to coat.
2. Place shrimp in microwave-safe container and microwave, covered, on HIGH for 2 minutes. Stir or rearrange shrimp so that shrimp in the center of the container are moved to the outside, and those on the outside are moved in. Continue microwaving on HIGH, stirring every 2 minutes, until shrimp are pink, about 4 minutes.
3. Serve with your favorite cocktail sauce.

{SERVES 6}

Who Knew?

To get the most juice possible out of your lemons (and limes and oranges), place them in the microwave and heat on HIGH for 30 seconds, then let stand for 2 minutes before squeezing. Rolling a lemon between your hand and the counter will also help maximize the amount of juice you get out of your citrus fruits.

407 Creamed Shrimp over Rice

3 (10 ounce) cans cream of shrimp soup

1 pint sour cream

1½ teaspoons curry powder

1 cup frozen, shelled shrimp, thawed

1. Combine all other ingredients in microwave-safe container. Microwave in 2–3 minute increments on HIGH, stirring each time, until heated through.
2. Serve over rice.

{SERVES 4}

408 Vegetarian Tacos

Even if you're not a vegetarian, eating meatless meals is a great way to save money—and lose weight!

8–10 taco shells
1 (12 ounce) can black or small red beans
1 cup diced tomato, drained
½ cup diced onion
1 cup chopped lettuce
1 (12 ounce) package shredded Cheddar cheese

1. Warm taco shells by microwaving on HIGH for 15 seconds.
2. Place beans in microwave-safe container and microwave on HIGH for approximately 2 minutes, stirring halfway through.
3. Fill each taco shell with beans, tomato, onion, lettuce and cheese. Serve with salsa.

{SERVES 4–6}

Who Knew?

Do you have a smell in your microwave that just won't quit? A tea bag in water (even a used one) placed in the microwave for a minute is all you need to eliminate the odor.

409 Sweet Potatoes with Black Beans

Make sure your kids eat the skins of these delicious sweet potatoes, which will provide them with plenty of fiber.

4 medium sweet potatoes
1 15-ounce can black beans, rinsed
2 medium tomatoes, diced
1 tablespoon extra-virgin olive oil
1 teaspoon ground cumin
¾ teaspoon salt
¼ teaspoon black pepper
¼ cup sour cream

1. Prick sweet potatoes with a fork in several places. Microwave on HIGH for 12–15 minutes, until tender and a toothpick or fork easily slides through to the center.
2. Meanwhile, in a medium microwaveable bowl, combine beans, tomatoes, oil, cumin, salt, and pepper; microwave on HIGH until just heated through, 2–3 minutes.
3. Cut each sweet potato lengthwise and spoon bean mixture into center. Top each with a dollop of sour cream and a sprinkle of cilantro.

{SERVES 4}

410 Broccoli Casserole

2 cups uncooked egg noodles
4 cups chopped broccoli
¼ cup (½ stick) butter or margarine
½ cup chopped onion
1 clove garlic, chopped
¼ cup flour
¾ teaspoon salt
¾ teaspoon dried basil
1½ cups milk
1½ cups shredded Gouda cheese, divided

1. Cook egg noodles according to package's microwave directions.
2. Place broccoli, onion, garlic, and butter in microwavesafe dish. Cover and microwave on HIGH for 3 minutes.
3. In separate container, mix flour, salt, basil, and milk. Pour over broccoli mixture and toss to combine. Microwave on HIGH, covered, for 4 minutes, stirring halfway through.
4. Stir pasta into broccoli mixture along with 1 cup Gouda cheese. Cook for 6 more minutes on HIGH, then sprinkle with the remaining cheese.
5. Cook on HIGH until cheese has completely melted, about 1 minute.

{SERVES 4}

Who Knew?

Believe it or not, cheese with a little mold on it is still perfectly safe to eat once you remove the offending areas. The easiest way to do this is to take a knife or cheese grater, dip it in vinegar, and slice the mold off. Dip the knife in vinegar after each slice–it kills the mold and prevents it from coming back.

411 Rice and More

You'll need a microwave rice cooker for this recipe. If you don't have one, it's worth purchasing! It will make it easy to make "fried" rice in the microwave.

1 teaspoon vegetable oil
½ teaspoon salt
1 cup long grain rice
¼ cup chopped onion
¼ cup diced sweet potato
¼ cup frozen or canned peas or lima beans
1½ cup water

1. Pour vegetable oil into bottom of microwave rice cooker. Add salt.
2. Add rice and all other ingredients except water to cook and mix.
3. Add water and cook on HIGH for 15 minutes or until rice is tender.

{SERVES 3 (OR A HUNGRY BACHELOR!)}

412 Mushroom Burgers

Adding nutrient-rich mushrooms to the meat in these burgers give them a great flavor. If you have any picky eaters, chop the mushrooms extra-fine and they'll never know they're there.

1 (4 ounce) can sliced mushrooms
3 tablespoons finely chopped onion
1 teaspoon garlic salt
¼ teaspoon black pepper
1 pound lean ground beef
2 tablespoons butter
4 hamburger buns Lettuce and sliced tomatoes for garnish

1. In microwave-safe container, combine mushrooms, onion, pepper, and garlic salt. Microwave on MEDIUM for 3 minutes. Let stand 3 minutes.
2. Add beef to mushroom mixture and shape into 4 tight patties.
3. Place on microwave-safe rack or pan and microwave on HIGH for 2 minutes. Let stand for 2 minutes, then turn patties over and microwave on HIGH until desired doneness, about 1½–2 minutes.
4. Serve on hot buns and garnish with tomato slices and lettuce.

{SERVES 4}

413 Speedy Zucchini and Fettuccini

1 (9 ounce) package refrigerated fresh fettuccini pasta
⅓ cup extra-virgin olive oil, divided
1 tablespoon minced garlic
4 small zucchini, grated
1 tablespoon lemon juice
½ cup pine nuts, toasted
¼ teaspoon salt
⅛ teaspoon black pepper
⅓ cup grated Parmesan cheese

1. Prepare pasta in microwave according to package directions. Drain.
2. Place garlic and zucchini in microwave-safe container with 2 tablespoons oil. Microwave on HIGH until tender, about 2 minutes. Drain any excess liquid.
3. Add zucchini mixture to pasta with lemon juice, pine nuts, salt, and pepper.
4. Stir in remaining olive oil and toss to combine. Sprinkle Parmesan cheese over top of dish before serving.

{SERVES 8–10}

CHAPTER 10

Microwave Meals

414 Creamy Microwave Macaroni and Cheese

2 cups dry elbow macaroni
4¼ cups chicken stock, divided
½ cup heavy cream
4 ounces cream cheese
8 ounces shredded cheddar cheese
Pinch of black pepper
Pinch of salt
Pinch of dry mustard (optional)

1. In a large microwave-safe bowl, combine 2 cups of dry macaroni, 2 cups of chicken stock, and a pinch of black pepper. Cover loosely with a lid or vented microwave-safe wrap.
2. Microwave on high for 12 minutes, stirring halfway through if possible.
3. Carefully remove from the microwave (the bowl will be hot). Stir well.
4. Add ½ cup heavy cream, ¼ cup more chicken stock, cream cheese, cheddar, salt, and dry mustard (if using).
5. Stir to combine, then return to the microwave and cook on high for 4 minutes.
6. Stir again until creamy and smooth. Serve hot.

{SERVES 4}

Who Knew?

For extra indulgence, top with crushed buttery crackers or breadcrumbs and microwave 1 minute more for a toasty finish.

415 Microwave Chicken and Yellow Rice

- **1 (10-ounce) package yellow rice mix**
- **Water or chicken stock and oil, as directed on package**
- **1 cup shredded rotisserie chicken**
- **½ cup frozen peas**
- **1 tablespoon diced Manzanilla olives**

1. In a large microwave-safe bowl, combine 2 cups of dry macaroni, 2 cups of chicken stock, and a pinch of black pepper. Cover loosely with a lid or vented microwave-safe wrap.
2. Microwave on high for 12 minutes, stirring halfway through if possible.
3. Carefully remove from the microwave (the bowl will be hot). Stir well.
4. Add ½ cup heavy cream, ¼ cup more chicken stock, cream cheese, cheddar, salt, and dry mustard (if using).
5. Stir to combine, then return to the microwave and cook on high for 4 minutes.
6. Stir again until creamy and smooth. Serve hot.

{SERVES 3-4}

Who Knew?

For extra flavor, squeeze a little fresh lemon juice over the top or sprinkle with chopped parsley before serving.

416 Microwave Pesto Rosé Penne

2 cups dry penne pasta
2 cups water
½ teaspoon chicken bouillon granules
4 ounces cream cheese
2 tablespoons pesto (bottled or homemade)
1 cup marinara sauce
½ cup grated parmesan
Fresh basil leaves, torn
Pinch of crushed red pepper flakes

1. In a large microwave-safe bowl, combine penne, water, and chicken bouillon. Cover loosely with a lid or vented plastic wrap.
2. Microwave on high for 12 minutes, or until the pasta is tender.
3. Carefully remove from the microwave and stir.
4. Add cream cheese, pesto, marinara, basil, and crushed red pepper flakes. Stir to combine.
5. Sprinkle with Parmesan cheese, then return to the microwave and cook on high for 3 minutes.
6. Stir again and serve hot.

{SERVES 3-4}

Who Knew?

For extra richness, drizzle a little olive oil over the top before serving, or add cooked chicken or shrimp for a heartier meal.

417 Microwave Shrimp Divine

1 pound raw shrimp (21–25 count), peeled and deveined
2 cloves fresh garlic, crushed
3 tablespoons butter, melted
1 tablespoon fresh lemon juice
1 tablespoon white wine
1 tablespoon chopped fresh parsley
¼ teaspoon black pepper
¼ teaspoon Old Bay seasoning

1. In a large microwave-safe dish, combine shrimp, garlic, butter, lemon juice, white wine, parsley, black pepper, and Old Bay. Stir well to coat the shrimp evenly.
2. Cover loosely with a vented lid or microwave-safe wrap.
3. Microwave on high for 10 minutes, stirring halfway through.
4. Stir again, then microwave 1 minute longer, or until the shrimp are pink and fully cooked.
5. Serve hot with rice, pasta, or crusty bread to soak up the sauce.

{SERVES 3-4}

Who Knew?

Add a pinch of crushed red pepper flakes for a spicy kick, or top with extra parsley and a drizzle of olive oil before serving.

418 Microwave Lemon Butter Salmon

- 1 salmon fillets (about 6 ounces each)
- 2 tablespoons butter
- 1 tablespoon lemon juice
- 1 teaspoon Dijon mustard
- 1 tablespoon fresh dill or parsley, chopped
- Pinch of salt and black pepper

1. Place salmon fillets in a microwave-safe dish.
2. In a small bowl, combine butter, lemon juice, and Dijon mustard. Spoon over the salmon.
3. Sprinkle with salt, pepper, and herbs.
4. Cover with vented wrap and microwave on high for 5–6 minutes, or until the fish flakes easily.
5. Serve with steamed rice or vegetables.

{SERVES 2}

Who Knew?

Add a spoonful of capers or a few cherry tomatoes before cooking for an elegant finish.

419 Microwave Thai Shrimp Noodles

- 1 (6-ounce) package rice noodles, cooked according to package directions
- 1 can coconut cream
- 2 tablespoons red Thai curry paste
- 2 tablespoons brown sugar
- 1 tablespoon fish sauce
- 1 tablespoon lime juice
- 1 cup shredded rotisserie chicken
- 1 red bell pepper, julienned
- 1 small onion, julienned
- 1 cup sugar snap peas
- Fresh Thai basil or regular basil, chopped, for garnish

1. In a microwave-safe bowl, combine 3 tablespoons coconut cream and Thai red curry paste. Microwave on high for 3 minutes.
2. Stir well, then add the remaining coconut milk, brown sugar, fish sauce, and lime juice. Mix to blend.
3. Add rotisserie chicken, red pepper, onion, and sugar snap peas. Stir to coat everything in the sauce.
4. Fold in the cooked rice noodles, tossing until evenly coated.
5. Cover and microwave on high for 10 minutes, stirring halfway through.
6. Top with fresh basil and serve hot.

{SERVES 4}

Who Knew?

For extra heat, add a few slices of fresh chili or a drizzle of sriracha before serving..

Measurement Equivalents

Measurement Conversions

3 teaspoons = 1 tablespoon

4 tablespoons = ¼ cup

2 cups = 1 pint

4 cups = 1 quart

1 gallon = 4 quarts

½ fluid ounce = 1 tablespoon

8 fluid ounces = 1 cup

Metric Equivalents

1 teaspoon = 5 milliliters

1 tablespoon = 15 milliliters

1 cup = 240 milliliters

1 quart (4 cups) = .95 liter

1 ounce = 28 grams

½ pound = 227 grams

1 pound = 454 grams

Oven Temperature Equivalents

225° F = 110° C = Gas mark ¼

250° F = 125° C = Gas mark ½

275° F = 140° C = Gas mark 1

300° F = 150° C = Gas mark 2

325° F = 165° C = Gas mark 3

350° F = 180° C = Gas mark 4

375° F = 190° C = Gas mark 5

400° F = 200° C = Gas mark 6

425° F = 220° C = Gas mark 7

450° F = 230° C = Gas mark 8

475° F = 240° C = Gas mark 9

Common Substitutions

IIngredient Called for	Substitute
Active dry yeast (one ¼-ounce envelope)	1 cake compressed yeast
Allspice (for baking only)	1 part ground cinnamon + 2 parts ground cloves or ground nutmeg
Anise seed	fennel seed
Apples (1 cup chopped)	1 cup firm chopped pears + 1 tablespoon lemon juice
Arrowroot	use 2 tablespoons flour for every 4 teaspoons arrowroot
Baking powder (1 teaspoon, double-acting)	5/8 teaspoon cream of tartar + ¼ teaspoon baking soda or ¼ teaspoon baking soda + ¼ cup sour milk or buttermilk (lessen other liquid in recipe)
Basil (dried)	tarragon or summer savory or thyme or oregano
Bay leaf	thyme
Black pepper	cayenne pepper (use much less; start with a pinch)
Brandy	cognac or rum
Broth,	1 cup 1 cup hot water + 1 cube or teaspoon bouillon
Bulgur	cracked wheat or kasha or brown rice or couscous or quinoa
Butter	hard margarine or shortening; or oil if it is not a baked good
Buttermilk	(1 cup) 1 cup milk + 1¾ tablespoons cream of tartar or 1 tablespoonlemon juice + milk to make 1 cup (let stand 5 minutes) or sour cream
Cake flour (1 cup)	1 cup minus 2 tablespoons unsifted all-purpose flour
Capers	chopped green olives
Caraway seed	fennel seed or cumin
Cardamom	cinnamon or mace
Chervil	parsley or tarragon or ground anise seed (use a bit less)
Chives	onion powder (small amount) or finely chopped leeks or shallots (small amount) or scallion greens
Chocolate, baking, unsweetened	3 tablespoons unsweetened cocoa powder + 1 tablespoon (one ounce or square) butter or 3 tablespoons carob powder + 2 tablespoons water
Chocolate, semisweet (6 ounces)	9 tablespoons unsweetened cocoa powder or squares + 7 tablespoons sugar + 3 tablespoons butter
Cilantro	parsley and lemon juice
Cinnamon	allspice (use less) or cardamom
Cloves (ground)	allspice or nutmeg or mace
Club soda	sparkling mineral water or seltzer
Cornmeal	polenta
Cornstarch	flour, as thickener
Corn syrup, light (1 cup)	1¾ cup granulated sugar + ¼ cup more of the liquid called for in recipe
Crème fraîche	sour cream in most recipes or ½ sour cream + ½ heavy cream in sauces. Note that crème fraîche can be boiled but sour cream cannot.
Creole seasoning	mixture of salt, black pepper, paprika, garlic powder, and a pinch of cayenne pepper

Cumin	1 part anise + 2 parts caraway or fennel seed (grind if necessary)
Dill seed	caraway or celery seed
Egg (1)	1 tablespoon cornstarch + 3 tablespoons water or 3 tablespoons mayonnaise or ½ of a mashed banana + ¼ teaspoon baking powder
Evaporated milk	half-and-half or cream
Flour	cornstarch or instant potato flakes or pancake mix
Garlic (1 medium clove)	¼ teaspoon minced dried garlic or 1/8 teaspoon garlic powder or ½ teaspoon garlic salt (omitting ½ teaspoon salt from recipe)
Ghee	clarified butter
Herbs, fresh (1 tablespoon)	1 teaspoon dried herbs
Honey (1 cup, in baked goods)	1¼ cups granulated sugar + ¼ cup more of the liquid called for in recipe
Italian seasoning	a blend of any of the following: oregano, basil, and rosemary
Lemongrass	lemon juice or lemon zest or finely chopped lemon verbena or lime zest
Lovage	celery leaves
Marjoram	oregano (use small amount) or thyme or savory
Masa harina	cornmeal
Mascarpone	8 ounces cream cheese whipped with 3 tablespoons sour cream and 2 tablespoons milk
Milk (in baked goods)	fruit juice + ½ teaspoon baking soda mixed in with the flour
Milk (1 cup)	½ cup evaporated milk + ½ cup water or ¼ cup powdered milk + 7/8 cup of water
Milk, whole	same as above + 2 ½ teaspoons melted and cooled butter
Milk, evaporated	half-and-half or cream
Molasses	honey
Mustard, dry (1 teaspoon)	I tablespoon prepared mustard
Nutmeg	allspice or cloves or mace
Oregano	marjoram or thyme
Pancetta	lean bacon (cooked) or very thinly sliced ham
Polenta	cornmeal or corn grits
Poultry seasoning	sage + a blend of any of these: thyme, marjoram, savory, black pepper, rosemary
Rosemary	thyme
Saffron	(1/8 teaspoon) 1 teaspoon dried yellow marigold petals or 1 teaspoon safflower petals
Sage	poultry seasoning or savory or marjoram
Scallions	white or Spanish onions, use 1/3 of amount listed
Self-rising flour	(1 cup) 1 cup all-purpose flour + 1½ teaspoons baking powder + 1/8 teaspoon salt
Shallots	scallions or leeks or yellow onions
Shortening (baked goods only)	butter or margarine

Sour cream	1 tablespoon white vinegar + milk (let stand 5 minutes before using) or 1 tablespoon lemon juice + evaporated milk or plain yogurt
Tahini	peanut butter
Tarragon	anise (use small amount) or chervil (use larger amount) or parsley (use larger amount) or a pinch of fennel seed
Tomato paste (1 tablespoon)	1 tablespoon ketchup or ½ cup tomato sauce (reduce some of the liquid in recipe)
Tomato sauce (2 cups)	¾ cup tomato paste + 1 cup water
Turmeric	mustard powder
Vanilla extract (baked goods only)	almond extract or any other extract
Vinegar	lemon juice for cooking and salads or wine in marinades
Yogurt	sour cream or crème fraîche or buttermilk or mayonnaise (in small amounts)